Praise from the Experts

"Sandra Schlotzhauer's *Elementary Statistics Using JMP*® provides a guide for doing what the title promises, getting basic statistical analyses from JMP. The book begins with descriptions of getting data into JMP, progresses through graphical and data summary methods, and moves into topics of statistical inference. Later chapters show analysis of variance and regression analysis. She clearly describes how to use the multitude of tools available in JMP in a way that takes the guesswork out of the software. The book is consistent in showing the right amount of material to get readers out of the woods, but not overwhelm them with details. Her long experience with using JMP in the real world is reflected by the presentation of the techniques that every data analyst needs. *Elementary Statistics Using JMP*® will be useful for practical statistical analysis and also as a companion to statistical text books for college and university courses."

Ramon C. Littell, Ph.D.
Professor of Statistics

"This book is a great overview of the use of JMP software to perform elementary statistical methods. It is packed with examples and takes the reader through the step-by-step menu clicks necessary to execute each analysis task. This book would be an excellent companion to the main text in an elementary statistics course in which JMP software was available to the students. It would also be of use to a wide range of researchers and scientists, both in academia and industry, who need to perform elementary statistical analyses on their data. One of the greatest strengths of the approach used in this book is that the reader gets an explanation of each statistical method, along with a contrast of the method with other similar statistical methods. This presentation strategy prevents the JMP user from applying statistical analysis techniques incorrectly.

"I would highly recommend this book to JMP users, and to those interested in learning JMP to analyze data. The book's contents are widely applicable to data in a number of research fields."

Dennis W. King, Ph.D.
Senior Statistician
STATKING Consulting, Inc.

"This book is a great tool for learning both statistics and JMP simultaneously. It could have also been titled "Elementary JMP Using Statistics." This book is ideal for those wanting to learn the power of JMP, along with learning the power of statistical data analyses. This book, used in conjunction with the powerful graphical features of JMP, will provide the reader the knowledge necessary to move to data-based decision making. It is a must for those who have data they'd like to analyze but don't know where to start."

Don Lifke, Certified Black Belt
Corporate Lean Six Sigma Office
Sandia National Laboratories

"This is a wonderful book. The prose is clear and uncluttered. I found it easy and fun to read. It would work as an introduction, as well as a guide for using JMP in data analysis courses beyond the introductory level. The summaries for each section and for each chapter are a really good idea, and the summaries of JMP steps for every operation discussed in a chapter is an even better idea. These are exactly what a software reference book needs. Users can find what they need without having to review the entire chapter. The author is to be congratulated on this material. I also liked the author's grasp of the logic of data analysis. The steps followed an order that I found intuitively satisfying, with no loose ends left hanging."

KW Taylor
Associate Professor, University of Manitoba

Elementary Statistics Using JMP®

Sandra D. Schlotzhauer

The correct bibliographic citation for this manual is as follows: Schlotzhauer, Sandra D. 2007. *Elementary Statistics Using JMP®*. Cary, NC: SAS Institute Inc.

Elementary Statistics Using JMP®

Copyright © 2007, SAS Institute Inc., Cary, NC, USA

ISBN 978-1-59994-375-6

All rights reserved. Produced in the United States of America.

SAS Institute Inc., SAS Campus Drive, Cary, North Carolina 27513.

1st printing, April 2007

SAS® Publishing provides a complete selection of books and electronic products to help customers use SAS software to its fullest potential. For more information about our e-books, e-learning products, CDs, and hard-copy books, visit the SAS Publishing Web site at **support.sas.com/pubs** or call 1-800-727-3228.

SAS® and all other SAS Institute Inc. product or service names are registered trademarks or trademarks of SAS Institute Inc. in the USA and other countries. ® indicates USA registration.

Other brand and product names are registered trademarks or trademarks of their respective companies.

Contents

Part 4   Fitting Lines to Data   305

Chapter 10   Correlation and Regression   307

Chapter 11   Basic Regression Diagnostics   359

Part 5   Data in Summary Tables   401

Chapter 12   Creating and Analyzing Contingency Tables   403

Acknowledgments

Most authors would tell you that writing a book involves a large support team, and this book is no exception. Many people contributed in many ways to this book. Thank you to the individuals and publishing companies who gave permission to use their data in the examples. In addition to the people listed here, I would like to thank the many students in my JMP classes over the years. Your feedback contributed to the approach used in this book, and taught me the importance of precision in speaking and writing about statistical software.

Special thanks goes to the reviewers who took time away from their jobs and families to provide detailed comments. I am grateful for your revisions to text, corrections to statistical and JMP discussions, and suggestions for topics to include or omit. Thanks to Paul Marovich, who clicked every mouse click in the book, provided his perspective as a JMP instructor, gave contributions to the "Further Reading" appendix, and provided key improvements for several topics. Thanks to Dr. Julie Jones, who also clicked every mouse click, and provided her perspective as a statistician and as a programmer new to JMP. Thanks to Jennifer Kendall, with her perspective as a longtime JMP instructor and statistician. Thanks to Dr. Ann Lehman, with her perspective as a JMP expert, statistician, and author of multiple JMP and SAS Press books. Thanks to Mark Bailey, both for his extensive review comments, and for his JMP scripts for the Chapter 10 figures on least squares regression. Thanks to Curt Hinrichs, for his review comments, information on JMP SE, and contributions to the "Further Reading" appendix. Thanks to Dr. Meimei Ma, who provided her perspective on how nonnative English speakers would interpret the text. Thanks to other SAS reviewers, who provided an insider's view in their comments: Nicole Jones, Marissa Langford, Tonya Mauldin, and Annie Zangi.

This book started as a JMP version of the *SAS System for Elementary Statistical Analysis,* which Dr. Ramon Littell coauthored. Initially, he planned to coauthor this book as well, but found that his position as Chairman of the University of Florida Department of Statistics demanded all of his time and energy. I first worked with him as a graduate student, and am, as ever, grateful for his insight and input on this book. He generously agreed to give permission to use the data from our previous book.

After all of the text is written, and all of the software screen captures are complete, a SAS Press book still involves the efforts of many people before it is published. Thanks to Stephenie Joyner, my acquisitions editor, for shepherding the book through every stage of the publishing process. Thanks to Amy Wolfe who corrected the mistakes (any remaining are mine, Amy!) and learned some statistics along the way. Thanks to Monica McClain and Denise Jones for production work, and to Jennifer Dilley for graphics work. Thanks to Patrice Cherry for the cover design, and to Bill Simmons and Galen Koch for producing the photo. Thanks to Liz Villani and Shelly Goodin for marketing the book, and to Mary Beth Steinbach, managing editor, for coordinating the project.

Finally, a special thank you goes to my husband, Galen Koch, for his patience and support.

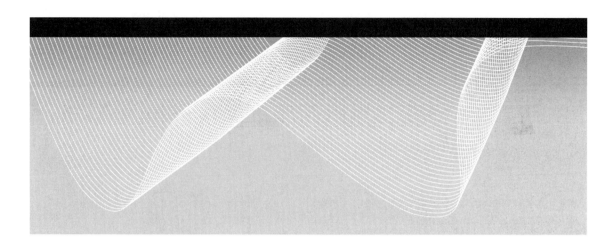

Part 1

The Basics

Chapter 1

Introduction

Elementary Statistics Using JMP helps you analyze your data in JMP. This chapter covers the following:

- the purpose of this book

- the audience for this book

- what this book is and isn't

- how this book is organized

- how to use this book

Purpose

This book shows how to use JMP for basic statistical analyses and explains the statistical methods used—when to use them, what the assumptions are, and how to interpret the results.

Audience

This book is for people who have minimal knowledge of JMP or statistics or both. You might be a manager, researcher, or analyst. Or, you might be a student or professor. The range of example data used in the chapters and sample data in the exercises is relevant to a broad audience. The book assumes only that you want to learn to use JMP to perform analyses.

What This Book Is and Isn't

Consider this book a task-oriented tool for basic data analysis. The book integrates analysis methods with JMP steps and then explains the results. Through the use of examples, the book describes how the analysis leads to decisions about the data.

This book is intended to be a companion to JMP. Because JMP software is interactive, the book is too. As you use the chapters, follow along with the examples. The book is in black and white, while JMP software is in color. The text refers to "the blue-shaded area," "the red line," and so on. Looking at the JMP results as you read through the book will help you learn.

If you are familiar with statistical terms, the book discusses descriptive summaries and graphs, testing for normality, hypothesis testing, two-sample *t*-tests, paired-difference *t*-tests, analysis of variance (ANOVA), basic regression, and basic contingency table analysis. The book does not discuss analysis of variance for designs other than completely randomized designs. It does not discuss multivariate analysis, time series methods, quality control, operations research analysis, or design of experiments.

The book concentrates on data analysis. Although you can perform analyses using only the information in this book, you might want to refer to statistical texts for more theory or details. The book includes very few formulas. Formulas for the statistical methods are available in many texts and in JMP documentation. See "Further Reading" at the end of the book for a list of references.

How This Book Is Organized

This book is divided into five parts.

Part 1: The Basics

Chapter 1, "Introduction"
Chapter 2, "Getting Started"
Chapter 3, "Using Data Tables"
Chapter 4, "Summarizing Data"
Chapter 5, "Graphing Data and Printing Results"

Part 2: Statistical Background

Chapter 6, "Understanding Fundamental Statistical Concepts"
Chapter 7, "Estimating the Mean"

Part 3: Comparing Groups

Chapter 8, "Comparing Two Groups"
Chapter 9, "Comparing More Than Two Groups"

Part 4: Fitting Lines to Data

Chapter 10, "Correlation and Regression"
Chapter 11, "Basic Regression Diagnostics"

Part 5: Data in Summary Tables

Chapter 12, "Creating and Analyzing Contingency Tables"

The first part of the book shows how to get your data into JMP and summarize it. The second part gives a statistical foundation for the analyses discussed in parts 3, 4, and 5. Parts 3, 4, and 5 show how to perform various analyses.

Using Part 1

Part 1 is essential for everyone. Chapters 1 and 2 give a brief introduction. Chapter 3 explains how to get your data into JMP. Chapters 4 and 5 show how to summarize your data with descriptive statistics and plots.

Starting with Chapter 2, there are two summaries for each chapter. The "Key Ideas" summary contains the main ideas of the chapter. The "JMP Steps" summary provides all the JMP activities for the chapter.

Using Part 2

Part 2 focuses on statistical concepts and provides a foundation for analyses presented in parts 3, 4, and 5. Topics include populations and samples, the normal distribution, the Empirical Rule, hypothesis testing, the effect of sample size and population variance on estimates of the mean, the Central Limit Theorem, and confidence intervals for the mean. Chapter 6 shows how to test for normality in JMP, and Chapter 7 shows how to get confidence intervals in JMP.

Using Part 3

Part 3 shows how to compare groups of data. Examples of problems are:

- New employees must take a proficiency test before they can operate a dangerous and expensive piece of equipment. Some new employees are experienced with this equipment and some are not. You want to find out if the average test scores for the two groups (experienced and inexperienced) are different.

- Heart rates of students are measured before and after mild exercise on a treadmill. You think the "before" heart rates are likely to be lower than the "after" heart rates. You want to know whether the changes in heart rates are greater than what could happen by chance.

- A study compared the effects of five fertilizers on potted geraniums. At the end of six weeks, you measured the height of the geraniums. Now, you want to compare the average heights for the geraniums that received the five different fertilizers.

- You recorded the number of defective items from an assembly line on the workdays Monday through Friday. You want to determine whether there are differences in the number of defective items made on different workdays.

Chapter 8 shows how to use JMP to summarize data from two groups, and how to perform the two-sample *t*-test, paired-difference *t*-test, Wilcoxon Signed Rank test, and Wilcoxon Rank Sum test.

Chapter 9 shows how to use JMP to summarize data from more than two groups, and how to perform the analysis of variance, Kruskal-Wallis test, and multiple comparison procedures.

Using Part 4

Part 4 shows how to fit a line or curve to a set of data. Examples of problems are:

- You want to determine the relationship between weight and age in children. You want to produce a plot showing the data and the fitted line or curve. Finally, you want to examine the data to find atypical points far from the fitted line or curve.

- You have varied the temperature of an oven in a manufacturing process. The goal is to estimate the amount of change in hardness of the product that is caused by an amount of change in temperature.

Chapter 10 shows how to use JMP for correlations, straight-line regression, polynomial regression (fitting curves), multiple regression, prediction intervals, and confidence intervals.

Chapter 11 shows how to use JMP to plot residuals and predicted values, residuals and independent variables, and residuals in a time sequence. Chapter 11 discusses investigating outliers and using lack of fit tests.

Using Part 5

Part 5 includes Chapter 12, which discusses how to analyze data in contingency tables. Examples of problems are:

- You want to know whether color preferences for shampoo are the same for men and women.

- You have conducted an opinion poll to evaluate how people in your town feel about the proposal for a new tax to build a sports arena. Do people who live close to the site for the proposed arena feel differently than people who live farther away?

- In conducting a test-market for a new product, your company used a survey that asked shoppers if they had bought the product. You asked other questions about the packaging of the product. Are the opinions on packaging different between people who have bought the new product and people who have not?

Chapter 12 shows how to use JMP for creating contingency tables, measuring association, and performing the Chi Square test of independence.

References

Appendix 1, "Further Reading," gives a list of references.

Typographic Conventions

The typographic conventions that are used in this book are:

regular	is used for most text.
italic	defines new terms.
bold	highlights points of special importance.
bold	identifies JMP choices. Choices such as **Basic→Distribution** mean you select **Basic** and then **Distribution**. This font also identifies items in JMP reports.
JMP	refers to JMP windows, such as JMP Starter. This font also identifies titles for JMP reports.

Chapters include "JMP Hints," which give hints that apply across JMP, not just for the topic being discussed.

Some chapters include "Technical Details," which give formulas or other details that add to the text, but aren't required for understanding the topic.

JMP Hint:

JMP is pronounced "jump".

How to Use This Book

If you have never used JMP, first read all of Part 1. Then, if you aren't familiar with statistics, read Part 2. Otherwise, you can skip to other parts of the book.

If you have used JMP, but you are not familiar with statistics, skim Part 1. Then, read Part 2, which gives an explanation of several statistical concepts. Then, skip to other parts of the book that best meet your needs.

If you have used JMP, and you are familiar with statistics, but don't know how to handle your particular problem, first skim Part 1. Then, go to the chapter that best meets your needs.

Caution: While the book shows how to use JMP to perform analyses and describes the statistical methods and JMP results, it is not a replacement for statistical texts.

Using JMP or JMP SE

JMP is the full-featured version of the software, and is available in industry and academia. JMP SE, or JMP Student Edition, has limited features, and is available only in academia.

JMP SE includes almost all of the features in this book. Specific exclusions for JMP SE are:

- With JMP SE, you can create JMP data tables up to 1000 rows and 100 columns. You can open any size existing JMP data table.

- Treemaps, discussed in Chapter 5, are not available in JMP SE.

- Journals, discussed in Chapter 5, are not available in JMP SE.

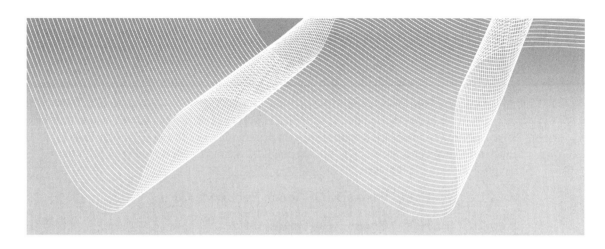

Chapter 2

Getting Started

This chapter discusses what you need to know before you use JMP; for example, it:

- describes how to start JMP, get help, and exit
- introduces JMP terminology
- shows a simple example

JMP and Your Computer

JMP is available for Windows, Linux, and Macintosh operating systems. While the features in JMP are the same for all of these operating systems, the menu choices might differ. The JMP documentation listed in "Further Reading" provides full detail on these differences. In addition, two quick reference cards are provided with JMP. If you don't have a paper version of these cards, you can print your own. The documentation and quick reference cards are in PDF, so you need the Adobe Reader to view or print them. To print the quick reference cards:

1. Click **Help→Books→JMP Quick Reference Card**.

2. Click **Help→Books→JMP Menu Card**.

The rest of this book uses Windows terminology and Windows choices, which simplifies the discussion and, for the most part, the terminology and choices are the same for Macintosh and Linux users. When a feature is available only for Windows, the book points that out.

The book assumes that you are familiar with the basics of using your computer. You should understand single-click, double-click, the CTRL key and click, and so on. The book assumes that you know how to print from your computer. Although the book discusses printing from JMP, it does not discuss how to install and set up a printer.

Releases of JMP

JMP is available in multiple releases. This book shows results and reports from Release 6.0.3. Earlier releases might have different appearances, and some features might not be available. Once you start JMP, here is how to find out what release you have:

1. Click **Help→About JMP**.

2. In the About JMP window, the first line shows the release number.

Explaining JMP Terms

JMP is very visual, combining graphs with summary information. It helps you learn about your data through interactivity and with a focus on data exploration. As a result, you can use JMP to do everything in this book without learning a programming language. However, you might find it helpful to learn basic terms that are unique to JMP.

As with most software, JMP provides a set of choices in a menu bar at the top of the JMP window. JMP refers to these choices as *commands*.

JMP displays data in a *data table*, which is similar to a spreadsheet. Chapter 3 discusses the data table in detail. For now, all you need to know is that JMP displays data in a row-and-column grid, and provides additional navigation features.

JMP groups related tasks into *analysis platforms*, which are referred to as *platforms*. The JMP Starter window shows the different analysis platforms by category. In addition, the platforms are available from menu bar commands. For example, the **Distribution** platform is available from the **Analyze** command, and from the **Basic** category in the JMP Starter window.

Once you have performed an analysis, JMP refers to the results as a *report*. This report can include both graphs and text summaries. The text summaries are called *report tables*.

Two key icons are best explained by example, but they are introduced here and later shown in an example in this chapter. First, *outline item icons* are blue diamonds. JMP refers to these as *disclosure diamonds*. Clicking on the blue diamond opens the associated item. Half of the diamond is blue—which half depends on whether the associated item is open or closed. Second, *hot spots* are red downward-pointing triangles. Clicking on a hot spot opens a menu or window that provides additional choices.

Starting JMP

JMP should be installed on your PC or you should access it over a network. Start JMP by double-clicking the JMP icon on your personal computer (PC). When JMP starts, you see:

1. A splash screen, which shows the JMP logo and your licensing information. This splash screen closes by itself.

2. The Tip of the Day window, which gives a tip about using JMP. The tip changes each time you start JMP. As you learn JMP, let the tips display at start-up for a while. Click the **Close** button to close this window.

3. The JMP Starter window, which is a navigation tool. Although you can access every JMP command from the menu bar, the JMP Starter window organizes analyses in a convenient way, and sometimes customizes choices to make the analysis easier to use. Use the JMP Starter window for analyses until you are familiar with JMP.

JMP Hint:

In the Tip of the Day window, click the check box for **Show tips at startup** so that it is deselected. The next time that JMP starts, tips will not display.

Displaying a Simple Example

This section shows you an example of a JMP data table and the results from an analysis.

One indicator of an individual's fitness is the percent of body fat, which is measured with a special set of calipers. (Calipers look like pliers that have a dial on them.) The calipers are placed at three or four different places on the body to measure the amount of skin that can easily be pinched. Women are measured on the triceps, the abdomen, and near the hips. Men are measured on the chest, the abdomen, near the hips, and at the midaxillary line. Skinfold measures are averaged across the different places to provide a measure of the percent of body fat. Depending on whose guidelines you look at, the normal range for men is 15–20% body fat, and the normal range for women is 20–25% body fat. Table 2.1 shows body fat percentages for several men and women[1]. These men and women participated in unsupervised aerobic exercise or weight training (or both) about three times per week for a year. Then, they were measured for their percentages of body fat.

Table 2.1 Body Fat Data

Group	Body Fat Percentage				
Male	13.3	8	20	12	12
	19	18	31	16	24
	20	22	21		
Female	22	16	21.7	21	30
	26	12	23.2	28	23

Figure 2.1 displays the data table and shows the navigation features discussed in Chapter 3. The areas labeled **bodyfat**, **Columns**, and **Rows** are *panels*. The panels have additional functionality available from the hot spot. The blue disclosure diamond in the upper-left corner of the data table gives you the ability to hide the panels. Clicking on the rows and columns hot spots in the data table displays menus with additional functionality.

---

[1] Data is from the Recreation & Fitness Center at SAS. Used with permission.

Figure 2.1 JMP Data Table for Body Fat Data

bodyfat				

bodyfat				Gender	Body Fat	
		1	Male	13.3		
		2	Male	19		
		3	Male	20		
		4	Male	8		
		5	Male	18		
		6	Male	22		
Columns (2/0)		7	Male	20		
il. Gender		8	Male	31		
◢ Body Fat		9	Male	21		
		10	Male	12		
		11	Male	16		
		12	Male	12		
		13	Male	24		
		14	Female	22		
		15	Female	26		
Rows		16	Female	16		
All rows	23	17	Female	12		
Selected	0	18	Female	21.7		
Excluded	0	19	Female	23.2		
Hidden	0	20	Female	21		
Labelled	0	21	Female	28		
		22	Female	30		
		23	Female	23		

Using the **Distribution** platform gives a quick summary of this data. Figure 2.2 illustrates how JMP combines graphs and summary information. Chapters 4 and 6 discuss the **Distribution** platform in detail. The JMP report has two hot spots, which open menus with additional functionality. The report has four disclosure diamonds—all are open. Clicking on a disclosure diamond hides the associated JMP report.

Figure 2.2 JMP Report Summarizing Body Fat Data

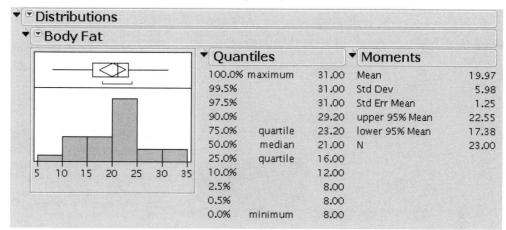

Getting Help

The easiest way to get help is by clicking **Help** in the menu bar. For Windows and Linux users, the usual choices for listing contents and searching are available. These choices don't appear for Macintosh. Figure 2.3 displays the **Help** choices in Windows, along with the Index window.

Figure 2.3 Windows Help Choices and Index Window

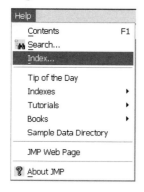
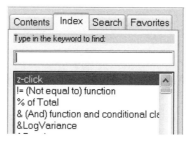

JMP provides several tutorials, some of which are used as exercises later in this book.

Under the **Help** menu, clicking **Indexes→Statistics** answers your question, "Does JMP do…?" because the index lists all of the statistical analyses and statistics generated by JMP. Figure 2.4 displays the menu choices and the **Statistics Index** window. Click in the list in the **Statistics Index** window and type the first letter of the statistical term of interest.

Figure 2.4 Menu Choices to View the Statistics Index Window

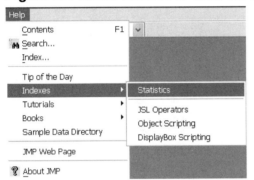
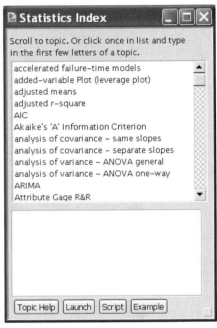

Within JMP windows, three additional features for help are available:

- Clicking the **?** tool on the toolbar opens context-sensitive help.
- Moving the mouse pointer in a small circle around an item sometimes reveals help about the item. "JMP Hints" highlight this feature.
- Positioning the mouse pointer over an item in a menu sometimes reveals help about the item. "JMP Hints" highlight this feature.

You can find help about JMP at www.jmp.com. Visit this site occasionally to view articles about and examples of using JMP. This is where you will learn about upgrades, new releases, and user conferences.

Exiting JMP

To exit JMP, click **File→Exit** in Windows and Linux, or use the **Quit** command in the JMP menu on the Macintosh. In addition, for Windows and Linux, you can click the **X** in the upper-right corner of the JMP window.

Most users, including the author, have had the experience of clicking to exit a software program and then saying, "Oops!" Fortunately, JMP gives you a chance to recover.

Suppose you have created new data tables in JMP and click to exit. Or, suppose you have made changes to existing data tables and click to exit. JMP displays the window in Figure 2.5.

Figure 2.5 JMP Close All Windows Window

This feature gives you a chance to save your new data before exiting. You can choose:

Save All   Displays a Save As window for each open data table.
                     Specify the name for each data table and save it.

Save None   Closes all open data tables and displays the Save Session
                     window (see Figure 2.6).

Save   Displays a Caution Alert window for each data table. In
Individually   this window, you answer a question about saving the data
                     table. Select **Yes** to open the Save As window. Select **No**
                     to close the data table without saving it. Select **Cancel** to
                     cancel the exit.

Cancel   Cancels the exit and leaves the data tables open.

Now, suppose you have handled the data tables and click to exit. Or, perhaps you didn't
have new or modified data tables. JMP displays the window in Figure 2.6.

Figure 2.6 JMP Save Session Window

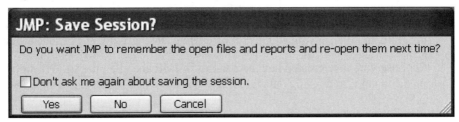

This feature gives you a chance to start your next JMP session with the same data tables
and reports open. (Some changes in the display will not be saved, but the basic data tables
and reports will be open.) You can choose:

Yes   Save the session.

No   Exit JMP without saving the session.

Cancel   Keep JMP open.

If you click the check box in the Save Session window, the window will not display in
future JMP sessions. As you are learning JMP, leave this check box deselected. It can be
helpful to have the chance to save all your in-progress work at the end of the day.

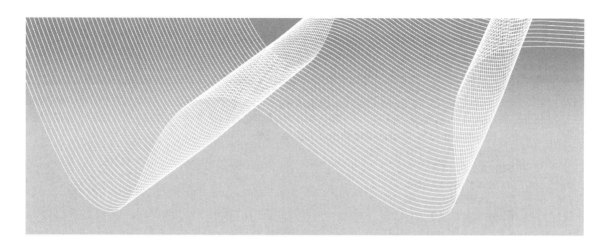

Chapter **3**

Using Data Tables

Using Data Tables

Your first step in using JMP to explore and analyze data is to create a JMP data table. If your data is available electronically, JMP can probably import it. This chapter discusses:

- creating a JMP data table

- importing data into JMP

- understanding features of JMP data tables

- sorting a JMP data table

- printing a JMP data table

What Is a Data Table?

Most of us work with data every day—in lists or tables or spreadsheets—on paper or on a computer. A data table is how JMP stores data in rows and columns. JMP data tables are similar to spreadsheets in appearance, but have additional features that are unique to JMP.

Table 3.1 shows the speeding ticket fines for driving 65 miles per hour (mph) in each of the 50 states. The information was collected when the speed limit on state and interstate highways was 55 mph. The next section shows how to create a JMP data table using this data as an example.

For convenience, the speeding ticket data is available in the **tickets** data table in the sample data for this book.

Table 3.1 Speeding Ticket Fines[1]

State	Fine	State	Fine
Alabama	$60	Hawaii	$35
Delaware	$31.50	Illinois	$20
Alaska	$20	Connecticut	$60
Arkansas	$47	Iowa	$33
Florida	$44	Kansas	$28
Arizona	$15	Indiana	$50
California	$50	Louisiana	$45
Georgia	$45	Montana	$5
Idaho	$12.50	Kentucky	$65
Colorado	$64	Maine	$40
Nebraska	$10	Massachusetts	$50
Maryland	$40	Nevada	$5
Missouri	$50	Michigan	$40
New Mexico	$20	New Jersey	$50
Minnesota	$44	New York	$28
North Carolina	$47.50	Mississippi	$39.50
North Dakota	$10	Ohio	$100
New Hampshire	$33	Oregon	$26
Oklahoma	$56	South Carolina	$45
Rhode Island	$30	Pennsylvania	$72.50
Tennessee	$40	South Dakota	$10
Texas	$48	Vermont	$35
Utah	$28	West Virginia	$60
Virginia	$40	Wyoming	$15
Washington	$38	Wisconsin	$44.50

[1] Data is from *Newsweek* (July 21, 1986). Used with permission.

Creating the Speeding Ticket Data Table

Suppose your data is only on paper. If the data is in a spreadsheet or other type of file, skip to "Importing Data." To create a data table in JMP:

1. Click **File→New**. In the JMP Starter window, you can click **File→New Data Table**.

2. JMP displays a new data table with one column and no rows in a window named Untitled.

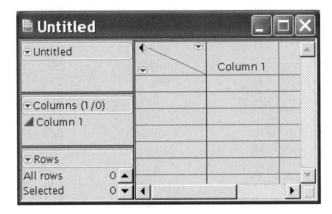

3. Double-click on the **Column 1** heading to display the following window.

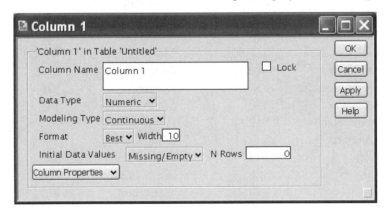

4. Enter the column name in the **Column Name** field. For the speeding ticket data, enter **State**. JMP allows column names up to 255 characters long.

5. Click the menu for **Data Type** and change it to **Character**. JMP changes the **Modeling Type** to **Nominal** (more on this later).

6. Enter **51** in the **N Rows** field. If you know in advance how many rows are in your data, this is an easy way to have JMP add the rows for you.

7. Compare your JMP window with Figure 3.1. Click **OK**.

Figure 3.1 Window for a New Character Column in a JMP Data Table

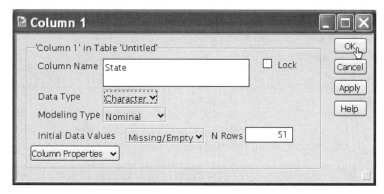

Continuing in JMP:

8. The columns panel now shows 1 column, and the rows panel shows 51 rows.

9. Double-click in the blank area to the right of your first column. JMP adds a new column and names it **Column 2**, as shown in the following window:

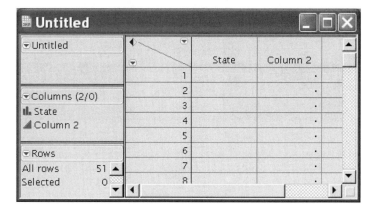

10. This new column will contain the speeding ticket fine amounts, so it will be numeric. JMP automatically creates numeric variables. Double-click on the **Column 2** heading.

11. Enter the column name in the **Column Name** field. For the speeding ticket data, enter **Amount** as shown in the following window:

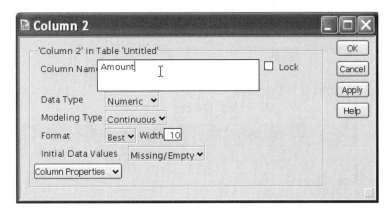

12. JMP automatically sets the format for numeric variables to **Best**, which means that JMP checks the data and selects a format. You can change the format by clicking the menu for **Format** as shown in the following window:

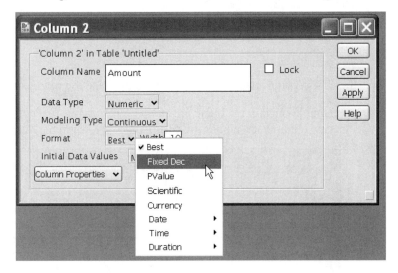

13. Select **Fixed Dec** for fixed decimal and accept the automatic values of a width of **10** with **2** places after the decimal point. These values work well for U.S. dollars. Figure 3.2 shows the completed window for the second column.

Figure 3.2   Window for a New Numeric Column in a
                  JMP Data Table

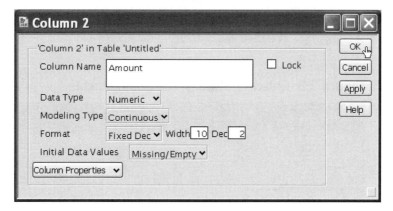

Continuing in JMP:

14. Click **OK**. The columns panel now shows 2 columns. The following window shows the empty data grid.

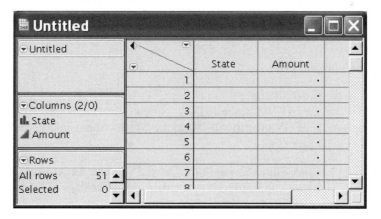

Continuing in JMP:

15. You are ready to enter data. Position your mouse pointer in the first row of the first column and enter data. After entering the first state in the data table (**Alabama**), click the TAB key and enter the speeding ticket fine amount (**60**). Click the TAB key again, and JMP moves the mouse pointer to the next row. Figure 3.3 shows the results after entering a few states. States not yet entered have blank fields because **State** is a character variable. Amounts not yet entered show a period (.) because this is how JMP displays missing values for a numeric variable.

Figure 3.3 Entering Data for Speeding Tickets

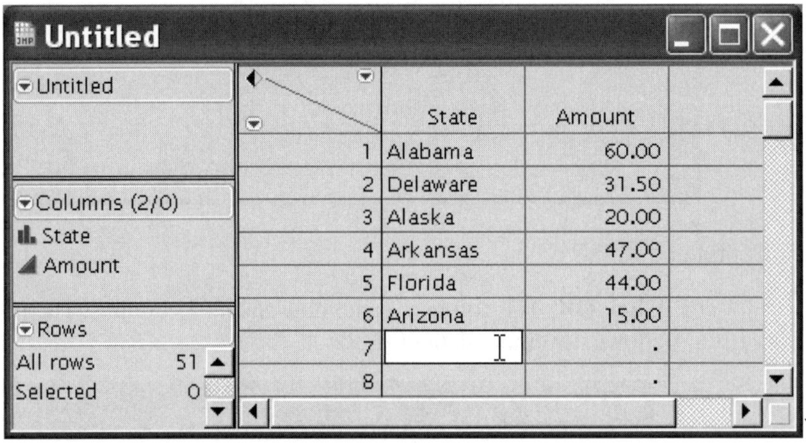

Continuing in JMP:

16. Enter all of the data in Table 3.1. Table 3.1 does not show the speeding ticket data for Washington, D.C., but you want to add this location to the data table. Enter **Washington DC** in the **State** column and leave the **Amount** column blank.

17. Click **File→Save**. In the Save JMP File As window, navigate to the location where you want to save the data, enter **Tickets** as the name, and click **Save**.

Opening an Existing JMP Data Table

Suppose your data is in a JMP file. To open a data table in JMP:

1. Click **File→Open**. In the JMP Starter window, you can click **File→Open Data Table**.

2. Navigate to the location of your data and click the data table.

3. Click **Open**.

JMP opens your data table.

Importing Data

If the data is in a spreadsheet or other type of electronic file, JMP can probably import it. Figure 3.4 shows the types of files that JMP imports in Windows on a specific PC. Your choices can vary, depending on the software that is installed on your PC.

Figure 3.4 File Types Available for JMP Import

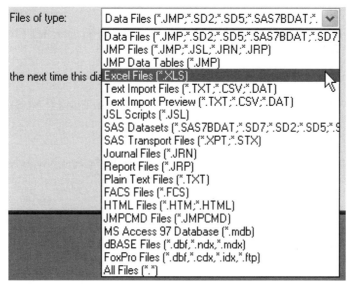

If the list in Figure 3.4 includes the file type that you want to import, then you can proceed with the following steps. If the file type you need is not included, try saving your file as either a plain text (TXT) file or Microsoft Excel (XLS) file first. Many software applications have options for saving to these two file types. If you can save your file to one of these file types, then JMP can import it. If your data is in electronic form, it's worth the extra time to investigate ways to import it, instead of entering the data in the file all over again. Importing data improves overall data quality because quality control checks that were previously performed on the data will not need to be performed again.

The steps for importing data in JMP depend on the file type. The following sections discuss two common file types—TXT and XLS. See the JMP Help or documentation for more detail on other file types, including importing data tables from Web pages. JMP imports TXT and XLS file types (and many others) on the Macintosh and in Linux, although the steps differ. See the JMP Help or documentation for more detail on these operating systems.

JMP has two limits for importing data. First, the imported file must fit in the memory on your computer—this is also a limit for any JMP file that you open or create. Second, the imported file can have a maximum of 10,000 columns and a maximum of 128 KB of information per row.[2]

Opening Microsoft Excel Spreadsheets

Importing data from Microsoft Excel is similar to opening an existing JMP data table. The steps are:

1. Click **File→Open**. In the JMP Starter window, you can click **File→Open Data Table**.

2. Navigate to the location of your data.

3. Click the menu for **Files of type** and select **Excel Files (*.XLS)**.

4. Click the name of the Microsoft Excel file you want.

5. If your Microsoft Excel file has column labels on the first line, select the check box for **Excel table has labels in row 1**.

---

[2] JMP SE has a size limit for creating JMP data tables. You can create JMP data tables up to 1000 rows and 100 columns. You can open any size existing JMP data table.

6. If your Microsoft Excel file has multiple worksheets and you want to select specific worksheets, select the check box for **Allow individual worksheet selection**. (JMP automatically opens all worksheets, so you might want to do this.) When you select this check box, JMP displays the Select sheets to import window. Select the check boxes for the worksheets you want to import and click **OK**.

7. If your Microsoft Excel file has a single worksheet, or if you want to open all worksheets in a Microsoft Excel file that has multiple worksheets, click **Open**.

JMP automatically uses the worksheet names from Microsoft Excel. If you changed the automatic names (Sheet 1, Sheet 2, and so on) in Microsoft Excel, JMP uses your new names.

JMP Hint:

You cannot open a file in JMP if the file is already open in Microsoft Excel. If the file is open in Microsoft Excel, you will get an error message when you try to open the file in JMP. If you must have the file open in both applications, open the file first in JMP. Then, open the file in Microsoft Excel. Use caution if you make any changes to this file. Save the open file in JMP as a .JMP file, and in Microsoft Excel file as an .XLS file.

Copy and Paste from Microsoft Excel

Suppose you have a Microsoft Excel spreadsheet open, and you want to copy only a portion of the spreadsheet to create a JMP data table. Suppose you want to copy the column headings so that they become variable names in JMP. The steps are:

1. In Microsoft Excel, select the rows and columns that you want to appear in the JMP data table. You can select a continuous block of cells, or you can hold down the CTRL key and click to select a complex block of cells.

2. In Microsoft Excel, click **Edit→Copy**.

3. In JMP, create an empty new data table either by clicking **File→New** in the menu bar or **File→New Data Table** in the JMP Starter window.

4. Hold down the SHIFT key and click **Edit→Paste** in the menu bar.

5. JMP pastes the selected cells into the new data table.

If your Microsoft Excel file doesn't have column headings that you want to use as variable names, you can click **Edit→Paste** in JMP. The cells are pasted, and variable names are **Column 1**, **Column 2**, and so on.

Importing Text Files

Text files can be in many forms, and JMP has three ways to import them. You can:

- Let JMP automatically detect columns and rows.

- Use your JMP file preferences.

- Use the preview option.

In Figure 3.4, JMP considers text files to have TXT, CSV, or DAT extensions.

To import a text file using automatic choices in JMP

1. Click **File→Open**.

2. Navigate to the location of your data.

3. Click the menu for **Files of type** and select **Text Import Files (*.TXT;*.CSV;*.DAT)**. Do not select **Text Import Preview**, which guides you through a preview process instead of using the automatic choices.

4. Click the name of the file you want.

5. Click the button for **Attempt to Discern Format**.

6. Click **Open**.

If JMP can identify column and row breaks, it opens the file. The next two topics discuss using JMP file preferences and using the preview option. Try using the automatic choices in JMP first, and only use one of these other approaches if necessary.

To import a text file using your JMP file preferences

1. Click **File→Preferences**.

2. Click the icon for **Text Data Files**. See Figure 3.5 for the JMP settings for importing text. Adjust the settings as needed for your text file.

   The **End Of Field** settings identify column breaks in the file, and the **End Of Line** settings identify row breaks. Select settings that reflect your data.

Strip enclosing quotes is automatically selected. If your data values are enclosed in quotation marks, this option removes the quotation marks. If they are not, leaving the check box selected does no harm.

The **Two-digit year rule** is automatically set to **10-90**. This setting works for most data; it assumes data values less than 90 are years in the current century, and data values of 90 or more are years in the previous century. For example, JMP interprets a value of 91 as 1991, and a value of 80 as 2080.

Table contains column headers is automatically selected. If your text data contains only the data, deselect this check box. JMP assigns column names of **Column 1**, **Column 2**, and so on. You can change these column names after importing the data.

If your data contains column headers, JMP assumes that the headers are in the first row and that your data starts in the second row. If your data has multiple rows of headers, editing the data so that it has a single row of headers will help in importing data to JMP.

3. Click **OK**.

4. Click **File→Open**.

5. Navigate to the location of your data.

6. Click the menu for **Files of type** and select **Text Import Files (*.TXT;*.CSV;*.DAT)**.

7. Click the name of the file you want.

8. Click the button for **Use Text Import Preferences**.

9. Click **Open**.

If JMP can read the data using the JMP preferences, it opens the file. If not, you might need to change the settings. Or, you can use the preview option, which immediately shows you the impact of your settings. JMP starts with your import settings when you use the Text Import Preview window, but does permit you to revise them.

Figure 3.5 JMP Import Settings

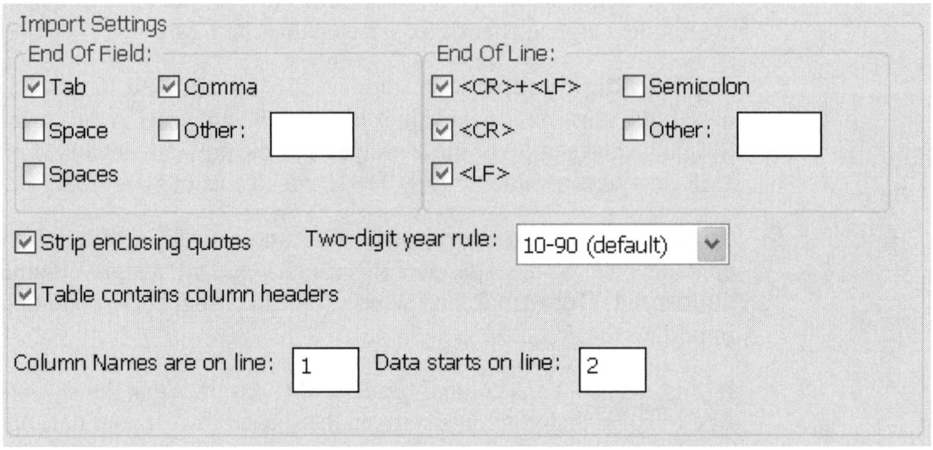

Import Settings
End Of Field:
☑ Tab   ☑ Comma   End Of Line:
☐ Space   ☐ Other: [   ]   ☑ <CR>+<LF>   ☐ Semicolon
☐ Spaces   ☑ <CR>   ☐ Other: [   ]
                              ☑ <LF>

☑ Strip enclosing quotes   Two-digit year rule: [10-90 (default) ▾]
☑ Table contains column headers

Column Names are on line: [1]   Data starts on line: [2]

To import a text file using the preview option in JMP

1. Click **File→Open**.

2. Navigate to the location of your data.

3. Click the menu for **Files of type** and select **Text Import Preview (*.TXT;*.CSV;*.DAT)**.

4. Click the name of the file you want.

5. Click **Open**.

6. JMP displays one of two windows, depending on whether it detects that your data is delimited (column breaks with tabs, for example) or fixed width (no characters used for column breaks). Figure 3.6 shows the Text Import Preview window for delimited data, using a text file of the speeding ticket data as an example.

7. Change the information in the Text Import Preview window until the preview area displays the data as you want it to appear when imported.

Figure 3.6 Text Import Preview Window for Delimited Data

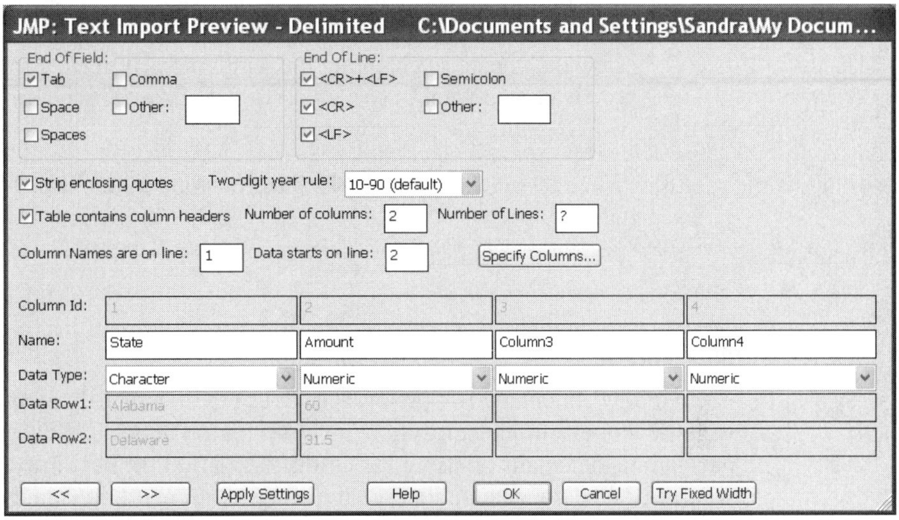

The preview area displays the **Column Id** and the first two rows of data. You cannot edit this information.

You can re-enter column names and use the menus to change the data types.

The preview area displays only a few columns. Use the **<<** and **>>** buttons to move left and right.

The top of the Text Import Preview window displays the same information as the window containing file preferences, plus some additional features. After you change any information in this part of the window, click the **Apply Settings** button to see the impact of your settings.

If your data has many columns and you want to import only a few of them, click the **Specify Columns** button. JMP displays a window in which you can select and deselect columns, specifying which columns you want to import.

If you cannot get the preview area to look like you want it to, click the **Try**

Fixed Width button. JMP displays a different preview window, with some of the same choices that are shown in the Text Import Preview window in Figure 3.6. A new choice is a **Field Width** column, in which you can enter values and view the impact of changing the width of each field. If these choices don't give you what you want to see, click the **Try Delimited** button, and continue working with the preview area.

8. When the preview area looks like you want it to, click **OK**. JMP opens the data table.

JMP Hints:

The window containing file preferences does not include help on the choices in the window. For electronic help, click the **Help** button in the File Open window, and navigate to the details on using the Understanding the Text Import Preview/Options window. In the documentation, see the section on importing data in the *JMP User Guide*.

Look back at Figure 3.4 and notice the choice for **Plain Text Files**. This might seem like a natural choice for importing text, but this opens a text file in an editing window. While you can edit the data and save it, you cannot perform any other data table or analysis platform tasks. This choice is not available in Linux.

Understanding Data Tables

Chapter 2 briefly introduced panels, disclosure diamonds, and hot spots in the data table. This section provides more detail using Figure 3.7, which shows the data table for the speeding ticket data.

Viewing Panels

JMP automatically displays the table, rows, and columns panels. Figure 3.7 shows the blue disclosure diamond. The diamond is a left-pointing triangle, indicating that the panels are revealed. When a disclosure diamond appears as a triangle, you are seeing everything that can be revealed in the table or report. When a disclosure diamond appears as a diamond, you can click it to reveal more details about the table or report.

In the data table, click the blue disclosure diamond to conceal the panels. The data table will change to look like a spreadsheet.

Figure 3.7 highlights two of the resizing borders. All double-line borders in the data table are resizing borders. Click and drag the border to change the size of the panel. If your data has a lot of columns, you will find it helpful to resize the columns panel so that you can see as many of the variable names as possible.

Columns Panel

Figure 3.7 shows the columns panel, which lists the columns in the data table. The terms "columns" and "variables" are interchangeable in this book.

The columns panel shows that the speeding ticket data has two columns, none of which is selected. The first number in parentheses in the columns panel heading identifies the number of columns in the data table. The second number identifies how many columns are selected.

Figure 3.7 highlights hot spots for the columns. The two columns hot spots include the same choices as the **Cols** menu. The hot spots simply provide another way to access these choices.

The columns panel lists each variable name, and displays the modeling type icon to the left of the variable name. See "Understanding Data Type and Modeling Type" for more discussion on modeling types.

Figure 3.7 Features of a Data Table

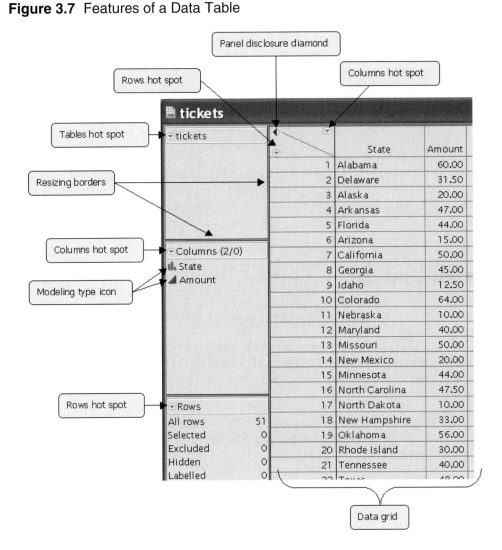

Rows Panel

Figure 3.7 shows the rows panel, which gives you information about the rows in the data table. The terms "rows," "observations," and "records" are interchangeable in this book.

Figure 3.7 highlights hot spots for the rows. The two rows hot spots include the same choices as the **Rows** menu. The hot spots simply provide another way to access these choices.

Figure 3.7 shows that the speeding ticket data has 51 rows, and that no rows are selected, excluded, hidden, or labeled.

Table Panel

Figure 3.7 highlights the table hot spot. For most data in this book, the table panel looks similar to what is shown in Figure 3.7—it shows the table name and a hot spot.

Figure 3.8 shows the choices from the table hot spot.

Figure 3.8 Table Hot Spot Choices

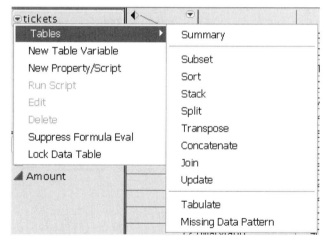

The hot spot includes the same choices as the **Tables** menu. See "Sorting a Data Table" for details on the **Sort** menu choice. Chapter 6 gives a brief example of the **Subset** menu choice. Chapter 8 gives a brief example of the **Split** menu choice. Chapter 12 gives a brief introduction to the **Summary** menu choice in the "Special Topic: Statistical Summary Tables" section at the end of the chapter. See the JMP Help or documentation for other **Tables** menu choices.

Adding Notes to Data Tables

New Table Variable is a helpful way to add notes about the data table. For the speeding ticket data in JMP:

1. Click the hot spot in the table panel.

2. Click **New Table Variable**.

3. Enter **Notes** in the field for **Name**.

4. Enter text in the **Value** field. See Figure 3.9 for an example.

5. Click **OK**.

The data table now shows the **Notes** variable and the start of the value (the text you entered). See Figure 3.10 for an example.

Figure 3.9 Adding Notes about a Data Table

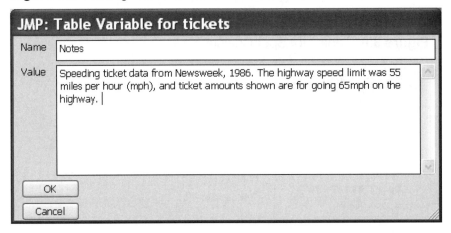

Figure 3.10 Data Table after Adding Notes

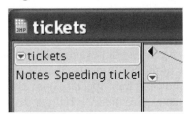

To see all of the text you entered, click on the text. JMP displays a pop-up window that shows all of the text. To edit the text, click in the pop-up window and enter your changes. To close the pop-up window, click outside of it.

Why is this useful? When working with data, you might create data tables with very similar names—tickets1, tickets2, and so on. After a short time, you might have a separate notebook with information on the data tables, or you might forget the distinction between the data tables. Table notes remind you of the details for each data table, and help create self-documenting data tables.

Additional Table Panel Choices

The **Run Script** menu choice cannot be selected in Figure 3.8 because there are no saved scripts for the data table. Although we don't actually save a script in this book, we do use the Sample Data Directory. Some of the sample data tables have saved scripts, or canned analyses, that are associated with them and can be rerun. The names of these scripts appear in the table panel.

The **Lock Data Table** menu choice prevents you from editing data values by mistake. Locked data tables have a padlock icon next to the table name in the table panel. When a data table is locked, you cannot edit the values in the table, add new rows or columns, or change the formatting of any column. But, you can change the modeling type of variables and run analyses. To unlock the data table, select **Lock Data Table** again, and the padlock icon disappears.

This book does not discuss the other choices in the table hot spot. See the JMP Help or documentation for details.

Working with Columns

This section describes several JMP features for working with columns. Read the first two topics, and then read other topics if they interest you. If your data table has only a few columns, the remaining topics might be less applicable.

Resizing Columns

To resize a column, position your mouse pointer on the column's right border. You can do this anywhere—in the column heading or on any row of the data table. The mouse pointer changes to a double-headed arrow. Click and drag to resize the column.

Selecting and Deselecting Columns

The following list summarizes the activities for selecting and deselecting columns. This list uses Windows choices (for example, holding down the CTRL key and clicking). When selecting or deselecting, you can click the column name in the columns panel or in the column heading.

Select a single column	Click the column name.
Deselect a single column	Hold down the CTRL key and click the column name.
Select or deselect multiple non-contiguous columns	Hold down the CTRL key and click the column names.
Select a range of columns	Click the first column name, hold down the SHIFT key, and click the column name at the end of the range. Or, click and drag to select all columns in the range.
Select all columns	Hold down the SHIFT key and click in the blank area near the columns hot spot in the upper-left corner of the data table (as shown in the window after this list).
Deselect all columns	Click in a blank area of the columns panel. Or, click in a blank area near the columns hot spot in the upper-left corner of the data table.

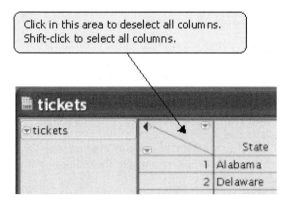

Many of the choices in the **Cols** menu are not available until you have selected a column in the data table.

Using Scroll Lock

When you scroll to the right in data tables with many columns, you lose sight of the identifying information that is typically in the first few columns. Scroll locking keeps the columns that you choose visible at all times. The easiest way to see this feature is with an example. In JMP:

1. Click **Help→Sample Data Directory**.

2. Click the disclosure diamond for **Exploratory Modeling**.

3. Click the **Cars 1993.jmp** link and JMP opens the data table.

4. Scroll to the right in the data table. The **Manufacturer**, **Model**, and **Vehicle Category** columns have been set as scroll lock columns, so they are always visible. (Leave the data table open for the next two topics.)

Scroll lock columns are italic in the columns panel. When you set a column as a scroll lock column, JMP moves it to the left of the data grid (and to the top of the columns panel).

To scroll lock a column, select the column in the columns panel. Right-click and select **Scroll Lock/Unlock**. To unlock a scroll lock column, select **Scroll Lock/Unlock** again.

Moving Columns

When your data has many columns, you often want to move columns around. This is especially true when you import data from elsewhere. JMP provides multiple ways to move columns. The easiest way is to use the columns panel. Using the Cars 1993 data table as an example:

1. Click the **City Mileage (MPG)** column in the columns panel.

2. Drag the column to just after the **Model** column. As you drag the column, JMP displays a thick black line that shows you where the column will be moved, as shown in the following display.

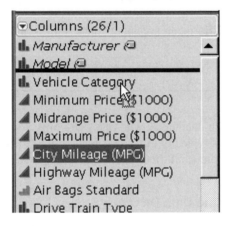

3. The **Vehicle Category** column is no longer a scroll lock column. When you move a column between two scroll lock columns, JMP unlocks the second scroll lock column.

4. Repeat steps 1 through 3 for **Highway Mileage (MPG)**, moving it just above **Vehicle Category**, as shown in the following display:

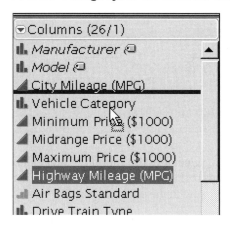

JMP Hints:

Click to select multiple contiguous columns in the columns panel. Then, you can drag all the columns to a new location.

Hold down the CTRL key and click to select separate columns in the columns panel. Then, you can drag all the columns to a new location.

If you move columns by mistake, click **Edit→Undo Move Columns** immediately. JMP remembers the move for one step backward. If you move columns and then do another action, you might not be able to undo the move.

Hiding Columns

When your data has many columns, you might have too many to view, even after moving them around. Hiding columns can be useful. The column names still appear in the columns panel, but they are hidden in the data grid. Using the Cars 1993 data table as an example:

1. Right-click the **Length (inches)** column in the columns panel.

2. Select **Hide/Unhide**. JMP displays a mask to the right of the column name in the columns panel. As you scroll to the right through the data table, you see that the column does not display, as shown in the following window.

⊞ Cars 1993						
▾Cars 1993	◀ 25/0 Cols ▾			Passenger	Wheel Base	
Note Robin H. Lock, "1993 New (	▾	Manufacturer	Model	Capacity	(inches)	(i
▾Distribution	1	Acura	Integra	5	102	
▾Overlay Plot	2	Acura	Legend	5	115	
	3	Audi	90	5	102	
▾Columns (26/0)	4	Audi	100	6	106	
◢ Fuel Tank Capacity	5	BMW	535i	4	109	
◢ Passenger Capacity	6	Buick	Century	6	105	
◢ Length (inches) ⚷	7	Buick	LeSabre	6	111	
◢ Wheel Base (inches)						

3. To unhide a column, select it in the columns panel and right-click and select **Hide/Unhide** again. JMP redisplays the column and removes the mask to the right of the column name in the columns panel.

4. Click **File→Close** to close the Cars 1993 data table. Click **No** in the Caution Alert window to close the data table without saving.

JMP lists hidden columns in windows for analyses and graphs. This reminds you that these columns exist.

JMP provides an **Exclude/Unexclude** menu choice. When you exclude a column, JMP continues to display it in the data grid, but excludes it in windows for analyses and graphs. JMP adds a Do Not Enter icon to the right of the column name in the columns panel, as shown in the following display:

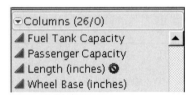

Hiding columns can be more useful than excluding columns in large data tables because columns still appear in windows, but are hidden in the data grid.

Avoid using both the **Hide/Unhide** and **Exclude/Unexclude** menu choices. Why? If you use both menu choices, then JMP hides the column in the data grid and in the dialog windows. JMP lists the column in the columns panel. But, in a data table with many columns, it's possible to forget that this column exists.

Viewing Column Information

JMP stores information about each variable and displays it in a column information window. You worked with this window when you created the tickets data table. To see column information for a variable in JMP:

1. Right-click on the column in the columns panel.

2. Select **Column Info**. JMP displays information about the column.

3. Click **OK** to close the window.

Figure 3.1 shows the column information window for **State** when it was a new column. Figure 3.11 shows the same window after the data table is created.

Figure 3.11 Column Information Window for State

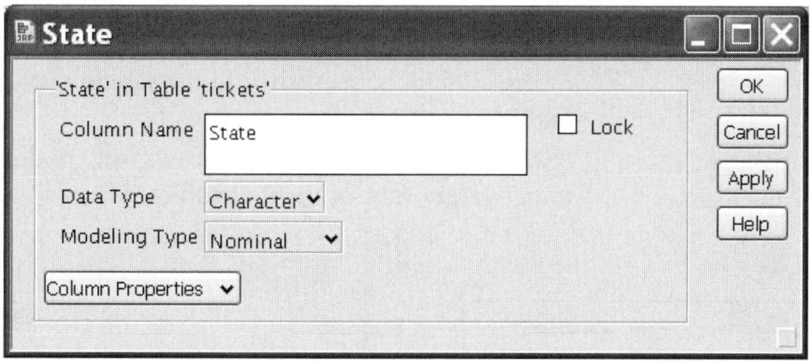

Working with Rows

This section describes how to select rows and how to move rows in a data table.

Selecting and Deselecting Rows

The following list summarizes the activities for selecting and deselecting rows. This list uses Windows choices (for example, holding down the CTRL key and clicking). When selecting or deselecting, you can click in the row number area. Clicking in a cell selects only that cell, not the entire row.

Select a single row	Click in the row number area.
Deselect a single row	Hold down the CTRL key and click the row number.
Select or deselect multiple non-contiguous rows	Hold down the CTRL key and click the row numbers.
Select a range of rows	Click the first row number, hold down the SHIFT key, and click the row number at the end of the range. Or, click and drag to select all rows in the range.
Select all rows	Hold down the SHIFT key and click in the blank area near the rows hot spot in the upper-left corner of the data table (as shown in the window after this list).
Deselect all rows	Click in a blank area near the rows hot spot in the upper-left corner of the data table.

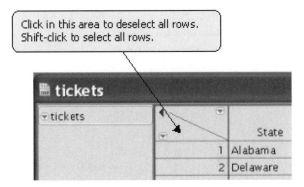

When you want to select rows, make sure that you do not have a column selected. If you have a column selected, JMP assumes that you want to select only the row-and-column combination (for example, a single cell), not all the variables for the rows.

Many of the choices in the **Rows** menu are not available until you have selected a row in the data table.

Moving Rows

If your data is not ordered the way you want, sorting is the best solution most of the time. See "Sorting a Data Table" for more information. Sometimes, you want to move specific rows to a specific location. In JMP:

1. Open the tickets data table.

2. Hold down the CTRL key and click to select the rows for **Alaska** and **Hawaii**. These might be your two favorite vacation states. They are the two states that are not part of the contiguous 48 states. Suppose you want to move these rows to the beginning of the data table. Sorting won't do this.

3. Click **Rows→Move Rows**.

4. Click **At start** in the Move Rows window. See Figure 3.12 to view other menu choices. If you click **After row**, JMP adds a field in which you can enter the row number.

5. Click **OK**.

JMP moves Alaska and Hawaii to the start of the data table.

Figure 3.12 Move Rows Window

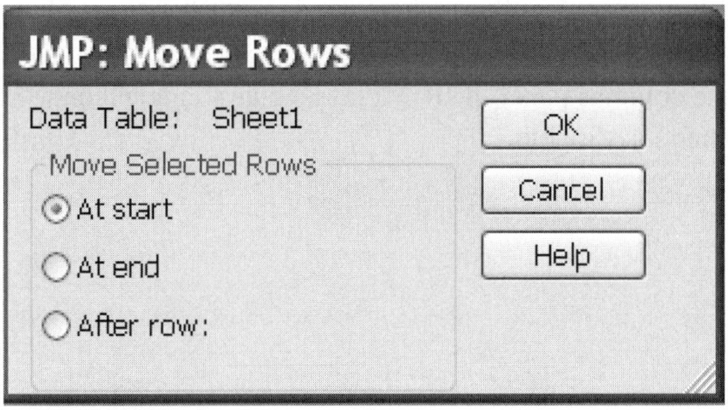

Understanding Data Type and Modeling Type

JMP classifies variables as either numeric or character, depending on their data type. Numeric variables can contain only numbers. Character variables can contain text, numbers, or both numbers and text.

JMP assigns a modeling type to each variable. Analysis platforms use the modeling type to make decisions about how to analyze the data. JMP provides three modeling types:

Nominal   Values of the variable provide names. These values have no implied order. Values can be character (Male, Female) or numeric (1, 2). If the value is numeric, then an interim value does not make sense. If gender is coded as 1 and 2, then a value of 1.5 does not make sense.

                 When you use numbers as values of a nominal variable, the numbers have no meaning, other than to provide names.

                 In the columns panel, JMP displays a red bar chart icon to the left of a nominal variable.

Ordinal   Values of the variable provide names and also have an implied order. Examples include High-Medium-Low, Hot-Warm-Cool-Cold, and opinion scales (Strongly Disagree to Strongly Agree). Values can be character or numeric. The distance between values is not important, but their order is. High-Medium-Low could be coded as 1-2-3 or 10-20-30, with the same result.

                 JMP uses numeric values to order numeric ordinal variables. JMP orders character ordinal variables according to their sorting sequence.

                 In the columns panel, JMP displays a green bar chart icon to the left of an ordinal variable.

Continuous   Values contain numbers, where the distance between values is important.

                 In the columns panel, JMP displays a blue triangle icon to the left of a continuous variable.

Figure 3.13 displays the icons for modeling types, using variables from the Cars 1993 data table. **Drive Train Type** is nominal, **Number of Cylinders** is ordinal, and **Engine Size (liters)** is continuous.

Figure 3.13 Icons for JMP Modeling Types

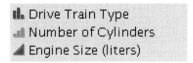

JMP allows character variables to be nominal or ordinal. Numeric variables can be any modeling type. For the graphs and analyses in this book, JMP treats nominal and ordinal variables the same way.

At first, you might think that numeric variables should always be continuous. However, think about age. If you want the average age, then you want the age variable to be continuous. If you want to create a table that classifies gender by age, then you want the age variable to be nominal or ordinal.

JMP automatically assigns a nominal modeling type to character variables, and a continuous modeling type to numeric variables. To change the modeling type, click the icon next to the variable. The current modeling type has a check mark next to it. Simply select a different modeling type. If a modeling type is gray, then you cannot select it. For example, **Continuous** cannot be selected for **Vehicle Category** in Figure 3.14.

Figure 3.14 Continuous Not Available for Character Variable

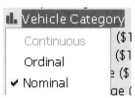

Technical Details: Interval and Ratio

Many statistical texts refer to interval and ratio variables. Here's a brief explanation.

Interval variables are numeric and have an inherent order. Differences between values are important. Think about temperature in degrees Fahrenheit (F). A temperature of 120°F is 20° warmer than 100°F. Similarly, a temperature of 170°F is 20° warmer than 150°F. Contrast this with an ordinal variable, where the numeric difference between values is not meaningful. For an ordinal variable, the difference between 2 and 1 does not necessarily have the same meaning as the difference between 3 and 2.

Ratio variables are numeric and have an inherent order. Differences between values are important and the value of 0 is meaningful. For example, the weight of gold is a ratio variable. The number of calories in a meal is a ratio variable. A meal with 2,000 calories has twice as many calories as a meal with 1,000 calories. Contrast this with temperature: it does not make sense to say that a temperature of 100°F is twice as hot as 50°F, because 0° on a Fahrenheit scale is just an arbitrary reference point.

JMP does not consider interval and ratio variables separately. Instead, JMP treats all continuous variables the same way in analyses. From a practical view, this makes sense. You would perform the same analyses on interval or ratio variables. The difference is how you would summarize the results in a written report. For an interval variable, it does not make sense to say that the average for one group is twice as large as the average for another group. For a ratio variable, it does.

Ordering Values

JMP automatically orders values in reports. JMP orders numeric variables from low to high, with low values appearing on the bottom or on the left, depending on the report or graph. JMP orders character values in alphabetical order, with values closer to the start of the alphabet appearing on the bottom or on the left, depending on the report or graph.

This automatic ordering might not meet your needs. Think about a variable with the values "excellent," "good," "fair," and "poor." Alphabetic ordering displays "fair" before "good," and is not as useful as the ordered values. JMP provides *value orders*, which assign an order to the values of a variable. JMP uses this order in reports and graphs.

JMP also provides *automatic value orders* for some commonly used values. JMP documentation lists some of these automatic value orders, including days of the week, months of the year, and opinion scales.

To assign value orders in JMP:

1. Open the tickets data table.

2. Double-click on the **State** column in the data table. JMP displays the State column information window.

3. Click **Column Properties→Value Ordering**.

4. JMP displays the values for the variable. Figure 3.15 displays the values for **State**.

5. To rearrange values, select a value. Then, click **Move Up** or **Move Down** repeatedly to move the value. After each click, JMP moves the value one position up or down.

6. To add a value, enter it in the blank field and click **Add**. The value will appear in the list, and you can move it to where you want it. This feature is useful when you know the full set of possible values, but don't yet have all of the data.

7. Click **OK**. JMP adds a heavy asterisk (✱) to the right of the variable name in the columns panel. The asterisk icon signifies that you have applied a special property to the variable.

Figure 3.15 Assigning Value Orders for a Column

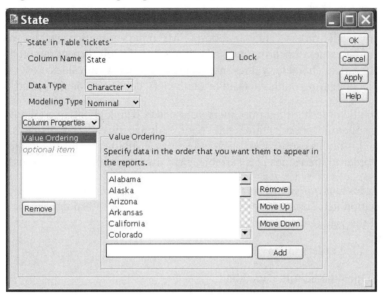

Figure 3.15 shows two **Remove** buttons. To remove your value order and use JMP's automatic value order, click the **Remove** button under **Column Properties**. To use the **Remove** button in the **Value Ordering** section, select a value, and click **Remove**. Caution: This removes the selected value from the list, but JMP still uses the value in graphs and reports.

Before you assign value orders for your data, read Chapter 4 and use **Distribution** to explore your variables. JMP might have automatic value orders that meet your needs. Also, sometimes JMP displays values in one order in the column information window, and in a slightly different order in **Distribution**. Figure 3.16 gives an example. The figure displays the first four rows of the data table, which give the complete set of values for **Q1 answer**. The column information window shows the automatic value order. However, the Distribution window shows the values as JMP actually orders them in reports and graphs. (Chapter 2 introduced **Distribution**, and Chapter 4 discusses it in detail.)

Figure 3.16 Example of Value Order

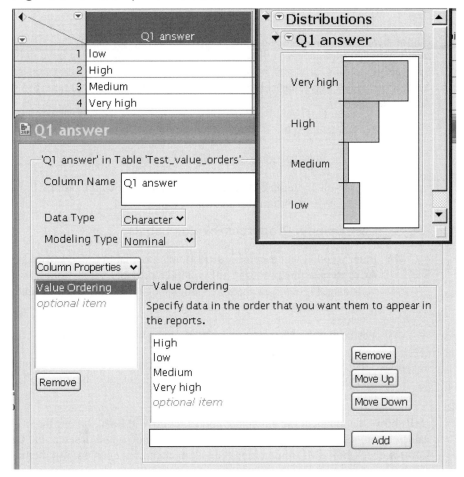

Chapter 5 discusses another way of assigning value orders when your data is sorted the way you want it. See "Creating Custom Bar Charts Using the Chart Platform" for an example of using row order levels in JMP.

Adding Value Labels

Suppose your data is coded, and you want to see the decoded values. JMP provides *value labels*, which assign labels to the codes. For example, suppose you have only the two-letter abbreviations for states, instead of the full names. The tickets_code sample data for this book uses two-letter abbreviations for state names, and contains the speeding ticket fine amounts.

To add value labels in JMP:

1. Open the tickets_code data table.

2. Double-click on the **State Code** column in the data table. JMP displays the State Code column information window.

3. Click **Column Properties→Value Labels**.

4. Enter a coded value in the **Value** field, and a label in the **Label** field. Click **Add**. Repeat this process until you have provided labels for all the values in your data. Figure 3.17 shows a value label added for Alabama, and a value label for Delaware ready to add.

5. Verify that the **Use Value Labels** check box is selected.

6. Click **OK**. JMP adds a heavy asterisk (✻) to the right of the variable name in the columns panel. The asterisk icon signifies that you have applied a special property to the variable.

JMP shows the labels in the data table and in report windows. To use the original coded values again, navigate to the column information window and deselect the **Use Value Labels** check box. JMP remembers the value labels, but does not use them.

If you need to change a value label, select it in the **Value Labels** section. The value and label appear in the two fields beneath this section. Update the label, and click **Change**. The updated label appears in the **Value Labels** section.

Instead of removing labels, select or deselect the check box for **Use Value Labels**. Although you can remove labels from the data table, this wastes the time and effort that you spent adding the labels. However, if you want to delete the labels from your data table, in the column information window, select **Value Labels** in the **Column Properties** section, and click **Remove** beneath the section.

Figure 3.17 Adding Value Labels for a Column

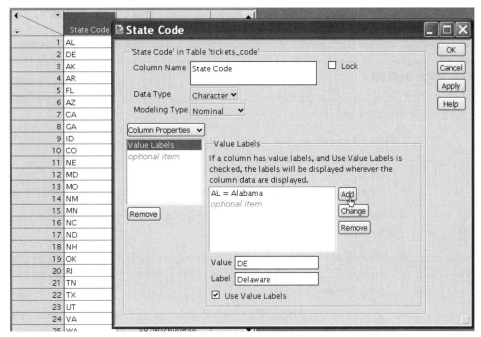

Printing a Data Table

To print the data table, click **File→Print**. JMP displays the Print window, in which you select the printer and options.

Printing Only Some of the Data

Sometimes you want to print only some of the data. JMP prints the data you select. If you don't have any rows or columns selected, JMP automatically prints the entire data table when you click **File→Print**.

To print only some of the columns, select the columns, and click **File→Print**. As needed, select the printer and number of copies in the Print window, and click **OK**.

To print only some of the rows, select the rows, and click **File→Print**.

To print only specific cells, select the cells, and click **File→Print**.

Print Preview

JMP provides a print preview choice in Windows. This choice is not available on the Macintosh or in Linux.

Click **File→Print Preview**. JMP displays a preview window with the data table's name as its title. Your choices are:

- **Print**—displays the Print window, in which you select the printer and options.

- **Next Page** and **Prev Page**—if your data will print on multiple pages. Click these choices to view other pages.

- **Two Page**—if your data will print on multiple pages. Click this choice to see two pages at once. The button will then change to **One Page**; click it to see only one page again.

- **Zoom In** and **Zoom Out**—magnifies the data. At first, **Zoom Out** will be unavailable because JMP shows the data at the maximum zoom out. After you zoom in as much as possible, **Zoom In** will be unavailable.

- **Close**—closes the preview window.

When you preview, you cannot see both the data table and the preview window. This is also true when printing results from analysis—you see either the analysis window or the preview window.

Printing to a Microsoft Word Table

Sometimes you want to list the data in a Microsoft Word table. Printing to Microsoft Word from JMP is a two-step process. First, save the data in a text file. Second, import the text file to Microsoft Word and convert it to a table. Using the tickets data as an example:

1. Open the tickets data table.

2. Click **File→Save As**.

3. Select **Text Export Files (*.TXT)** in **Save as type**.

4. Click **Options**.

5. Select **Tab** as **End Of Field**, **<CR>+<LF>** as **End Of Line**, and **Yes** for **Export Column Names to Text File**. See Figure 3.18.

6. Click **OK**.

7. Either accept the automatic JMP filename, or enter your own. Click **Save**.

8. Click **Yes** in the Caution Alert window, in which JMP tells you that formulas and some formatting might be lost.

9. In Microsoft Word, open the text file. You might need to decrease the font size or change the formatting to landscape to see all of the columns. Click **Edit→Select All**.

10. Click **Table→Convert→Text to Table**. Make sure that **Tabs** are identified as the column separator, and confirm the number of columns for your data. Click **OK**.

As different versions of Microsoft Word are released, the exact steps can change.

Figure 3.18 Exporting a JMP Data Table to a Text File

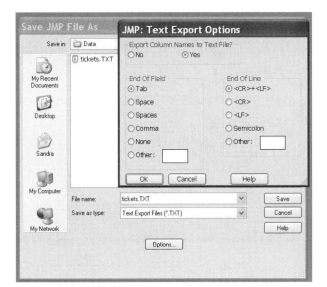

Sorting a Data Table

JMP automatically prints the data as it appears in the data table. Suppose you want to print the data in a sorted order. To sort the tickets data by state in JMP:

1. Open the tickets data table.

2. Click **Tables→Sort**.

3. Click **State→By**.

4. Enter a name for the output data table.

5. Click **OK**.

Figure 3.19 shows the Sort window. The triangle to the left of **State** indicates that the variable will be sorted minimum to maximum (A to Z in this case), or in ascending order. To change to descending order, select the variable in the **By** section and click the maximum to minimum triangle beneath the list of **By** variables.

Figure 3.19 Sort Window

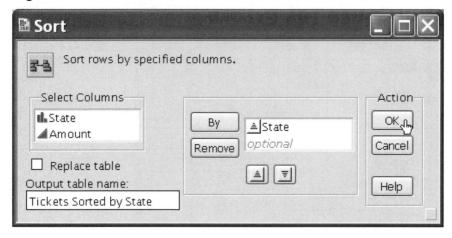

JMP Hints:

Always provide a name for the output data table. If you don't, JMP automatically provides names using Untitled 1, then Untitled 2, and so on. Descriptive names are more useful.

Use caution with the Replace table check box. This feature overwrites your existing data table. It is safer to create a new data table, and then you will have both versions.

You can select more than one **By** variable. Select the variables in the order you want JMP to use. For example, select **State**, then **County** for a data table that contains per-county sales tax information for every state.

Figure 3.20 shows the first few rows of the sorted data table.

Figure 3.20 Data Table Sorted by State

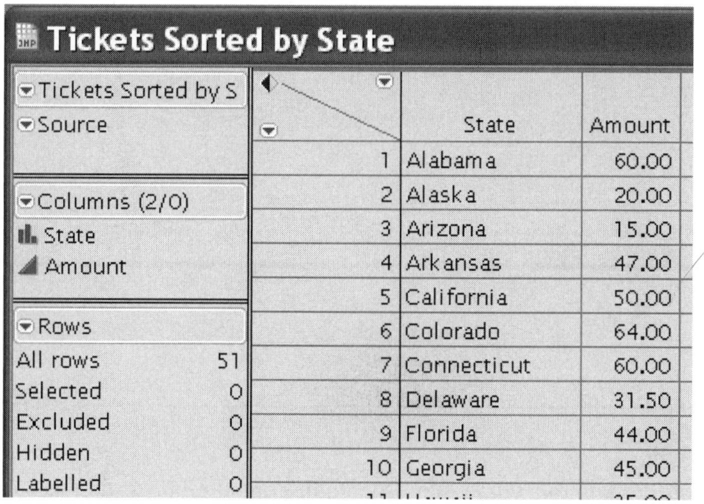

You can sort the data table by the amount of the speeding ticket fine. Figure 3.21 shows the results of sorting by **Amount** in descending order.

Figure 3.21 Data Table Sorted by Descending Amount

Tickets Sorted by Amount			
▼Tickets Sorted by A ▼Source		State	Amount
	1	Ohio	100.00
▼Columns (2/0)	2	Pennsylvania	72.50
Il. State	3	Kentucky	65.00
◢ Amount	4	Colorado	64.00
	5	Alabama	60.00
▼Rows	6	Connecticut	60.00
All rows 51	7	West Virginia	60.00
Selected 0	8	Oklahoma	56.00
Excluded 0	9	California	50.00
Hidden 0	10	Missouri	50.00
Labelled 0			

Summary

Key Ideas

- JMP stores data in a data table. Data tables are similar to spreadsheets, but have additional features that are unique to JMP.

- You can create JMP data tables by entering your data. JMP can import data in many formats. Importing from Microsoft Excel takes only a few clicks. For importing text files, you can use JMP's automatic choices, apply your file preferences, or use the preview option.

- Data tables include table, rows, and columns panels. These panels display the name of the data table, the number of rows (observations), and the number of columns (variables). JMP features include hot spots (that provide quick access to menu choices), the ability to resize borders, and disclosure diamonds (that show or hide detail).

- JMP uses the modeling type to identify nominal, ordinal, and continuous variables. Numeric variables can be any modeling type. Character variables can be nominal or ordinal.

- Add notes to your data tables to store details about the data with the data table.

- You can select single columns, a range of columns, or multiple non-contiguous columns. Click the column name in the column heading or in the columns panel. Similarly, select rows by clicking the row number in the row number area of the data grid.

- When your data table has many columns, helpful JMP features include:

  □ scroll lock, to keep selected columns visible at all times

  □ moving columns, to place the columns where you want

  □ hiding columns, to keep columns visible in the columns panel, but to hide them in the data grid

  □ viewing column information, to display details

- When data is not ordered as you want, sorting is the best solution most of the time. You can sort using multiple variables. You can sort each variable in either ascending or descending order. When you want to place specific rows in a specific location, you can move rows.

- JMP automatically orders values in reports and graphs. Numeric variables are ordered from low to high. Character variables are ordered alphabetically. With a value order, you can change the automatic order to meet your needs.

- When your data is coded, you can use value labels to see decoded values.

- Printing JMP data tables is similar to printing in other software. In Windows, you can preview the printed data table. With a two-step process, you can save a data table that you can import as a table in Microsoft Word.

JMP Steps

To create a JMP data table:

1. Click **File→New**. In the JMP Starter window, you can click **File→New Data Table**.

2. JMP displays a new data table with one column and no rows in a window named Untitled.

3. Double-click on the **Column 1** heading. Enter the column name in the **Column Name** field. If necessary, click the menu for **Data Type** and change it to **Character**. JMP changes the **Modeling Type** to **Nominal**. If necessary, change the format for numeric variables.

4. If you know in advance how many rows are in your data, enter the number in the **N Rows** field. Click **OK**.

5. Repeat step 3 as needed for the rest of the columns in your data.

6. You are ready to enter data. Position your mouse pointer in the first row of the first column and enter data. Enter the values for the first column in the first row. Click **Tab** to enter the remaining columns. Continue to click **Tab** through the rows and columns until you have entered all data.

7. Click **File→Save**. In the Save JMP File As window, navigate to the location where you want to save the data, enter a name, and click **Save**.

To open a JMP data table:

1. Click **File→Open**. In the JMP Starter window, you can click **File→Open Data Table**.

2. Navigate to the location of your data and click the data table.

3. Click **Open**.

To open Microsoft Excel spreadsheets:

1. Click **File→Open**.

2. Navigate to the location of your data.

3. Click the menu for **Files of type** and select **Excel Files (*.XLS)**.

4. Click the name of the Microsoft Excel file you want.

5. If your Microsoft Excel file has column labels on the first line, select the check box for **Excel table has labels in row 1**.

6. If your Microsoft Excel file has multiple worksheets and you want to select specific worksheets, select the check box for **Allow individual worksheet selection**. (JMP automatically opens all worksheets, so you might want to do this.) When you select this check box, JMP displays the Select sheets to import window. Select the check boxes for the worksheets you want to import and click **OK**.

7. If your Microsoft Excel file has a single worksheet, or if you want to open all worksheets in a Microsoft Excel file that has multiple worksheets, click **Open**.

To import text files with JMP's automatic choices:

1. Click **File→Open**.

2. Navigate to the location of your data.

3. Click the menu for **Files of type** and select **Text Import Files (*.TXT,*.CSV,*.DAT)**.

4. Click the name of the file you want.

5. Click the button for **Attempt to Discern Format**.

6. Click **Open**. If JMP can identify column and row breaks, it opens the file.

To import text files using your file preferences:

1. Click **File→Preferences**.

2. Click the icon for **Text Data Files**. Adjust the settings as needed for your text file. You can adjust **End Of Field, End Of Line, Strip enclosing quotes, Two-digit year rule, Table contains column headers**, and more. Click **OK**.

3. Click **File→Open**.

4. Navigate to the location of your data.

5. Click the menu for **Files of type** and select **Text Import Files (*.TXT,*.CSV,*.DAT)**.

6. Click the name of the file you want.

7. Click the button for **Use Text Import Preferences**.

8. Click **Open**. If JMP can read the data using the JMP import settings, it opens the file.

To import text files using JMP's preview option:

1. Click **File→Open**.

2. Navigate to the location of your data.

3. Click the menu for **Files of type** and select **Text Import Preview (*.TXT,*.CSV,*.DAT)**.

4. Click the name of the file you want.

5. Click **Open**.

6. JMP displays one of two windows, depending on whether it detects that your data is delimited (column breaks with tabs, for example) or fixed width (no characters used for column breaks). Change the information in the Text Import Preview window until the preview area displays the data as you want it to appear when imported. When the preview area looks like you want it to, click **OK**. JMP opens the data table.

To resize, show, and hide panels in the data table:

1. To resize panels in the data table, click and drag any double-line border.

2. To hide panels in the data table, click the blue disclosure diamond.

3. For data tables that look like a spreadsheet, click the blue disclosure diamond to reveal the panels.

To add notes to a data table:

1. Click the hot spot in the table panel.

2. Click **New Table Variable**.

3. Enter **Notes** in the field for **Name**.

4. Enter text in the **Value** field.

5. Click **OK**.

To scroll lock a column:

1. Right-click the column in the columns panel.

2. Select **Scroll Lock/Unlock**.

To move a column:

1. Select the column in the columns panel.

2. Drag the column to the new location.

To hide a column:

1. Right-click the column in the columns panel.

2. Select **Hide/Unhide**.

To view column information:

1. Right-click the column in the columns panel.

2. Select **Column Info**. JMP displays information about the column.

3. Click **OK** to close the window.

To move rows:

1. Click to select the rows you want to move.

2. Click **Rows→Move Rows**.

3. Select **At start** in the Move Rows window to move the rows to the beginning of the data table. Select **At end** to move the rows to the end. If you click **After row**, JMP adds a field in which you can enter the row number.

4. Click **OK**.

To assign value orders:

1. Double-click on the column name in the data table. JMP displays the column information window.

2. Click **Column Properties→Value Ordering**.

3. JMP displays the values for the variable. To rearrange values, select a value. Then, click **Move Up** or **Move Down** repeatedly to move the value. After each click, JMP moves the value one position up or down.

4. To add a value, enter it in the blank field and click **Add**. The value will appear in the list, and you can move it to where you want it. This feature is useful when you know the full set of possible values, but don't yet have all of the data.

5. Click **OK**. JMP adds a heavy asterisk (✱) to the right of the variable name in the columns panel. The asterisk icon signifies that you have applied a special property to the variable.

To add value labels:

1. Double-click on the coded column name in the data table. JMP displays the column information window.

2. Click **Column Properties→Value Labels**.

3. Enter a coded value in the **Value** field, and a label in the **Label** field. Click **Add**. Repeat this process until you have provided labels for all the values in your data.

4. Verify that the **Use Value Labels** check box is selected.

5. Click **OK**. JMP adds a heavy asterisk (✱) to the right of the variable name in the columns panel. The asterisk icon signifies that you have applied a special property to the variable.

To print a data table:

1. Select rows and columns to print. To print the entire data table, do not select individual rows or columns.

2. Select **File→Print**. JMP displays the Print window, in which you select the printer and options.

3. In Windows, select **File→Print Preview** to preview results before printing.

To print data to a Microsoft Word table:

1. Click **File→Save As**.

2. Select **Text Export Files (*.TXT)** in **Save as type**.

3. Click **Options**.

4. Select **Tab** as **End Of Field**, **<CR>+<LF>** as **End Of Line**, and **Yes** for **Export Column Names to Text File**. Click **OK**.

5. Either accept the automatic JMP filename, or enter your own. Click **Save**.

6. Click **Yes** in the Caution Alert window, in which JMP tells you that formulas and some formatting might be lost.

7. In Microsoft Word, open the text file. You might need to decrease the font size or change the formatting to landscape to see all the columns. Click **Edit→Select All**.

8. Click **Table→Convert→Text to Table**. Make sure that **Tabs** are identified as the column separator, and confirm the number of columns for your data. Click **OK**.

To sort a data table:

1. Click **Tables→Sort**.

2. Click the first sort variable and then **By**. If necessary, click the triangle to change from ascending order to descending order.

3. Repeat step 2 for additional sort variables.

4. Enter a name for the output data table.

5. Click **OK**.

Exercises

1. The sample data for this book includes the speeding ticket data in a Microsoft Excel spreadsheet. Use the information in this chapter to open the spreadsheet in JMP. Confirm that the data table has 51 rows and 2 columns.

2. The sample data for this book includes the speeding ticket data in a text file. Use the information in this chapter to import the text file to JMP. Confirm the correct number of rows and columns. Use the column information window and change the format of the **Amount** column to **Fixed Dec** with **2** decimal places.

3. Open the Cars 1993 data table. Sort the data table in descending order by **Maximum Price**. Print the data table, but print only the three scroll lock columns, **Maximum Price**, and **Highway Mileage**.

4. Click **Help→Sample Data Directory** and click the disclosure diamond for **Medical Studies**. Click the link for **Diet.jmp** and open the data table. Confirm that the data table has 500 rows and 2 columns. Click to view the table notes. Observe how JMP displays missing values for the numeric variable.

5. JMP provides sample import data. For Windows, it is installed in the directory: C:\Program Files\SAS\JMP6\Support Files English\Sample Import Data. Navigate to this directory on your PC. In JMP, open the **Bigclass.xls** spreadsheet. Confirm that the data table has 40 rows and 5 columns.

6. Create a data table using your own data and explore the ideas in this chapter.

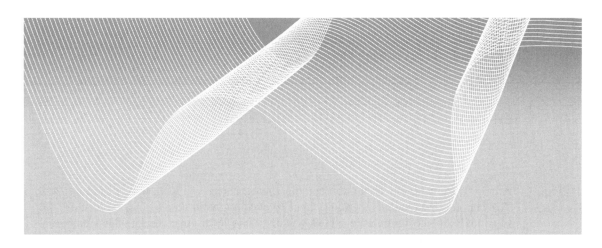

Chapter **4**

Summarizing Data

After you know how to create a data table, the next step is to learn how to summarize it. This chapter first explains the importance of checking your data for errors. You use the same JMP tools to summarize data as you do to check for errors in data. Depending on the modeling type, JMP summarizes a variable with:

- descriptive statistics, such as the average

- frequencies or counts of values for a variable

- graphs that are appropriate for the modeling type

JMP provides a basic summary for variables and several options for enhancing the summary.

The chapter explains many JMP features and enhancements that you can use in other JMP platforms. Working with results, the chapter shows how to interact with JMP graphs and reports. The interactivity of JMP might be its most valuable feature in summarizing data.

Checking Data for Errors

As you summarize your data, you can also check it for errors.

For small data tables, you can print the data table and compare it with the original data source.

This process is difficult for larger data tables, where it's easier to miss errors when checking manually. Here are some other ways to check:

- For continuous variables, look at the maximum and minimum values. Are there any values that seem odd or wrong? For example, you don't expect to see a value of 150° for a person's temperature.

- For nominal and ordinal variables, are there duplicate values that are misspellings? For example, do you have both "test" and "gest" as values for a variable? Do you have both "TRue" and "True" as values for a variable?

- For nominal and ordinal variables, are there too many values? If you have coded answers to an opinion poll with numbers 1 through 5, all of your values should be either 1, 2, 3, 4, or 5. If you have a 6, you know it's an error.

For each of the JMP tools, this chapter discusses how to use the tool to check data for errors.

Using Distribution for a Continuous Variable

In JMP, **Distribution** provides reports and graphs for variables. Before starting a detailed analysis of any data table, use **Distribution** to explore your data and check it for errors.

Distribution shows different results depending on whether a variable is continuous, nominal, or ordinal. For the speeding ticket data, the following steps summarize the speeding ticket fine amounts. In JMP:

1. Open the tickets data table discussed in Chapter 3.

2. In the JMP Starter window, click **Basic→Distribution**. Figure 4.1 shows the JMP Starter window with the **Basic** category selected.

When you first open JMP, the **File** category is selected in the JMP Starter window. If you open JMP and the JMP Starter window does not display, click **View→JMP Starter**.

Figure 4.1 JMP Starter Window with Basic Selected

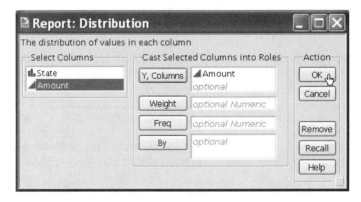

Continuing in JMP:

3. Click **Amount→Y, Columns**. Compare your window with the following window.

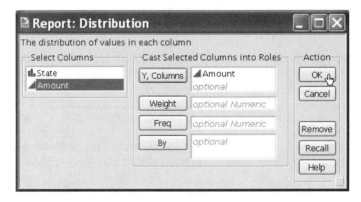

4. Click **OK**. Figure 4.2 shows the results.

Figure 4.2 Distribution Results for a Continuous Variable

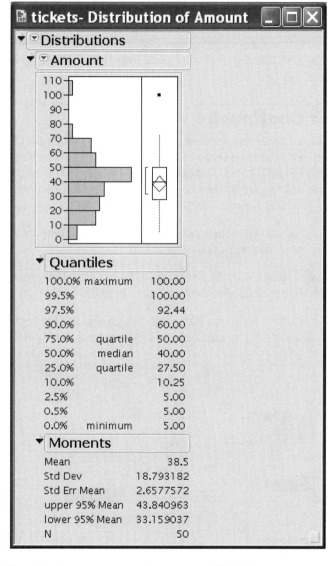

JMP identifies the data table name (in this case, tickets) in the title of the Distribution window. When you select only one variable, JMP also identifies the variable (in this case, **Amount**) in the title of the Distribution window.

JMP uses disclosure diamonds in reports. As in the data table, clicking the disclosure diamond shows or hides the report. You can show or hide individual report tables, the entire Amount report, or the entire Distributions report.

JMP uses hot spots in reports. Figure 4.2 shows a hot spot for the Distributions report and the Amount report. Clicking the hot spots reveals additional options.

JMP often displays one or more graphs with the reports. **Amount** is a continuous variable, so JMP displays a histogram, outlier box plot, and the Quantiles and Moments reports. The next four topics discuss these items and the JMP options for each.

Histogram for Continuous Variables

JMP displays a histogram for continuous variables. Histograms are similar to bar charts in that they both show the shape of the distribution of values. The **Amount** variable has a somewhat mound-shaped distribution, with one bar separated from the other bars. As a general rule, investigate irregularities like this to check for an error in the data. For this data, you know that the separate bar is a valid data point for Ohio, with a value of 100.

JMP labels the boundaries between bars. The first bar shows data between 0 and 10, and the last bar shows data between 100 and 110.

JMP lets you interact with the histogram to learn more about your data. In addition, you can control the appearance of the histogram. In JMP:

1. Click on a bar in the histogram to highlight it. JMP highlights the rows in the data table that are in the bar. Highlighting is shown in the following display.

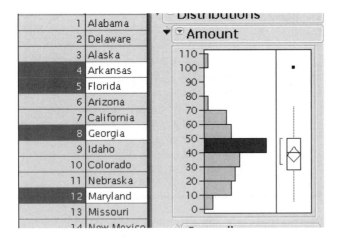

2. Hold down the SHIFT key and click on different bars to highlight them. Again, JMP highlights the rows in the data table that are in the bars.

3. With multiple bars selected, hold down the CTRL key and click to deselect one of the bars. JMP removes the highlighting of the bar's corresponding rows in the data table.

4. Double-click on a bar and JMP creates a data table that contains only the rows in that bar. This is a quick way to explore the data behind a bar in a large data table.

5. Click in an area with no bars to deselect all bars. In the Amount histogram, click in the blank area between 80 and 100. Or, click in the box plot area.

6. Click the hand tool 🖐 in the JMP toolbar. JMP Help also calls this the grabber tool. Drag the hand left to right across the histogram to increase the number of bars. Drag it right to left to decrease the number of bars. With large data tables, increasing the number of bars can reveal subgroups in the data. Figure 4.3 shows the hand tool, and the results of clicking on the original 40-to-50 bar and dragging the hand to the right. Dragging to the right increased the number of bars so these data points now appear in two bars.

Figure 4.3 Selecting Histogram Bars and Using the Hand Tool

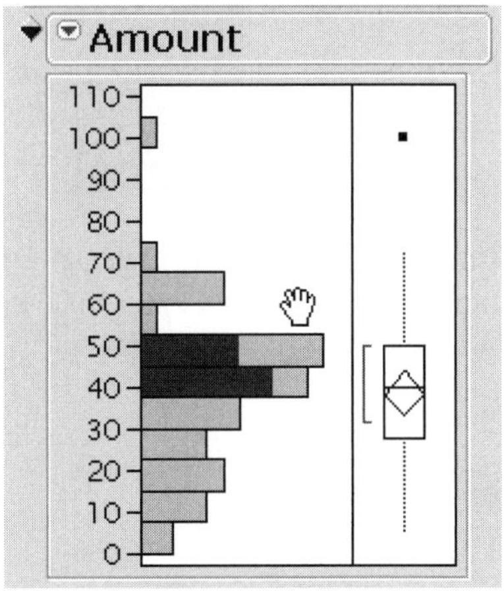

7. Drag the hand vertically to shift the boundaries of the bars. If you try this and it does not seem to work, first, drag the hand right to left until you see fewer bars. Then, drag the hand vertically. When you maximize the number of bars that are displayed, JMP cannot shift the bar boundaries.

8. When you are finished, click the arrow tool ⬚ on the JMP toolbar.

9. Right-click in the histogram. Select **Histogram Color** and a color you like. JMP changes the entire histogram to the new color. (Chapter 5 discusses how to use bar charts and how to change colors for specific bars.) Figure 4.4 shows how to select a color, and Figure 4.5 shows the results of changing colors.

Figure 4.4 Changing the Histogram Color

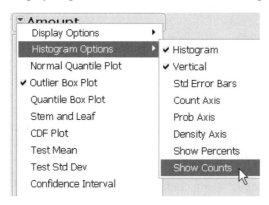

10. Click the hot spot for Amount and select **Histogram Options**. Click **Show Counts** to add the count to the end of each bar, as shown in the following display. Figure 4.5 shows the results of adding counts.

You can add percents, but be careful. JMP uses the number of rows with non-missing values in the percent calculation, not the total number of rows. In data tables with many missing values, the percentages based on the number of rows with non-missing values can be very different from the percentages based on the total number of rows. When you add percents, JMP displays the percent at the end of the bar (above the count if both are displayed).

Figure 4.5 Changed Histogram Color with Counts Added

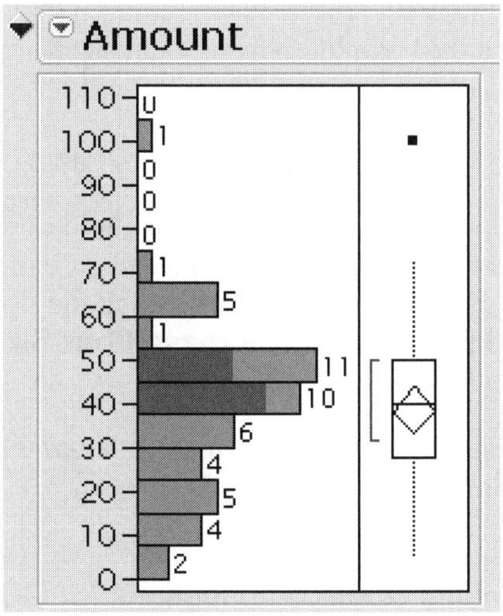

JMP Hint:

Position your mouse pointer over an option in **Histogram Options** and JMP displays pop-up help about that option. This feature is available for many menu choices and is faster than going to the Help.

You can resize the graph and the text in reports. In JMP:

1. Position your mouse pointer in the lower-right corner of the histogram or box plot. Click and drag to resize while maintaining the vertical-to-horizontal ratio.

    Or, position your mouse pointer on the lower border of a box plot. Click and drag to resize the box plot vertically.

    Or, position your mouse pointer on the right border of a box plot. Click and drag to resize the box plot horizontally.

    If you want to return the box plot to its original size, click **Edit→Undo** as many times as needed.

    Figure 4.6 shows examples of all three of these resizing options.

2. To increase the text size in Windows or Linux, hold down the CTRL key and the SHIFT key, and then click the + key. To decrease the text size, hold down the CTRL key and the SHIFT key, and then click the - key. This is faster than clicking **Window→Font Sizes→Increase Font Sizes** or **Window→Font Sizes→Decrease Font Sizes**.

    To change the text size on the Macintosh, click **View→Make Text Bigger** or **Make Text Smaller**.

Figure 4.6 Examples of Resizing Options for Graphs

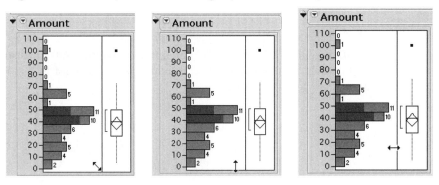

JMP provides several other options when you right-click the histogram or click the hot spot. This section discussed the basic options that are often most helpful in exploring data. Later sections discuss **Uniform Scaling** and **Stem and Leaf**. Chapter 6 discusses **Normal Quantile Plot** and **Fit Distribution**. Chapter 8 discusses **By** variables and **Horizontal Layout**. See JMP Help for explanations of other options.

Box Plot

In Figure 4.2, JMP displays an outlier box plot to the right of the histogram. The bottom and top of the box are the 25th percentile and the 75th percentile. The length of the box is the *interquartile range*, which is sometimes used as a measure of variability.

The line inside the box is the 50th percentile, or *median*. Half of the data values are above the median, and half are below it. The median is not exactly in the middle of the box, which indicates a small amount of skewness or sidedness to the data values. When estimating the center of a distribution, the median is less sensitive to skewness than the average is. For ordinal data, the median is often used instead of the average.

The dotted vertical lines that extend from the box are *whiskers*. Each whisker extends up to 1.5 interquartile ranges from the end of the box. Values outside the whiskers are potential outlier points and appear as small squares. The potential outlier point for the **Amount** variable matches the value of $100 for Ohio and is valid.

The diamond inside the box is a *means diamond*. Chapter 9 discusses means diamonds in detail. The center of the diamond is the mean, and the top and bottom of the diamond are the ends of 95% confidence intervals for the mean. When the mean and the median are equal, the diamond has the median line running through its center.

The red line outside the box is the *shortest half*. This is the densest 50% of the data.

The means diamond and red shortest half line are unique features of JMP. For some presentations and papers, you might want to omit them. In JMP:

1. Right-click on the box plot.

2. Click to deselect **Mean Confid Diamond**, **Shortest Half Bracket**, or both. See the following display.

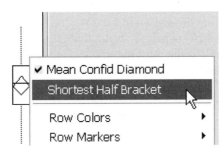

To add these features back, follow the previous steps again.

You can enhance the appearance of the box plot. Suppose you want to highlight the potential outlier point so that it prints in a different color and uses a larger marker. In JMP:

1. Right-click on the small square, select **Row Colors**, and a color you like. The point changes color. JMP adds a colored marker in the row number of the data table for this point.

2. Right-click on the small square again, select **Row Markers**, and a marker you like. The point uses the new marker, as does the data table.

3. Right-click on the small square again, select **Marker Size**, and a size you like. The marker uses the larger size, as does the data table.

JMP provides several other options when you right-click the box plot. This section discussed some favorite options. See JMP Help for explanations of other options.

JMP Hint:

After exploring the box plots and histograms, you might have set many colors and markers. To remove these changes from your data table, click **Rows→Clear Row States**. Or, you can wait until you exit JMP and choose to save the data table without the changes.

Quantiles Report

In Figure 4.2, the Quantiles report gives more detail about the distribution of values. The 0th percentile is the lowest value and is labeled as the **minimum**. The 100th percentile is the highest value and is labeled as the **maximum**. The difference between the highest and lowest values is the range.

The 25th, 50th, and 75th percentiles are shown in the box plot. The Quantiles report provides the actual values. The 25th percentile is the first quartile and is greater than 25% of the values. The 75th percentile is the third quartile and is greater than 75% of the values. The difference between these two percentiles is the interquartile range, which is the length of the box. The 50th percentile is the median.

JMP shows several other quantiles, which are interpreted in a similar way. For example, the 90th percentile is 60, which means that 90% of the values are less than 60.

JMP provides an option to display a quantile box plot that shows all of the numbers listed in the Quantiles report. In JMP:

1. Click the hot spot for Amount.

2. Select **Quantile Box Plot**.

JMP adds a quantile box plot between the histogram and outlier box plot. To remove it, follow the previous steps again.

Moments Report

In Figure 4.2, the Moments report gives the most commonly used summary statistics. These are:

Mean	Average of the data. It is calculated as the sum of values, divided by the number of non-missing values. The mean is the most common measure used to describe the center of a distribution.
Std Dev	Standard deviation, which is the square root of the variance. The standard deviation is the most common measure used to describe dispersion, or variability, around the mean. When all values are close to the mean, the standard deviation is small. When the values are scattered widely from the mean, the standard deviation is large. Chapter 6 gives the formula for standard deviation.
Std Err Mean	Standard error of the mean. It is calculated as the standard deviation, divided by the square root of the sample size. It is used in calculating confidence intervals. Chapter 7 gives more detail.
upper 95% Mean **lower 95% Mean**	Confidence intervals for the mean. Chapter 7 gives more detail.
N	Number of rows with non-missing values for the variable. This number might not be the same as the number of rows in the data. The Amount data table has 51 rows, but N is 50 because the value for Washington, D.C. is missing. JMP uses N in calculating other statistics, such as the mean.

JMP provides an option to add more statistics to this report. In JMP:

1. Click the hot spot for **Amount**.

2. Select **Display Options→More Moments**.

Figure 4.7 shows the new report.

Figure 4.7 Moments Report after Adding More Moments

▼ Moments	
Mean	38.5
Std Dev	18.793182
Std Err Mean	2.6577572
upper 95% Mean	43.840963
lower 95% Mean	33.159037
N	50
Sum Wgt	50
Sum	1925
Variance	353.18367
Skewness	0.4468142
Kurtosis	1.1336825
CV	48.813459
N Missing	1

JMP adds statistics to the bottom of the report. To remove them, follow the previous steps again. The statistics are:

Sum Wgt
Sum of weights. When you don't use a Weight column, Sum Wgt is the same as N. When you do use a Weight column, Sum Wgt is the sum of that column. JMP uses Sum Wgt instead of N in calculations.

Sum
Sum of values for all rows.

Variance
Square of the standard deviation. The Variance is never less than zero, and is zero only if all rows have the same value.

Skewness	Measure of the tendency for the distribution of values to be more spread out on one side than the other side. Positive skewness indicates that values located to the right of the mean are more spread out than values to the left. Negative skewness indicates the opposite.
	For **Amount**, skewness is caused by the outlier point at 100, which pulls the distribution to the right of the mean, and spreads out the right side more than the left side.
Kurtosis	Measure of the shape of the distribution of values. Think of kurtosis as measuring how peaked or flat the shape of the distribution of values is. Large values for kurtosis indicate that the distribution has heavy tails or is flat. This means that the data contains some values that are very distant from the mean, as compared to most of the other values in the data.
	For **Amount**, the right tail of the distribution of values is heavy because of the outlier point at 100.
CV	Coefficient of variation. It is calculated as the standard deviation, divided by the mean and multiplied by 100; or **(Std Dev/Mean)*100**.
N Missing	Number of missing values.

JMP Hint:

If you see an unfamiliar statistic in a JMP report, click **Help→Indexes→Statistics**. In the **Statistics Index**, find the name of the statistic. JMP displays a brief definition. Click **Topic Help** for more detail.

This index is useful when you want to find out if JMP calculates a statistic. Click **Launch** to identify the platform that calculates the statistic. Click **Example** to see how JMP displays the statistic in a report or graph.

Click the **X** in the upper-right corner to close the **Statistics Index**.

Figures 4.2 and 4.7 show most statistics to six or seven decimal places. For presentations, this is too much detail—especially for a variable that is measured to only two decimal places. You can control the number of decimal places displayed in almost all JMP reports. In JMP:

1. Position your mouse pointer over a statistic in the Moments report and double-click. (Position your mouse pointer over the numbers, not the name of the statistic.)

2. Click the menu for **Format** and select **Fixed Dec**.

3. Change the number of decimal places to **2**, if needed. (It might be automatically set to 2.) Compare your window with Figure 4.8.

4. Click **OK**.

JMP changes the appearance of statistics in the Moments report.

Figure 4.8 Changing Decimal Places for Statistics in Reports

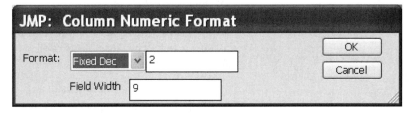

Stem-and-Leaf Plots

The histogram groups values into categories and displays them on a graph. This type of display is especially useful for summarizing large data tables. Sometimes, particularly for smaller data tables, you want to see the individual values in each bar. Stem-and-leaf plots are designed to do this. In JMP:

1. Click the hot spot for Amount.

2. Select **Stem and Leaf**.

Figure 4.9 shows the results.

Figure 4.9 Stem-and-Leaf Plot

Stem	Leaf	Count
▼ **Stem and Leaf**		
10	0	1
9		
8		
7	3	1
6	00045	5
5	000006	6
4	000000445555788	15
3	0233558	7
2	0006888	7
1	000355	6
0	55	2

0|5 represents 5

The stem is on the left side of the vertical line, and the leaves are on the right. The instructions at the bottom tell you how to interpret the stem-and-leaf plot. Figure 4.9 says that the stems are the 10s and the leaves are 1s. So, a stem-and-leaf value of 0|5 corresponds to a data value of 5. A stem-and-leaf value of 7|3 corresponds to a data value of 73. For your data, follow the instructions to determine the values of the variable.

The stem boundaries depend on your data. For the **Amount** variable, JMP creates 10 stems. The first stem, labeled 0, contains values from 0 to 9. The second stem contains values 10 to 19, and so on.

The stem-and-leaf plot is interactive. Clicking on a value highlights the point in the plot, all other graphs, and the data table. This is especially useful because the plot might round data to display it. The speeding ticket data doesn't have a value of 73, but it does have a value of 72.5. The stem-and-leaf plot rounds the value. JMP's interactivity is a big help here—click the data point and you can check it in the data table.

The stem-and-leaf plot shows the distribution of values and points out unusual values in the data. As with other plots, the outlier point at 100 is separated from the other data points. The plot is roughly mound-shaped, like the histogram. The highest part of the mound is in the 40s, which makes sense given the mean and median. The plot shows a slight skewness or sidedness. The values near 100 are more spread out than the values near 0. The data is slightly skewed to the right—in the direction where more values trail at the end of the distribution of values. This slight skewness is seen in the box plot and **Moments** report.

The column labeled **Count** identifies how many values appear in each stem. For example, there are 2 values in the stem labeled 0.

The stem-and-leaf plot is one way to show the individual values in a graph. Chapter 5 shows another way that uses bar charts.

Checking for Errors in Continuous Variables

In checking your data for errors, investigate points that are separated from the main group of data—either above it or below it—and confirm that the points are valid. In the histogram, click on bars that are separated from other bars. In the box plot, click on the outlier points. For large data tables, you might not be able to see the bars with very small counts, but the box plot always shows outlier points.

Use the **Quantiles** report to check the minimum and maximum values. See if these values make sense for your data. For the speeding ticket data, a minimum value of 0 is expected. For other types of data, negative values might make sense.

Use the **Moments** report to check the data against what you expect. For example, if your data consists of scores on a test, you have an idea of what the average should be. If it's very different from what you expect, investigate the data for outlier points or for mistakes in data values.

Also, look at the number of missing values. If it is large, you might need to check your data for errors. For example, in clinical trials, some data (such as age) must be recorded for all patients. Missing values are not allowed. For the speeding ticket data, the missing value for Washington, D.C. could mean that the researcher didn't collect this data.

Use stem-and-leaf plots to identify outlier points and to check the minimum and maximum values.

Using Distribution for Multiple Variables

JMP creates different reports and graphs for nominal or ordinal variables. Also, JMP is valuable in exploring multiple variables at one time. Interacting with JMP graphs helps provide insight about the possible relationships among variables. This section uses the Cars 1993 data table to discuss these ideas. In JMP:

1. Click **Help→Sample Data Directory**.

2. Click the disclosure diamond for **Exploratory Modeling**.

3. Click **Cars 1993.jmp** and JMP opens the data table.

4. Click the **X** in the upper-right corner of the Sample Data Directory window to close it.

5. In the data table, move down in the columns panel until you see **Passenger Capacity**. This is a numeric variable, so JMP automatically sets it to be continuous. Because 4.5 passengers in a car does not make sense, you need to change the type to ordinal. Click the icon for **Passenger Capacity** (in the columns panel) and select **Ordinal** from the pop-up window. Compare your columns panel with Figure 4.10. JMP changes the icon to a green bar chart.[1]

Figure 4.10 Changing the Modeling Type for a Variable

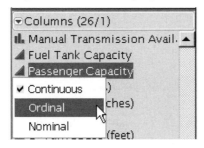

6. In the JMP Starter window, click **Basic→Distribution**.

---

[1] If you close and reopen JMP as you work through this chapter, JMP asks if you want to save the Cars 1993 data table changes. Either select No or save the data table in a folder other than Sample Data Directory.

7. Hold down the CTRL key and click **Vehicle Category**, **Midrange Price ($1000)**, **City Mileage (MPG)**, and **Passenger Capacity**, and then **Y**, **Columns**. Compare your window with Figure 4.11.

Figure 4.11 Distribution Window with Multiple Variables Selected

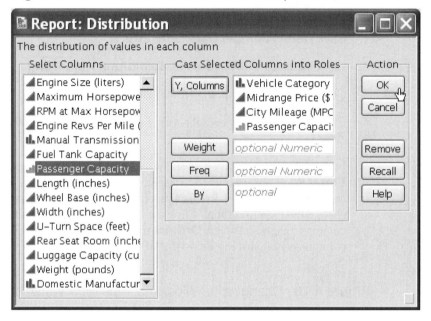

8. Click **OK**.

Figure 4.12 shows the results.

JMP Hint:

When you hold down the CTRL key and click variables in the **Select Columns** section, JMP uses the data table order of variables to display them in the Distributions report. Compare the order of variables in Figures 4.11 and 4.12—the order is the same.

If you want a specific order for variables, click the first variable and then **Y**, **Columns**. Repeat this step until you have selected all of the variables you want to summarize.

Figure 4.12 Distribution Results for Cars 1993 Data

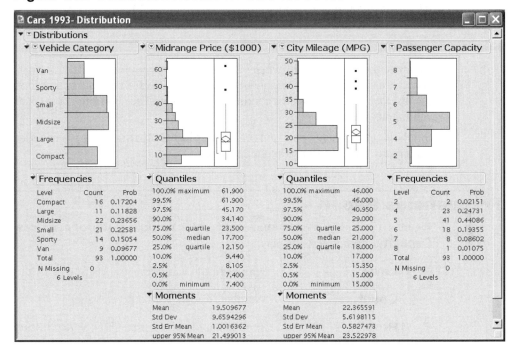

For **Vehicle Category** (nominal) and **Passenger Capacity** (ordinal), JMP displays a histogram and the Frequencies report in Figure 4.12. The next two topics discuss these items and some favorite options. For other options, see JMP Help.

Histogram for Nominal and Ordinal Variables

Figure 4.12 shows histograms for the selected variables. For the nominal and ordinal variables, the histograms show all values of the variable. For the continuous variables, JMP groups values into categories.

When you right-click on the histograms for nominal or ordinal variables, JMP has the same options as it does for continuous variables.

Similarly, when you click the hot spot for a nominal or ordinal variable, and select **Histogram Options**, JMP has the same options as it does for a continuous variable.

You can use the features described for histograms and reports for the continuous variable **Amount** for all four variables displayed in Figure 4.12.

JMP Hint:

Compare the list of options when you click the hot spot for nominal, ordinal, and continuous variables. JMP displays the same options for nominal and ordinal variables, but displays more options for continuous variables. The additional options make sense for continuous variables only.

Similarly, click the hot spot and select **Display Options**. The options reflect the reports and graphs for the different modeling types.

Frequencies Report

Figure 4.12 displays a Frequencies report for **Vehicle Category** and **Passenger Capacity**. Both reports display:

Level	Values of the variable.
Count	Number of rows with a given value.
Prob	Proportion of rows with a given value. It is calculated as the Count divided by the Total, which appears at the bottom of the report.
Total	Total frequency count for the variable. It is the number of rows in the data table that have a value for the variable.
N Missing	Number of rows in the data table that have a missing value for the variable.

The Frequencies report displays **Prob** to five decimal places. As in the Moments report, you can double-click on a value of a statistic in the column and change the number of decimal places. Or, you can hide the column. In JMP:

1. Right-click in the Frequencies report for **Passenger Capacity** and select **Columns**.

2. Click **Prob** to hide the **Prob** column. Figure 4.13 shows the three columns that are automatically displayed and the two columns without check marks.

To display the **Prob** column again, repeat the previous steps.

Figure 4.13 Hiding Columns in the Frequencies Report

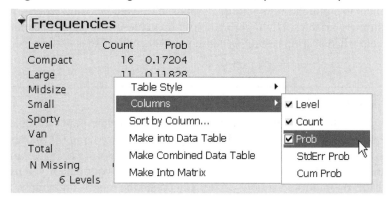

Figure 4.13 shows two additional columns that can appear in the Frequencies report. These are:

StdErr Prob	Standard error of the proportions.
Cum Prob	Cumulative sum of the proportions. This is most useful for ordinal variables. For example, display the **Cum Prob** column and have JMP add the proportions. This would show that about 71% of the cars can carry five or fewer passengers.

JMP Hint:

Hide columns in most JMP reports by right-clicking in the report and selecting **Columns**. Sometimes, JMP lists columns by their headings, such as in the Frequencies report. Other times, JMP lists columns only as **Column 1**, **Column 2**, and so on. Although you can hide columns in the Moments and Quantiles reports, the reports are not useful without all of the columns displayed.

Checking for Errors in Nominal or Ordinal Variables

This Frequencies report lists all the values for a variable and can be used to check for unusual or unexpected values. The histograms also show all the values and are another option for checking your nominal or ordinal variables for errors.

Interacting with Distribution Results

This section discusses useful features when working with multiple variables. These features include highlighting in multiple graphs, hiding and closing reports, and scaling axes for similar variables. Highlighting helps you explore your data. The other two features help when sharing results, because you can emphasize specific reports or graphs.

Highlighting in Multiple Graphs

Interacting with the graphs in **Distribution** helps you explore your data quickly. When you click on a point in any graph, JMP highlights the selected point in all other graphs and in the data table. While this feature is useful when exploring a single variable, such as **Amount**, you can gain a much better understanding of your data if you use **Distribution** on multiple variables. After you create the reports and graphs for the Cars 1993 data table in JMP:

1. Click the **Compact** bar in the **Vehicle Category** histogram. All of these cars have midrange prices from around $10,000 to over $30,000. These cars get between 20 and 30 miles per gallon in the city. They hold between four and six passengers. Figure 4.14 shows the results.

Figure 4.14 Interacting with Histograms

2. Click the **6** bar in the **Passenger Capacity** histogram. These cars are **Compact**, **Midsize**, or **Large**. These cars have midrange prices from under $15,000 to near $40,000. The cars get between 15 and 25 city miles per gallon.

3. Click the lasso tool 🔾 on the toolbar. Click and drag a circle around the three outlier points in the City Mileage (MPG) box plot.

4. Right-click in the box plot for City Mileage (MPG). Select **Row Colors** and a color you like, and select **Row Markers** and a marker. Figure 4.15 shows green asterisks for these outlier points. The cars are small and inexpensive, but none can carry more than four people.

Figure 4.15 Highlighted Outliers after Changing Appearance

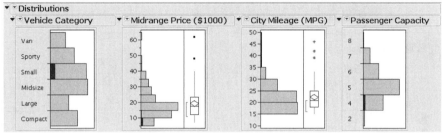

Hiding Reports and Graphs

When working with many variables, you can hide reports or graphs one at a time. JMP provides a shortcut to hide all reports or graphs of the same type. For a Distributions report in JMP:

1. Right-click the disclosure diamond for a report. For example, right-click the disclosure diamond for the Frequencies report for **Vehicle Category**.

2. Select **Close All Like This**. Compare your window with the window in Figure 4.16.

JMP closes all Frequencies reports in this Distribution window. If you have multiple Distribution windows open, JMP closes reports only in the active Distribution window.

Figure 4.16 Closing Reports

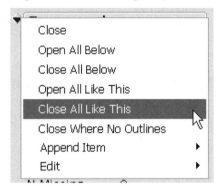

To re-display the reports, right-click the disclosure diamond and select **Open All Like This**. Or, you can open reports individually.

The options for **Open All Below** and **Close All Below** apply to sub-reports. These options do not apply to separate reports that are below the report you select. For example, clicking **Close All Below** on the Quantiles report doesn't also close the Moments report. Later chapters have examples of sub-reports, where these two options will make sense.

Right-click on the disclosure diamond for any JMP report to see the options in Figure 4.16. If a JMP graph has a disclosure diamond, you can hide the graph.

Closing Reports and Graphs

When a report is hidden, JMP still displays the report title with the disclosure diamond. Keep in mind that many graphs don't have disclosure diamonds. If you want to omit the report entirely, you can do so for variables one at a time. Similarly, you can omit graphs one variable at a time. JMP provides a useful shortcut when you have multiple variables. For the Cars 1993 Distribution report in JMP:

1. Hold down the CTRL key and click the hot spot for a report, and then click **Display Options**. For example, hold down the CTRL key and click the hot spot for **Midrange Price ($1000)**.

2. Select a report to omit (close the report and remove its title). Figure 4.17 shows the **Quantiles** report being selected.

JMP omits all the reports like the one you selected and their titles.

Figure 4.17 Omitting a Report

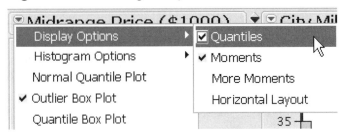

This shortcut works with other options in the hot spot. For example, suppose you want to remove the outlier box plot for all continuous variables. In JMP:

1. Hold down the CTRL key and click the hot spot for a report. For example, hold down the CTRL key and click the hot spot for **Midrange Price ($1000)**.

2. Select a report to omit. For example, select **Outlier Box Plot**.

JMP closes all the graphs or reports like the one you selected. Figure 4.18 shows the results of hiding all of the Frequencies reports, omitting all of the Quantiles reports, and omitting all outlier box plots for the Distributions report.

Figure 4.18 Results from Hiding and Omitting

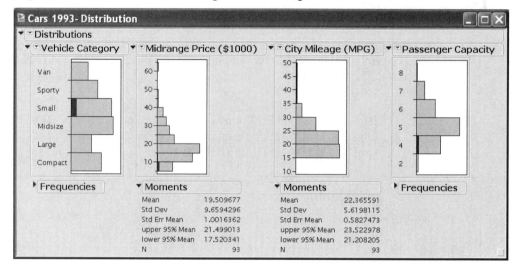

Scaling Axes

When creating histograms, JMP uses the range of data values to choose the scale for the axis. If your data table has variables with similar meanings, it makes sense for the histograms to use the same scale. You can change the scale for variables one at a time. (Chapter 5 provides an example.) JMP provides a shortcut to change multiple axes.

The Cars 1993 data has variables for both city and highway mileage (MPG). Suppose you create a Distributions report for these two variables. JMP scales the histogram for **City Mileage (MPG)** from **10** to **50**, and for **Highway Mileage (MPG)** from **15** to **55**. To scale both axes at once in JMP:

1. Click the hot spot for the Distributions report.

2. Select **Uniform Scaling**, as shown in Figure 4.19.

    In Figure 4.19, you see that JMP displays the variable names in the window title. You saw this earlier for the **Amount** variable in the speeding ticket data. JMP tries to list the data table name and variable names in the window title. When there are too many variables names to list, JMP lists just the data table name.

    Figure 4.19 shows how JMP carries previous highlighting over to new reports. Because you created this report after Figure 4.15, JMP shows highlighting from the previous report.

    The Quantiles and Moments reports are both hidden in Figure 4.19.

Figure 4.19 Selecting Uniform Scaling

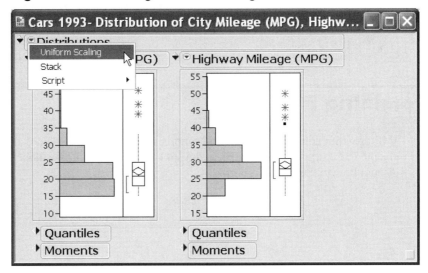

JMP uses the combined range for both variables and rescales the histograms. Figure 4.20 shows the results.

Figure 4.20 Results from Uniform Scaling

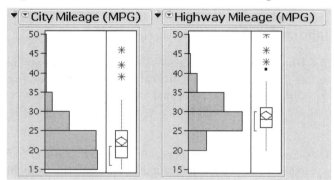

Uniform scaling is available in many JMP reports. When you select it, JMP scales as many plots and histograms as possible to be on the same scale. For example, in a Distributions report with the two MPG variables and three price variables, JMP scales all histograms as 0 to 80. This might not meet your needs, so you can either scale the histograms individually, or you can create separate reports for the MPG and price variables, and use the **Uniform Scaling** option in those two separate reports.

Customizing Reports

JMP provides automatic titles for all reports and all column headings in reports. You can change these titles. Also, you can add a sticky note to explain results. The next two topics discuss how to customize reports.

Changing Report Titles and Column Headings

Suppose you want to change the title of the Moments report to Statistics. In JMP:

1. Double-click in the title area.

2. Enter the new title. See Figure 4.21 for an example with the Cars 1993 data.

3. Press the ENTER key or click outside the title area. JMP displays the new title.

Figure 4.21 Changing a Report Title

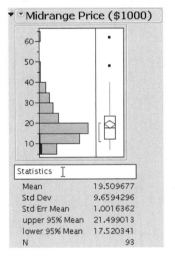

You can change column headings. Suppose you want to change the heading in the Frequencies report for **Vehicle Category** from **Prob** to **Proportion**. In JMP:

1. Double-click on the column heading.

2. Enter the new name. For this example, enter **Proportion**.

3. Press the ENTER key or click outside the column heading. JMP displays the new column heading. Figure 4.22 shows the results.

You can change any report title in JMP, including variable names and the overall report. You can change most column headings. Figure 4.22 is a continuation of Figure 4.18. It shows the results of changing both **Moments** report titles, changing the title for City Mileage (MPG) to City MPG, and changing the title for the **Distributions** report. Figure 4.22 also shows the results after changing the **Prob** column heading in the **Frequencies** report for **Vehicle Category**.

Figure 4.22 Results after Changing Multiple Titles

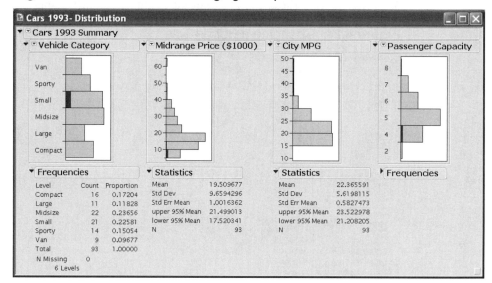

Adding Sticky Notes

Just as sticky notes are helpful with paper reports, they are helpful with electronic reports. Suppose you want to add a note that says the data is valid or explains an outlier point. Continuing with Figure 4.22 in JMP:

1. Click the annotate tool in the toolbar. This is the yellow block with an "A" as shown in the following display.

2. JMP changes the mouse pointer to a block with an "A". Move the pointer to where you want to place the sticky note.

3. Click and drag the pointer to create the sticky note, and then release the mouse button. While dragging, JMP shows the sticky note as a yellow box.

4. JMP changes the sticky note to a white box and moves the pointer inside the box. Enter your text. You can enter multiple paragraphs just like you would in word processing software. Press the ENTER key to go to the next line, and press it again to insert a blank line between paragraphs. JMP does not provide special formatting options for line spacing.

5. When you are finished, click outside the sticky note area. JMP displays the sticky note as a yellow box.

6. Depending on how much text you entered, JMP might not display all of it. Click a border of the sticky note, and JMP changes the sticky note outline to a blue box. You can then click and drag the borders to resize the sticky note so that all text is displayed.

Figure 4.23 shows the results of adding a sticky note to the report in Figure 4.22.

Figure 4.23 Adding a Sticky Note to a Report

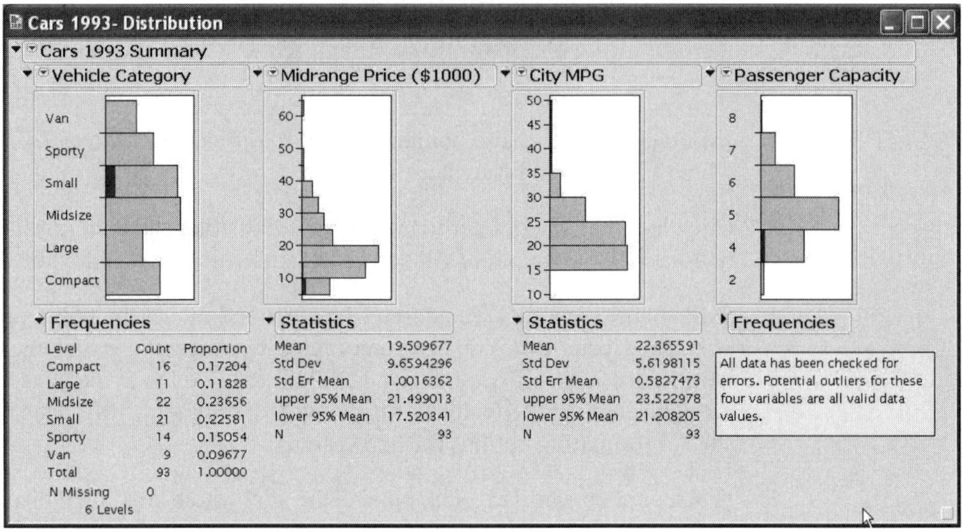

You can use sticky notes on any report or graph in JMP.

Summaries

Key Ideas

- As you summarize your data, check it for errors. For continuous variables, look at the maximum and minimum values and look at potential outlier points. Also, check the data against your expectations—do the values make sense? For nominal and ordinal variables, check for unusual or unexpected values. For all types of variables, confirm that the number of missing values is reasonable.

- JMP displays reports and graphs when summarizing data. By interacting with the graphs and reports, you can gain insight into your data. Some of the unique tools in JMP are the hand and lasso tools.

- Histograms show the distribution of data values and help you see the center, spread (dispersion or variability), and shape of your data. Histograms are available for all modeling types.

- Box plots show the distribution of continuous data. Like histograms, they show the center and spread of your data. Box plots highlight outlier points and display skewness (sidedness) by showing the mean and median in relationship to the dispersion of data values. JMP provides box plots only for continuous variables.

- Stem-and-leaf plots are similar to histograms because they show the shape of your data. Stem-and-leaf plots show the individual data values in each bar, which provides more detail. JMP provides stem-and-leaf plots only for continuous variables.

- With all types of graphs, using different colors or markers can highlight important features in your data. Depending on the graph, JMP provides different options for enhancing the appearance.

- With all types of reports, JMP provides features for controlling the details of the report, hiding the report, omitting the report, changing report titles and column headings, and adding sticky notes.

- The mean (or average) is the most common measure of the center of values for a variable. The median (or 50th percentile) is another measure. The median is less sensitive to skewness and is often preferred for ordinal variables.

- Standard deviation is the most common measure of the variability of values for a variable. Standard deviation is the square root of the variance. The interquartile range, which is the difference between the 25th percentile and the 75th percentile, is another measure. The length of the box in an outlier box plot is the interquartile range.

- For nominal and ordinal variables, frequency counts of the values are the most common way to summarize the data.

JMP Steps

This topic first summarizes JMP steps for activities that apply to any JMP report or graph. Then, the topic summarizes JMP steps for activities in the Distributions report.

To resize graphs and text in any JMP report:

1. Position your mouse pointer in the lower-right corner of the histogram or box plot. Click and drag to resize while maintaining the vertical-to-horizontal ratio.

   Or, position your mouse pointer on the lower border of a plot. Click and drag to resize the plot vertically.

   Or, position your mouse pointer on the right border of a plot. Click and drag to resize the plot horizontally.

   If you want to return the plot to its original size, click **Edit→Undo** as many times as needed.

2. To increase the text size in Windows or Linux, hold down the CTRL key and the SHIFT key, and then click the + key. To decrease the text size, hold down the CTRL key and the SHIFT key, and then click the – key. This is faster than clicking **Window→Font Sizes→Increase Font Sizes** or **Window→Font Sizes→Decrease Font Sizes**.

   To change the text size on the Macintosh, click **View→Make Text Bigger** or **Make Text Smaller**.

To show and hide any JMP report:

1. Right-click the disclosure diamond for a report.

2. Select **Close All Like This** to hide all similar reports. JMP still displays the disclosure diamond and report title.

3. To re-display the reports, right-click the disclosure diamond and select **Open All Like This**.

To change report titles or column headings in any JMP report:

1. Double-click in the title area of the report.

2. Enter the new title. Press the ENTER key or click outside the title area. JMP displays the new title.

3. Double-click on the column heading for a report. If you can change the column heading, JMP displays a field where you enter the new heading.

4. Enter the new name. Press the ENTER key or click outside the column heading. JMP displays the new column heading.

To add a sticky note to any JMP report:

1. Click the annotate tool in the toolbar. This is the yellow block with an "A".

2. JMP changes the pointer to a block with an "A". Move the pointer to where you want to place the sticky note.

3. Click and drag the pointer to create the sticky note, and then release the mouse button. While dragging, JMP shows the sticky note as a yellow box.

4. JMP changes the sticky note to a white box and moves the pointer inside the box. Enter your text. You can enter multiple paragraphs just like you would in word processing software. Press the ENTER key to go to the next line, and press it again to insert a blank line between paragraphs. JMP does not provide special formatting options for line spacing.

5. When you are finished, click outside the sticky note area. JMP displays the sticky note as a yellow box.

6. Depending on how much text you entered, JMP might not display all of it. Click a border of the sticky note, and JMP changes the sticky note outline to a blue box. You can then click and drag the borders to resize the sticky note so that all text is displayed.

To hide columns in any JMP report:

1. Right-click in the report and select **Columns**.

2. Click on a column name to hide it. Columns might be listed by their headings, or as **Column 1**, **Column 2**, and so on.

3. To re-display the columns, repeat the previous steps.

To change decimal places in any JMP report:

1. Position your mouse pointer over a statistic in the report and double-click.

2. Click the menu for **Format** and select the option you need. For example, select **Fixed Dec** and change the number of decimal places to **2**.

3. Click **OK**.

To summarize variables in the Distributions report:

1. In the JMP Starter window, click **Basic→Distribution**.

2. Click your variables and then click **Y, Columns**. Hold down the CTRL key and click to select several variables and to create a report that displays the variables in the order they appear in the data table. Click each variable and then click **Y, Columns** to control the order of variables in the report.

3. Click **OK**.

To explore histograms in the Distributions report:

1. Click on a bar in the histogram to highlight it. JMP highlights the rows in the data table that are in the bar.

2. Hold down the SHIFT key and click on different bars to highlight them. Again, JMP highlights the rows in the data table that are in the bars.

3. Double-click on a bar and JMP creates a data table that contains only the rows in that bar. This is a quick way to explore the data behind a bar in a large data table.

4. Click in an area with no bars to deselect all bars. Or, click in the box plot area.

5. Click the hand tool in the JMP toolbar. Drag the hand left to right across the histogram to increase the number of bars. Drag it right to left to decrease the number of bars.

6. Drag the hand vertically to shift the boundaries of the bars. If you try this and it does not seem to work, first, drag the hand right to left until you see fewer bars. Then, drag the hand vertically. When you maximize the number of bars that are displayed, JMP cannot shift the bar boundaries.

7. Right-click in the histogram. Select **Histogram Color** and a color you like. JMP changes the entire histogram to the new color.

8. Click the hot spot for a variable and select **Histogram Options**. As you move down the list of options, JMP displays pop-up help about that option. Click **Show Counts** to add the count to the end of each bar.

9. Click the hot spot for the Distributions report and select **Uniform Scaling**. JMP changes the histogram axes to use the same scale.

To explore box plots in the Distributions report:

1. Right-click on the box plot. Click to deselect **Mean Confid Diamond**, **Shortest Half Bracket**, or both to remove these features. To add these features back, follow this step again.

2. Right-click on an outlier point to select it. To select multiple outlier points, click the lasso tool on the toolbar. Click and drag a circle around the outlier points.

3. Select **Row Colors** and a color you like. The point changes color. JMP adds a colored marker in the rows area of the data table for this point.

4. Right-click on the outlier point again, select **Row Markers**, and a marker you like. The point uses the new marker, as does the data table.

5. Right-click on the outlier point again, select **Marker Size**, and a size you like. The marker uses the larger size, as does the data table.

6. Click the hot spot for the variable and select **Quantile Box Plot**. JMP adds a quantile box plot between the histogram and outlier box plot.

To add statistics to the Moments report in the Distributions report:

1. Click the hot spot for the variable.

2. Select **Display Options→More Moments**.

To add a stem-and-leaf plot to the Distributions report:

1. Click the hot spot for the variable.

2. Select **Stem and Leaf**.

To omit a report and its title in the Distributions report:

1. Click the hot spot for a report and click **Display Options**. JMP displays a list of reports that can be omitted.

2. Select a report to omit. JMP omits the report and its title.

3. To omit all instances of the same report, hold down the CTRL key and click the hot spot for a report. Next, select **Display Options** and then select a report. JMP omits all the reports like the one you selected and their titles.

Exercises

1. Click **Help→Tutorials** from the JMP menu. Work through the **One Means** tutorial.

2. For the Cars 1993 data, apply value ordering to **Vehicle Category** so that JMP displays the categories as **Compact**, **Small**, **Sporty**, **Midsize**, **Large**, and **Van**. Then, summarize the variables **Vehicle Category**, **Highway Mileage (MPG)**, **Maximum Price**, and **Passenger Capacity**. Discuss your results. Include your assessment of how value ordering impacts the appearance of the reports and graphs. (Hint: See Chapter 3 for JMP steps on value ordering.)

3. Using the Candy Bars data in the Sample Data Directory (under the Food and Nutrition heading), create a **Distribution** summary on **Brand**, **Calories**, **Sugars**, and **Protein**. Do the potential outlier points correspond to real candy bars? What brands of candy bars contain more than 7 grams of protein? Are there any candy bars with fewer than 200 calories and more than 5 grams of protein? Explore the data and discuss any insights from the report.

4. Using the Children's Popularity data in the Sample Data Directory (under the Psychology and Social Science heading), create a **Distribution** summary. First, review the information in the table notes and look at the variables. Should **Grade** stay a continuous variable? Summarize **Gender**, **Urban/Rural**, **Grade**, and **School**. Do all schools have students in all grades? Are both boys and girls in all schools, grades, and urban/rural categories? Identify which schools are in each of the three urban/rural categories. Discuss any insights from the report.

5. Using the On-time Arrivals data in the Sample Data Directory (under the Business and Demographic heading), create a **Distribution** summary of the four variables in the data table. Use **Uniform Scaling** and click the top bar in each of the histograms for the different time periods. Identify the airlines (if any) that are selected for all three time periods. Click the bottom bar in each of the histograms for the different time periods. Identify the airlines (if any) that are selected for all three time periods. Discuss the box plots and histograms and whether skewness exists in the data for the three time periods.

6. Using the Companies data in the Sample Data Directory (under the Business and Demographic heading), create a **Distribution** summary of **Type**, **Size Co**, and **profit/emp**. Describe common features for companies with negative profits per employee. Describe common features for companies with more than $40,000 in profits per employee. Discuss any additional insights from the results.

7. Using the Movies data in the Sample Data Directory (under the Business and Demographic heading), create a **Distribution** summary of **Type**, **Rating**, and **Domestic $**. Describe G-rated movies in terms of their money-making capability and their type of movie. Discuss action movies in terms of their money-making capability and their ratings. Identify the movies that earned over $400 million and discuss common features.

8. For your own data, use the **Distribution** features discussed in this chapter. Summarize the data and explain any insights from your results.

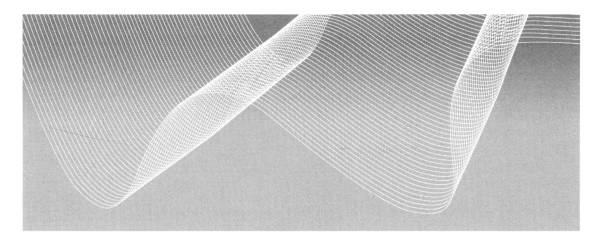

Chapter 5

Graphing Data and Printing Results

This chapter extends the ideas from Chapter 4. Histograms are useful for summarizing variables, but JMP has other options that are helpful. This chapter discusses:

- Creating custom bar charts to summarize a variable.

- Using treemaps to summarize multiple variables.

- Printing JMP results.

- Using JMP journals.

The features and tools in this chapter apply to all types of data.

Creating Custom Bar Charts

The most frequently used graph of values for a variable is the bar chart. Bar charts are very similar to histograms. For nominal and ordinal variables, you usually want a bar for each value of the variable. For continuous variables, you usually want to group values. In most cases, the histogram in **Distribution** is a better choice than the bar chart in **Graph**.

Sometimes you want a customized bar chart for presenting results, and the histogram does not meet your needs. For example, for the speeding ticket data, suppose you want a bar chart of the speeding ticket fine amounts with each bar labeled according to the state. Also, you want the bars to be in descending order so that the highest fine amounts appear at the top, and the lowest at the bottom. Last of all, you want to highlight Ohio (the highest fine amount) with a red bar and use a different color for all of the other bars. You can do all of this in JMP.

First, sort the data by **Amount** in ascending order (see Chapter 3 for more information). Second, apply row order levels to **State**, which tells JMP to display the data according to the order in the data table. Third, use **Graph** and apply appearance options to get the bar chart you want. In JMP:

1. Open the tickets data table.

2. Click **Tables→Sort**.

3. Click **Amount** and then **By**. Accept the automatic choice for an ascending sort (the upward-pointing triangle).

4. Enter **Tickets Sorted** as the name of the output data table. Compare your window with Figure 5.1.

5. Click **OK**.

Figure 5.1 Sort Window for Tickets Data

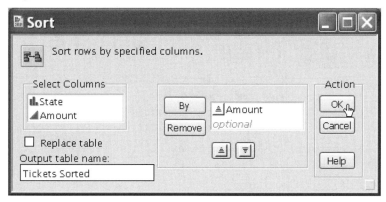

This completes the first task of sorting the data. (For your convenience, the Tickets Sorted data table is available in the sample data for this book.)

Next, apply row order levels. Continuing in JMP:

6. Click on the Tickets Sorted data table to make it the active data table.

7. Double-click on **State** in the data table. JMP displays the column information window.

8. Click the menu for **Column Properties** and select **Row Order Levels**. Compare your window with Figure 5.2.

9. Click **OK**. JMP adds a heavy asterisk (✱) to the right of **State** in the columns panel. The asterisk icon signifies that you have applied a special property to the variable.

Figure 5.2 Applying Row Order Levels

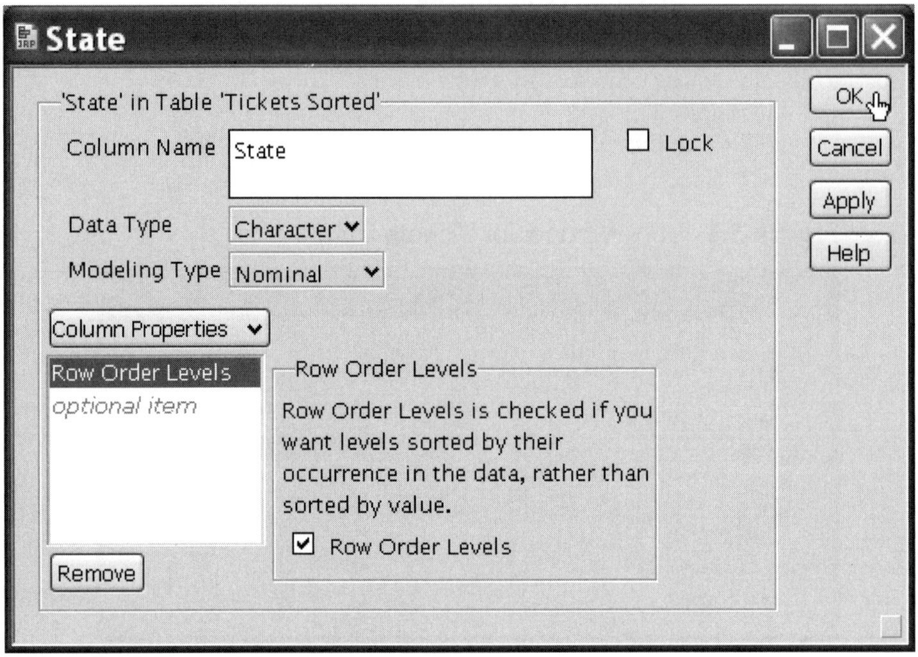

This completes the second task of choosing how to display the data. The third task is to create the bar chart and apply appearance options. Continuing in JMP:

10. In the JMP Starter window, click **Graph→Chart**. Figure 5.3 shows the window before clicking **Chart**.

Figure 5.3 JMP Starter Window with Graph Category Selected

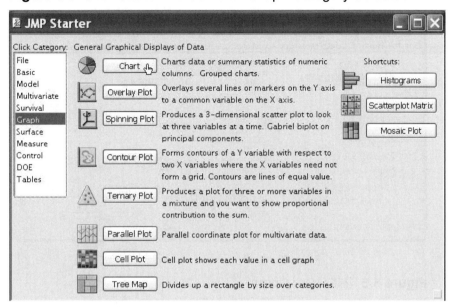

11. Click **Amount** and then **Statistics→Data**.

12. Click **State** and then **Categories**, **X**, **Levels**.

13. Click the menu for **Vertical** and change it to **Horizontal**. Compare your window with Figure 5.4.

14. Click **OK**.

This completes the task of creating the bar chart. Figure 5.5 shows the initial bar chart with a portion of the legend. Next, apply appearance options to finish the bar chart.

Figure 5.4 Chart Window with Selections

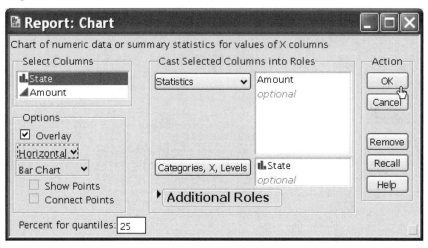

Figure 5.5 Initial Bar Chart

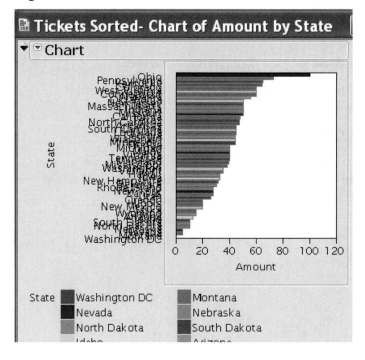

Figure 5.5 shows the fine amounts in descending order. It includes a legend that is not needed, uses different colors for every bar, uses an axis scaled to 120, and needs resizing to show all of the state names.

In JMP:

15. Click the hot spot for Chart and select **Show Level Legend** as shown in the following display. JMP hides the legend that appears at the bottom of the bar chart.

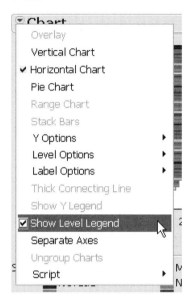

16. In the JMP menu, click **Rows→Row Selection→Select All Rows**.

17. Click the hot spot for Chart again, select **Level Options→Colors**, and a color you like. This is similar to changing the histogram color (see Figure 4.5 in the Chapter 4).

18. Position your mouse pointer in the lower-right corner of the bar chart. Click and drag to resize the bar chart until you can read the names of all of the states. Figure 5.6 displays the results.

Figure 5.6 Resized Bar Chart with Legend Hidden and Row Colors Applied

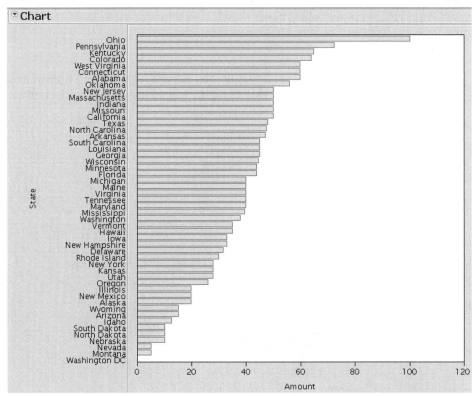

Continuing in JMP:

19. To change the color of the bar for Ohio only, click on the bar. Then, click the hot spot for Chart again, select **Level Options→Colors**, and a color you like.

20. To change the scale of the axis, position your mouse pointer on an axis label and double-click.

21. Enter **110** in the **Maximum** field in the Axis Specification window. Compare your window with Figure 5.7.

22. Click **OK**.

Figure 5.7 Axis Specification Window

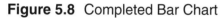

Figure 5.8 displays the results.

Figure 5.8 Completed Bar Chart

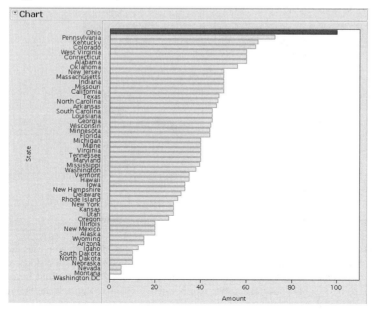

Creating Treemaps

Treemaps[1] are another tool for presenting data, especially complex data. Treemaps help show patterns among groups. For example, look closely at the bar chart of speeding ticket fine amounts and you will notice that most of the low amounts are in Western states. Most of the higher amounts are in the Midwest or in the East. Treemaps can help highlight these patterns. In this section, the examples start with two treemaps for the tickets data, which use the only two variables in the data table. The third and last example is a treemap using multiple variables with the Cars 1993 data. In JMP:

1. Open the tickets data table. (Or, you can open the Tickets Sorted data table.)

2. In the JMP Starter window, click **Graph→Tree Map**.

3. Click **State→Categories**. This is the only required role, and you could create a treemap with only the categories role. However, a treemap with other features would be more useful.

4. Click **Amount→Ordering**.

5. Click **Amount→Coloring**. Compare your window with Figure 5.9.

6. Click **OK**.

Figure 5.9 Creating a Treemap

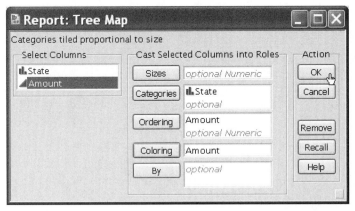

---

[1] As discussed in JMP Help, treemaps were developed by Ben Schneiderman, who uses the single word "treemap" to describe them. Treemaps were first used to show file structures on disk drives, but now have many uses. JMP uses two words—"tree map"—in its interface. The text of this book uses one word when referring to the general concept, and two words when referring to items in the JMP interface. JMP SE does not include treemaps.

Figure 5.10 displays the treemap.

Figure 5.10 Treemap of State Colored and Ordered by Amount

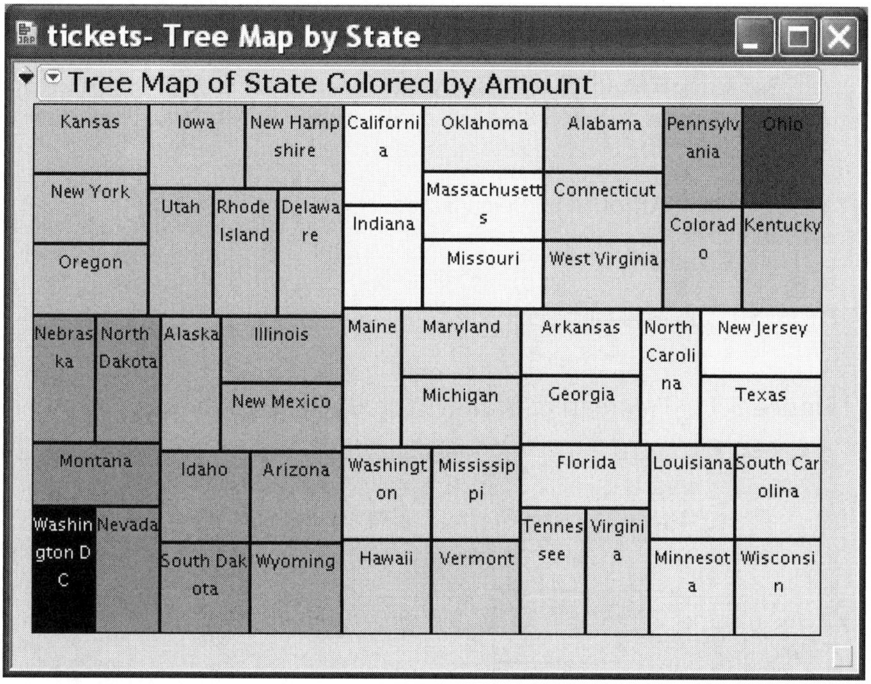

JMP treemaps use a coloring scheme from green to red. As you look from the left to the right across the treemap, the values of **Amount** change from low to high. Darker green indicates low values that are further from the mean. Lighter green indicates values that are less than the mean, but closer to the mean. Lighter red indicates values that are higher than the mean, but closer to the mean than darker red values. Black indicates categories that have a missing value for the **Coloring** role. Washington, D.C. has a missing value for **Amount**, so it's black in the treemap.

Figure 5.10 shows the impact of choosing **Ordering**. Without it, JMP orders the rectangles alphabetically. This creates a red and green checkerboard effect. With **Amount** as the **Ordering** variable, JMP creates the green-to-red ordering as you look from the left to the right.

Using Figure 5.10, it's easier to see that most of the low amounts (darker green rectangles) are in the West. Colorado is an exception; it is the only Western state with a fine amount above the mean.

You can resize the treemap. Position your mouse pointer on the border and click and drag.

JMP uses internal programming to size the rectangles. You can change the size. In JMP:

1. In the JMP Starter window, click **Graph→Tree Map**.

2. Click **Recall**. JMP fills in your choices from the previous treemap. (This assumes you are in the same JMP session. If you have exited and restarted JMP, then create a new treemap.)

3. Click **Amount** and then **Sizes**.

4. Click **OK**.

Figure 5.11 displays the treemap.

Figure 5.11 Treemap of State Colored, Ordered, and Sized by Amount

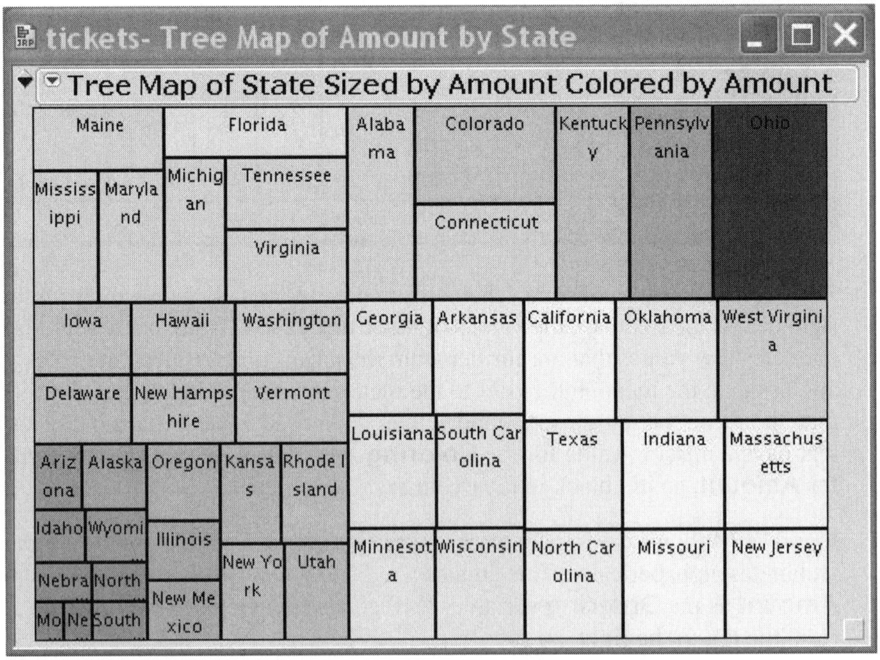

Figure 5.11 highlights the much lower amounts for the Western states, and highlights how much higher the amount for Ohio is. The ordering and red-to-green coloring are the same as they are in Figure 5.10, because the two treemaps use the same variables for **Ordering** and **Coloring**. However, Figure 5.11 cannot display Washington, D.C. because it cannot size the rectangle for a missing value. When you create a JMP treemap with **Sizes**, it will not show **Categories** with a missing value.

Compare the titles for the treemaps in Figures 5.10 and 5.11. JMP includes the **Sizes** and **Coloring** variables in the title, but does not include the **Ordering** variable. For many data tables, it is useful to use the same variable for **Coloring** and **Ordering**.

JMP Hint:

Recall is available in many JMP analysis windows. When you are exploring data tables, using the **Recall** button is a quick way to fill in choices.

These two treemaps use two variables. Treemaps are most useful when exploring data tables with many variables. In JMP:

1. Click **Help→Sample Data Directory**.

2. Click the disclosure diamond for **Exploratory Modeling**.

3. Click **Cars 1993.jmp** and JMP opens the data table.

4. Click the **X** in the upper-right corner of the Sample Data Directory window to close it.

5. In the JMP Starter window, click **Graph→Tree Map**.

6. Click **Model** and then **Categories**.

7. Click **Minimum Price ($1000)** and then **Ordering**.

8. Click **Minimum Price ($1000)** and then **Coloring**.

9. Click **Highway Mileage (MPG)** and then **Sizes**.

10. Click **OK**.

Figure 5.12 displays the treemap.

Figure 5.12 Using Multiple Variables in a Treemap

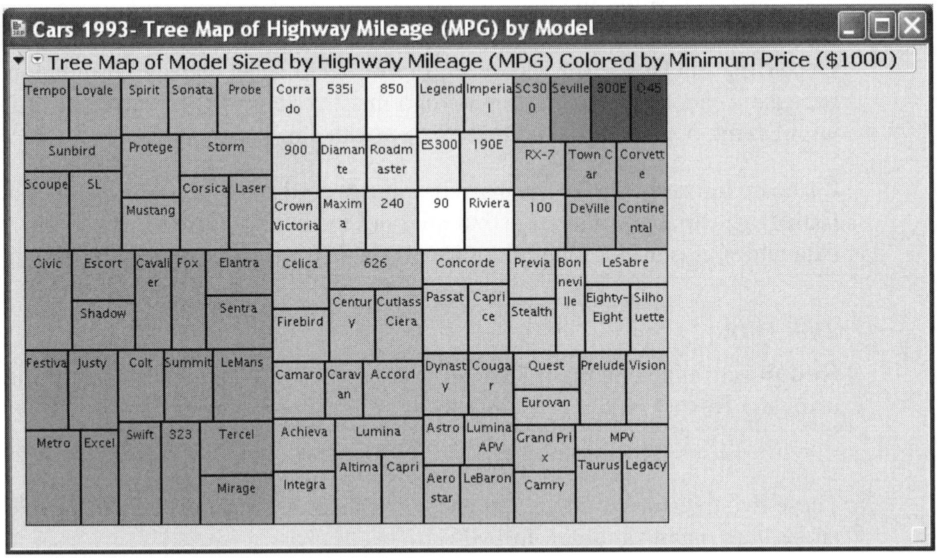

It's hard to imagine a bar chart that displays as much information as this treemap. Inexpensive, high-mileage cars have small, darker green rectangles. Expensive cars have red rectangles.

Treemaps are interactive. In JMP:

1. Click on a rectangle in the treemap. JMP displays the values of the **Categories** and **Sizes** variables. (Without a **Sizes** variable, JMP displays the number of rows represented by the rectangle.)

2. Click the hot spot for the treemap and select **Change Color Column**.

3. Select a different variable. For example, select **Domestic Manufacturer**, which is the last variable in the data table.

4. Click **OK**.

Figure 5.13 displays the treemap.

Figure 5.13 Using Different Coloring Variables

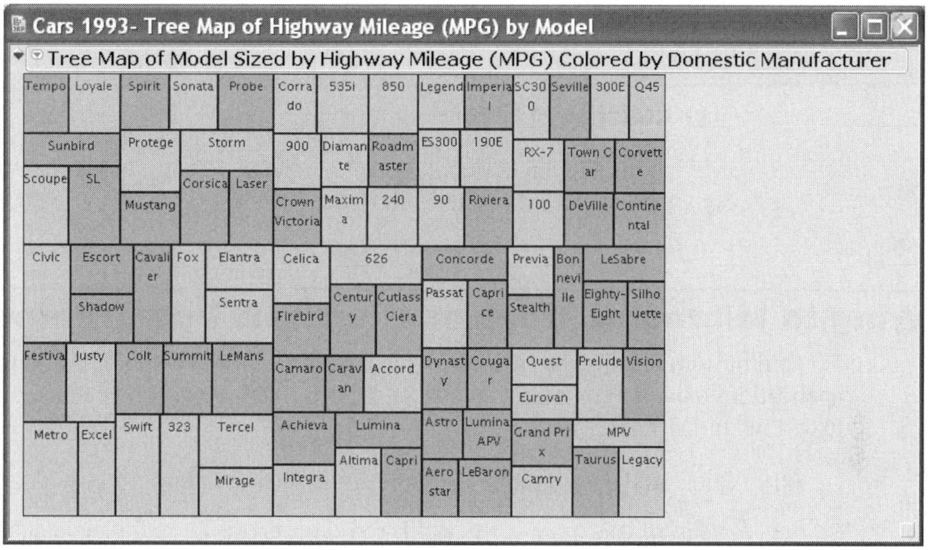

JMP changes the title of the treemap to reflect the new **Coloring** variable.

Figures 5.12 and 5.13 have the same ordering because the **Ordering** variable is the same. Figure 5.13 has two colors for **Domestic Manufacturer**, which has only two values. If you wanted an inexpensive, high-mileage domestic car, the Festiva would have been a good choice in 1993.

Exploring data with treemaps can lead you to insights about your data and help with what-if analyses.

Printing Results

After exploring your results, customizing reports and graphs, adding annotations, and highlighting important issues, you might want to print the results. Chapter 3 discussed printing data tables and **Print Preview** (for Windows only). Printing JMP results is similar. Suppose you have created a report and want to print it. In JMP:

1. Click on the report to make it the active JMP window.

2. Click **File→Print**.

3. Select the printer and number of copies in the Print window, and click **OK**.

JMP prints the results. You can insert page breaks; however, once you insert a page break, it cannot be removed. To insert a page break:

1. Right-click on the disclosure diamond where you want to insert the page break.

2. Click **Edit→Page Break**.

3. JMP inserts a green horizontal line to indicate the page break. In Windows, you can view the printed results with **Print Preview**.

Copying to Microsoft Word or Microsoft PowerPoint

You might want to copy the JMP results to a document or slide deck. Although software applications exist for copying windows or regions in windows, you can use JMP features to do this. In JMP:

1. Click on the report to make it the active JMP window.

2. Click the selection tool in the JMP toolbar. This tool looks like an oversized plus sign, as shown in the following display. Position your mouse pointer over a menu option and JMP displays a tip about the option.

3. For report tables, click the title, and JMP selects the entire report table. You can select individual reports, such as the Moments or Quantiles report. You can select all of the results for a variable by clicking the title. Or, you can select an entire report, such as Distributions, by clicking the title.

4. Right-click and select **Copy**.

5. In the other software application, such as Microsoft Word or Microsoft PowerPoint, position your mouse pointer where you want the JMP results to appear.

6. Click **Edit→Paste Special**.

7. Select the pasting format. Either a **Picture** or a **Bitmap** works well. With these formats, the JMP results appear as you see them in JMP and cannot be edited. If you choose formatted or unformatted text, the results can be edited.

8. Click **OK**. The other application displays the JMP results.

For graphs, use these same steps. After clicking the selection tool, position your mouse pointer over the graph. Click and drag to select some or all of the graph. JMP allows you to copy just the graphic portion, such as the bars of a histogram or a box plot, or to copy the entire graph, including the axes and labels.

JMP Hints:

After pasting the JMP results, you can resize them the same way you resize any other picture in your document or slide presentation.

For graphs, you can use **Paste** and the JMP graph is imported as a picture. However, if you use **Paste** for report tables, they are imported as formatted text, and thus can be edited. For this reason, using **Paste Special** is usually better.

Saving Results to Journals

In addition to copying results to Microsoft Word or Microsoft PowerPoint, JMP provides a way for you to save your results in a JMP journal.[1] A JMP journal is a special JMP file format, in which you can change the appearance of JMP reports. Journals can be opened in JMP, or you can save them as formatted text files that can be opened by other applications.

Look again at Figure 4.23. Suppose you want to save this report as a journal, because you want to save the customized report titles and column headings for future use. In JMP:

1. Click on the report to make it the active window.

2. Click **Edit→Journal**.

Figure 5.14 displays the results.

JMP Hints:

If you click **Edit→Journal** and a data table is the active window, JMP creates a journal that contains a view of the data table. However, most of the time, you want the journal to contain the results instead of the data table.

If you click **File→New Journal** in the JMP Starter window, JMP opens a blank Journal window. You can create a journal of your results in this window. For this activity, using the JMP menu bar is faster than using the JMP Starter window.

---

[1] JMP SE does not include journals.

Figure 5.14 Creating a JMP Journal

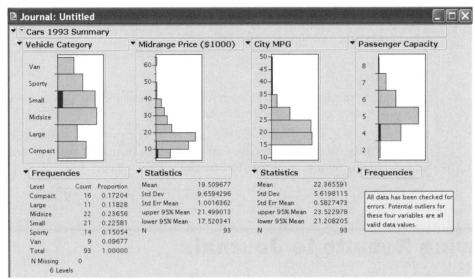

Compare Figures 4.23 and 5.14—they are very similar. When you create a journal from an entire report, it is an exact copy of all of the reports and graphs in the JMP report window.

Modifying JMP Journals

JMP journals are interactive. You can change the appearance of anything that is not linked to the data. For example, you can show and hide reports, change report titles, change column headings, edit the sticky note, change decimal places, or change axis scaling. JMP can perform all of these tasks in the journal without linking to the data table. You cannot highlight bars or points, because JMP links to the data table to perform these tasks. You cannot add more reports or graphs, because JMP creates them from the data table when you click to add them to the report. Look closely at Figure 5.14 and you will see that the hot spots next to each variable name (in Figure 4.23) do not appear. To interact with a JMP journal:

1. Double-click in the **Proportion** column in the Frequencies report for **Vehicle Category**.

2. In the Column Numeric Format window, change the **5** for **Fixed Dec** to **2**.

3. Click **OK**. Compare your results with Figure 5.15.

4. Click the disclosure diamond for the Statistics report for **Midrange Price ($1000)**. JMP hides the report. Figure 5.15 displays the results.

5. Click in the sticky note and add text to explain that the highlighted points are high values for **City MPG**. Click outside the sticky note and resize it as needed. Figure 5.15 displays the results.

6. You can add text to journals. Double-click at the bottom of the journal. JMP displays a field in which you can enter text. Enter your text and click outside the field. Figure 5.15 displays the text at the bottom of the window.

Figure 5.15 Modifying a JMP Journal

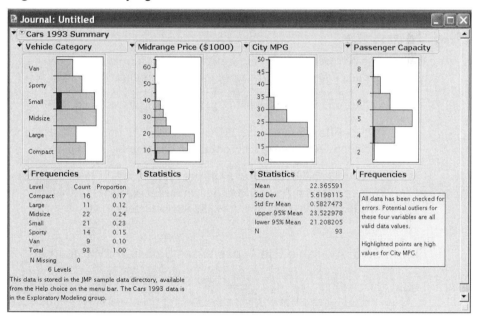

Look at either Figure 5.14 or Figure 5.15. The Distributions report, which is retitled Cars 1993 Summary, has a hot spot next to it. In the journal, this hot spot has different options than what is available in the JMP results. In JMP:

1. Click the hot spot next to Cars 1993 Summary in the Journal window.

2. Select **Rerun in new window**.

3. If the data table is open, JMP creates a new Distributions report.

   If the data table is not open, JMP prompts you to open it. For data tables in the Sample Data Directory, it's easier to open the data table using **Help**. For your own data tables, locate the file for the data table and open it.

JMP creates a new Distributions report that looks similar to the report in the journal. In this example, the Distributions report includes the Frequencies and Moments reports, but not the Quantiles report because it was omitted. The Distributions report does not have any of the changes that you made to titles, column headings, or decimal places. The report does not include the sticky note. The report will have the same highlighting as the journal only if the points are already selected in the data table.

Saving Journals

Journals can be saved in different formats. The best format depends on how you plan to use the journal. You can save the same journal in multiple formats. In JMP:

1. Click on the journal window to make it the active window.

2. Click **File→Save** in the JMP menu bar. JMP opens the Save Journal As window. Navigate to where you want to save the journal.

3. Click the menu for **Save as type**. Figure 5.16 displays the bottom of the Save Journal As window. Accept the automatic choice of **Journal Files (*.JRN)**, which lets you open the journal later in JMP.

Figure 5.16 Available File Types When Saving a JMP Journal

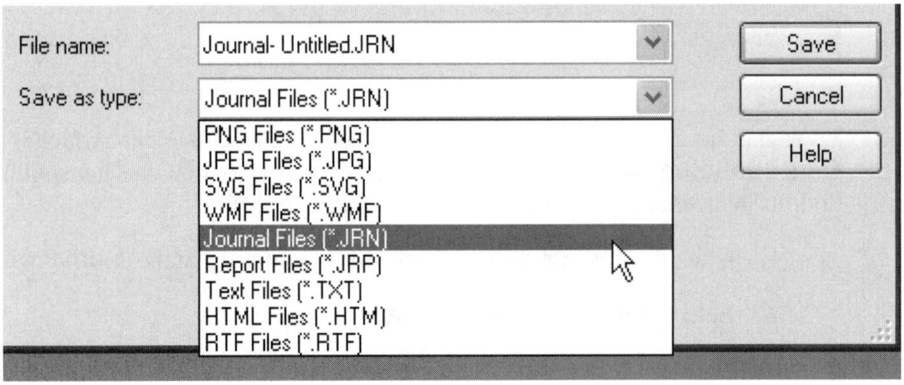

4. Enter a name in the **File name** field.

5. Click **OK**.

6. JMP saves the journal and leaves it open. JMP changes the name of the journal window to the filename that you entered.

Because the journal is open, you can add more results to it. Click on another report and select **Edit→Journal**. To close the journal, click the **X** in the upper-right corner.

Figure 5.16 displays a list of available file types when saving a journal. If you want to:

- Open the journal later in JMP, then save it as a JRN file.

- Display the journal on an intranet, then save it as an HTM file.

- Work with the journal in a document, then save it as an RTF file. Use this file type with caution. After inserting the RTF file in a document, you will be able to double-click it and edit the text. This might not be what you want.

- Include the journal as an image in a document or presentation, then save it as a JPG file. If you want to save the journal in multiple file types, choose JPG last. After you save the journal as a JPG file, it remains open in JMP, but your file types are limited for future saves.

Printing Journals

Print a journal as you would print any JMP report. In Windows, clicking **Print Preview** and right-clicking and selecting **Edit→Page Break** are available.

Summaries

Key Ideas

- Custom bar charts are useful for presentations, where you want to reorder the bars or highlight specific bars.

- Treemaps are a tool for presenting complex data. Treemaps let you view multiple variables in a single, two-dimensional graph. By using different variables for ordering, coloring, and sizing the rectangles of a JMP treemap, a single graph can provide much detail about your data.

- Journals are a useful way to save JMP results for later use.

- Journals are interactive. You can change the appearance of anything that is not linked to the data.

JMP Steps

This topic first summarizes JMP steps for activities that apply to any JMP report or graph. Then, the topic summarizes JMP steps for activities in **Graph**.

To scale axes in any JMP graph:

1. Position your mouse pointer on an axis label and double-click. (This is easier than positioning your mouse pointer exactly on the axis.)

2. Enter values in the fields for **Maximum**, **Minimum**, and **Increment** in the Axis Specification window.

3. Click **OK**.

To recall your choices in any JMP analysis window:

1. JMP remembers your choices during a session. In any window where you select analysis variables, click **Recall** and JMP fills in your previous choices.

To insert a page break in any JMP report:

1. Right-click on the disclosure diamond where you want to insert the page break.

2. Click **Edit→Page Break**.

To copy JMP reports or graphs to Microsoft Word or Microsoft PowerPoint:

1. Click on the report to make it the active JMP window.

2. Click the selection tool in the JMP toolbar. (This tool looks like an oversized plus sign.) Position your mouse pointer over a menu option and JMP displays a tip about the option.

3. For report tables, click the title, and JMP selects the entire report table. You can select individual reports, or all of the results for a variable by clicking the title, or an entire report (such as Distributions) by clicking the title. For graphs, click and drag to select some or all of the graph.

4. Right-click and select **Copy**.

5. In the other application, such as Microsoft Word or Microsoft PowerPoint, position your mouse pointer where you want the JMP results to appear.

6. Click **Edit→Paste Special**.

7. Select the pasting format. Either a **Picture** or a **Bitmap** works well. With these formats, the JMP results appear as you see them in JMP and cannot be edited. If you choose formatted or unformatted text, the results can be edited.

8. Click **OK**. The other application displays the JMP results.

To save results to a journal for any JMP report:

1. Click on the report to make it the active window.

2. Click **Edit→Journal**.

To modify, print, and save journals:

1. Modify the journal by clicking the disclosure diamond and changing report titles, changing column headings, changing decimal places, scaling axes, and adding sticky notes. You can change the appearance of anything that is not linked to the data. You cannot add new analyses or highlight bars or points.

2. To rerun the report shown in the journal, click the hot spot in the report and select **Rerun in new window**. JMP creates as similar a report as possible.

3. Print the journal as you would print any JMP report.

4. Click **File→Save** to save the journal in one of several file types. Select a file type, enter a filename, and click **OK**.

To create and enhance custom bar charts in Graph:

1. In the JMP Starter window, click **Graph→Chart**.

2. Click a continuous variable and then **Statistics→Data**.

3. Click a nominal or ordinal variable and then **Categories, X, Levels**.

4. Click the menu for **Vertical** and change it to **Horizontal**.

5. Click **OK**. JMP creates the bar chart.

6. Click the hot spot for **Chart** and select **Show Level Legend**. JMP hides the legend that appears at the bottom of the bar chart.

7. To change the color for all of the bars in the chart:

   ▪ In the JMP menu, click **Rows→Row Selection→Select All Rows**.

   ▪ Click the hot spot for **Chart**, select **Level Options→Colors**, and a color you like.

8. To change the color for a single bar, click on the bar, select **Level Options→Colors**, and a different color you like.

Steps 1 through 5 create a graph that displays the value of the continuous variable for each level of the nominal or ordinal variable. For example, using **Amount** as the continuous variable and **State** as the categorical variable creates a bar chart in which the length of the bar for each state is the fine amount. Steps 6 through 8 enhance the appearance of the graph.

To apply row order levels to bar charts in Graph:

Apply row order levels before creating the bar chart.

1. First, sort the data and save the sorted data as a new data table. (See Chapter 3 for JMP steps on sorting.)

2. Double-click on the column heading in the data table. JMP displays the column information window.

3. Click the menu for **Column Properties** and select **Row Order Levels**.

4. Click **OK**. JMP adds a heavy asterisk (✱) to the right of the variable name in the columns panel. This asterisk icon signifies that you have applied a special property to the variable.

To create and enhance treemaps in Graph:

1. In the JMP Starter window, click **Graph→Tree Map**.

2. Click a nominal or ordinal variable and then click **Categories**. This is the only required role, and you could create a treemap with only **Categories**. However, a treemap with other features would be more useful. Steps 3 through 5 describe additional options.

3. Click a numeric variable and then click **Ordering**. JMP orders the rectangles in the treemap according to the values of the numeric variable.

4. Click a variable and then click **Coloring**. This can be any variable. JMP colors the rectangles in the treemap according to the values of the variable. When learning treemaps, use the same variable for **Coloring** and **Ordering**.

5. Click a numeric variable and then click **Sizes**. JMP sizes the rectangles in the treemap according to the values of the numeric variable.

6. Click **OK**. JMP creates the treemap.

7. Click on a rectangle in the treemap. If you selected a **Sizes** variable, JMP displays the values of the **Categories** and **Sizes** variables. Otherwise, JMP displays the number of rows represented by the rectangle.

8. Click the hot spot for the treemap and select **Change Color Column**. This option is available even if you created the treemap without a **Coloring** variable.

9. Select a variable and click **OK**.

Exercises

1. For the Cars 1993 data, create a treemap using the **Vehicle Category**, **Highway Mileage (MPG)**, **Maximum Price ($1000)**, and **Passenger Capacity** variables. Explore different treemaps with different choices for the **Ordering**, **Coloring**, and **Sizes** variables. Discuss your insights about the data.

2. Using the Presidential Elections data in the Sample Data Directory (under the Business and Demographic heading), create a bar chart for the 1996 results. Hint: Follow similar steps as you would for the speeding ticket data; first, sort the data table, apply **Row Order Levels**, and then graph the data. Discuss your insights about the data.

3. For the Presidential Elections data, create a treemap using **State** as the **Categories** variable. Use the 1996 results for other choices. Discuss your insights about using the 1996 results as the **Sizes**, **Ordering**, and **Coloring** variable.

4. Using the Movies data in the Sample Data Directory (under the Business and Demographic heading), create a treemap using **Movie** as the **Categories** variable. Use **Domestic $** as the **Sizes**, **Ordering**, and **Coloring** variable. Discuss your insights and identify common features among the high-income movies.

5. For your own data, use the **Graph** features discussed in this chapter. Summarize the data and explain any insights from your results.

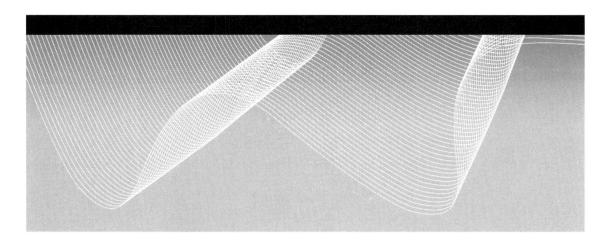

Part 2

Statistical Background

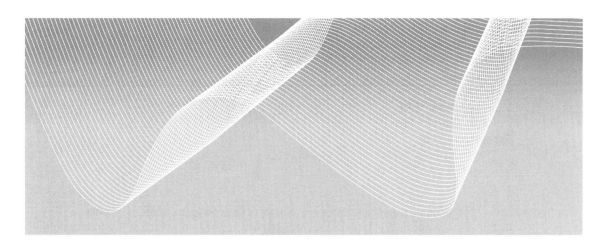

Chapter 6

Understanding Fundamental Statistical Concepts

This chapter focuses more on statistical concepts than on using JMP. It discusses using JMP to test for normality. It also discusses hypothesis testing, which is the foundation of many statistical analyses. The major topics are:

- understanding populations and samples

- understanding the normal distribution

- defining parametric and nonparametric statistical methods

- testing for normality

- building hypothesis tests

- understanding statistical and practical significance

Testing for normality is appropriate for continuous variables. The other concepts in this chapter are appropriate for all types of variables.

Populations and Samples

Definitions

A *population* is a collection of values that has one value for every member in the group of interest. For example, consider the speeding ticket data. If you consider only the 50 states (and ignore Washington, D.C.), the data table contains the speeding ticket fine amounts for the entire group of 50 states. This collection contains one value for every member in the group of interest (the 50 states), so it is the entire population of speeding ticket fine amounts.

This definition of a population as a collection of values might be different from the definition you are more familiar with. You might think of a population as a group of people, as in the population of Detroit. In statistics, think of a population as a collection of measurements on people or things.

A *sample* is also a collection of values, but it does not represent the entire group of interest. For the speeding ticket data, a sample could be the collection of values for speeding ticket fine amounts for the states located in the Southeast. Notice how this sample differs from the population. Both are collections of values, but the population represents the entire group of interest (all 50 states), and the sample represents only a subgroup (states located in the Southeast).

Consider another example. Suppose you are interested in estimating the average price of new homes sold in the United States during 2006, and you have the prices for a few new homes in several cities. This is only a sample of the values. To have the entire population of values, you would need the price for every new home sold in the United States in 2006.

Figure 6.1 shows the relationship between a population and a sample. Each value in the population appears as a small circle. Filled-in circles are values that have been selected for a sample.

Figure 6.1 Relationship between a Population and a Sample

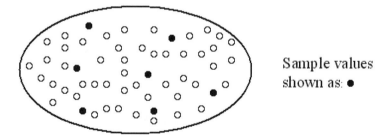

Sample values
shown as: ●

For a final example, think about opinion polls. You often see the results of opinion polls in the news, yet most people have never been asked to participate in a poll. Rather than ask every person in the country (collect a population of values for the group of interest), the companies that conduct these polls ask a small number of people. They collect a sample of values for the group of interest.

Random Samples

Most of the time, you cannot collect the entire population of values. Instead, you collect a sample. To make a valid decision about the population based on a sample, the sample must be representative of the population. This is usually accomplished by collecting a random sample.

A sample is a *simple random sample* if the process that is used to collect the sample ensures that any one sample is as likely to be selected as any other sample. For example, the companies that conduct opinion polls often collect random samples. Any group of people (and their associated sample values) is as likely to be selected as any other group of people. In contrast, the collection of speeding ticket fine amounts for states located in the Southeast is not a random sample of the entire population of speeding ticket fine amounts for the 50 states. This is because the Southeastern states were deliberately chosen to be in the sample.

In many cases, the process of collecting a random sample is complicated and requires the help of a statistician. Simple random samples are only one type of sampling scheme. Other sampling schemes are often preferable. Suppose you conduct a survey to find out students' opinions of their professors. At first, you decide to randomly sample students on campus, but then realize that seniors might have different opinions from freshmen, sophomores from juniors, and so on. Over the years, seniors have developed opinions about what they expect in professors, and freshmen haven't yet had the chance to do so. With a simple random sample, the results could be affected by the differences between the students in the different classes. Thus, you decide to group students according to class and to get a random sample from each class (seniors, juniors, sophomores, and freshmen). This *stratified random sampling* is a better representation of the students' opinions and examines the differences in opinions for the different classes. Before conducting a survey, consult a statistician to develop the best sampling scheme.

Describing Parameters and Statistics

Another difference between populations and samples is the way summary measures are described. Summary measures for a population are called *parameters*; summary measures for a sample are called *statistics*. As an example, suppose you calculate the average for a set of data. If the data set is a population of values, the average is a parameter, which is called the *population mean*. However, if the data set is a sample of values, the average is a statistic, which is called the *sample average* (or the *average*, for short). The rest of this book uses the word "mean" to indicate the population mean and the word "average" to indicate the sample average.

To help distinguish between summary measures for populations and samples, different statistical notation is used for each. In general, population parameters are denoted by letters of the Greek alphabet. For now, consider only three summary measures: the mean, the variance, and the standard deviation.

Recall that the mean is a measure that describes the center of a distribution of values, the variance is a measure that describes the dispersion around the mean, and the standard deviation is the square root of the variance. The average of a sample is denoted with $\overline{X}$ and is called x bar. The population mean is denoted with μ and is called Mu. The sample variance is denoted with s^2 and is called s-squared. The population variance is denoted with σ^2 and is called sigma-squared. Because the standard deviation is the square root of the variance, it is denoted with s for a sample and σ for a population. Table 6.1 summarizes the differences in notation.

Table 6.1 Symbols Used for Populations and Samples

	Average	Variance	Standard Deviation
Population	μ	σ^2	σ
Sample	$\overline{X}$	s^2	s

For the average or mean, the same formula applies to calculations for the population parameter and the sample statistic. This is not the case for other summary measures, such as the variance. See the box labeled "Technical Details: Sample Variance" for formulas and details. JMP automatically calculates the sample variance, not the population variance. Because you almost never have measurements on the entire population, JMP gives summary measures, such as the variance, for a sample.

Technical Details: Sample Variance

To calculate the sample variance for a variable:

1. Find the average.
2. For each value, calculate the difference between the value and the average.
3. Square each difference.
4. Sum the squares.
5. Divide by $n-1$, where n is the number of differences.

For example, suppose your sample values are 10, 11, 12, and 15. The sample size is 4, and the average is 12. The variance is calculated as:

$$s^2 = \frac{(10-12)^2 + (11-12)^2 + (12-12)^2 + (15-12)^2}{4-1}$$

$$= 14/3 = 4.67$$

More generally, the formula is:

$$s^2 = \frac{\sum (X_i - \overline{X})^2}{(n-1)}$$

where $\sum$ stands for sum, X_i represents each sample value, $\overline{X}$ represents the sample average, and n represents the sample size.

The difference between computing the sample variance and the population variance is in the denominator of the formula above. The population variance uses n instead of $n-1$.

The Normal Distribution

Definition and Properties

Many methods of statistical analysis assume that the data is a sample from a population with a normal distribution. The *Normal distribution* is a theoretical distribution of values for a population. The normal distribution has a precise mathematical definition. Rather than describing the complex mathematical definition, this book describes some of the properties and characteristics of the normal distribution.

Figure 6.2 shows several normal distributions. Notice that μ (the population mean) and σ (the standard deviation of the population) are different. The two graphs with μ=100 have the same scaling on both axes, as do the three graphs with μ=30.

Figure 6.2 Graphs of Several Normal Distributions

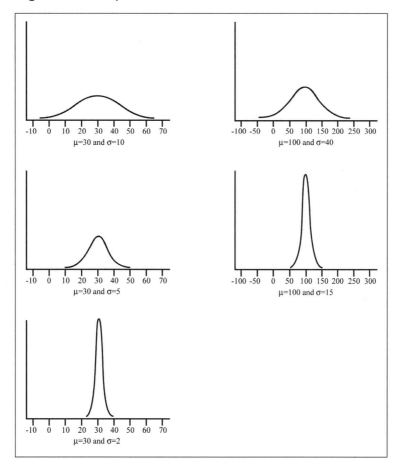

The normal distribution:

- **is completely defined by its mean and standard deviation**. For a given mean and standard deviation, there is only one normal distribution whose graph you can draw.

- **has mean=mode=median**. The mode is the most frequently occurring value, and the median is greater than half of the values, and less than half of the values. If you draw a graph of the normal distribution and then fold the graph in half, the center of the distribution (the fold) is the mean, the mode, and the median of the distribution.

- **is symmetric**. If you draw a graph of the normal distribution and then fold the graph in half, each side of the distribution looks the same. A symmetric distribution has a skewness of 0, so a normal distribution has a skewness of 0. The distribution does not lean to one side or the other, it is even on both sides.

- **is smooth**. From the highest point at the center of the distribution, out to the ends of the distribution (the tails), there are no irregular bumps.

- **has a kurtosis of 0** as calculated in JMP. (There are different formulas for kurtosis; in some formulas, a normal distribution has a kurtosis of 3.) Kurtosis describes the heaviness of the tails of a distribution. Extremely non-normal distributions can have high positive or high negative kurtosis values, while nearly normal distributions will have kurtosis values close to 0. Kurtosis is positive if the tails are heavier than they are for a normal distribution, and negative if the tails are lighter than they are for a normal distribution.

Because the plots of the normal distribution are smooth and symmetric, and the normal distribution resembles the outlines of a bell, the normal distribution is sometimes said to have a bell-shaped curve.

You might be wondering about the use of the word "normal." Does it mean that data from a non-normal distribution is abnormal? The answer is no. Normal distribution is one of many distributions that can occur. For example, the time to failure for computer chips does not have a normal distribution. Experience has shown that computer chips fail more often early (often on their first use), and then the time to failure slowly decreases over the length of use. This distribution is not symmetrical.

The Empirical Rule

If data is from a normal distribution, the Empirical Rule gives a quick and easy way to summarize the data. The Empirical Rule says:

- About 68% of the values are within one standard deviation of the mean.

- About 95% of the values are within two standard deviations of the mean.

- More than 99% of the values are within three standard deviations of the mean.

Figure 6.3 shows a normal distribution. About 68% of the values occur between $\mu - \sigma$ and $\mu + \sigma$, corresponding to the Empirical Rule.

Figure 6.3 The Normal Distribution and the Empirical Rule

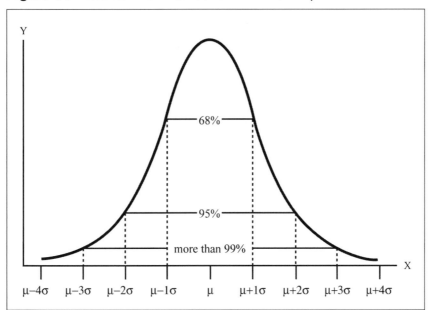

To better understand the Empirical Rule, consider an example. Suppose the population of the individual weights for 12-year old girls is normally distributed with a mean of 86 pounds and a standard deviation of 10 pounds. Using the Empirical Rule, you find that:

- About 68% of the weights are between 76 and 96 pounds.

- About 95% of the weights are between 66 and 106 pounds.

- More than 99% of the weights are between 56 and 116 pounds.

Parametric and Nonparametric Statistical Methods

Many statistical methods rely on the assumption that the data values are a sample from a normal distribution. Other statistical methods rely on an assumption of some other distribution of the data. Statistical methods that rely on assumptions about distributions are called *parametric methods*.

There are statistical methods that do not assume a particular distribution for the data. Statistical methods that don't rely on assumptions about distributions are called *nonparametric methods*.

This distinction is important in later chapters, which explain both parametric and nonparametric methods for solving problems. Use the parametric method if your data meets the assumptions, and use the nonparametric method if it doesn't. These later chapters provide details about the assumptions.

Testing for Normality

A normal distribution is the theoretical distribution of values for a population. Many statistical methods assume that the data values are a sample from a normal distribution. For a given sample, you need to decide whether this assumption is reasonable. Because you have only a sample, you can never be absolutely sure that the assumption is correct. What you can do is test the assumption and, based on the results of this test, decide whether the assumption is reasonable. This testing and decision process is called *testing for normality*.

Statistical Test for Normality

When testing for normality, you start with the idea that the sample is from a normal distribution. Then, you verify whether the data agrees or disagrees with this idea. Using the sample, you calculate a statistic and use this statistic to try to verify the idea. Because this statistic tests the idea, it is called a *test statistic*. The test statistic compares the shape of the sample distribution with the shape of a normal distribution.

The result of this comparison is a number called a *p*-value, which describes how doubtful the idea is in terms of probability. A *p*-value can range from 0 to 1. A *p*-value close to 0 means that the idea is very doubtful and provides evidence against the idea. If you find enough evidence to reject the idea, you decide that the data is not a sample from a normal distribution. If you cannot find enough evidence to reject the idea, you proceed with the analyses based on the assumption that the data is a sample from a normal distribution.

JMP provides the formal test for normality in the **Distribution** platform. To illustrate the test, Table 6.2 shows data values for the heights of aeries, or nests, for prairie falcons in North Dakota[1].

Table 6.2 Prairie Falcons Data

Aerie Height in Meters				
15.00	3.50	3.50	7.00	1.00
7.00	5.75	27.00	15.00	8.00
4.75	7.50	4.25	6.25	5.75
5.00	8.50	9.00	6.25	5.50
4.00	7.50	8.75	6.50	4.00
5.25	3.00	12.00	3.75	4.75
6.25	3.25	2.50		

This data is available in the Falcons data table in the sample data for this book. To see the test for normality in JMP:

1. Open the Falcons data table.

2. In the JMP Starter window, click **Basic→Distribution**.

3. Click **Aerieht→Y, Columns**.

4. Click **OK**.

5. In the Distribution window, click the hot spot for Aerieht and select **Fit Distribution→Normal**.

6. Click the hot spot for Fitted Normal and select **Goodness of Fit**.

Figure 6.4 shows the results, with the Quantiles and Moments reports hidden. Chapter 4 discusses these reports.

---

[1] Data is from Dr. George T. Allen, U.S. Fish & Wildlife Service, Arlington, Virginia. Used with permission.

Figure 6.4 Testing for Normality of Falcons Data

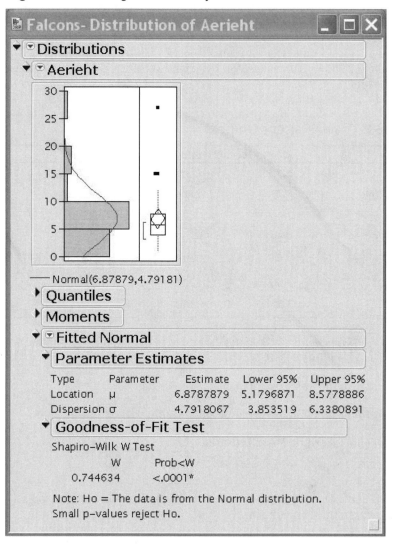

The Goodness-of-Fit Test report shows the results of the formal test for normality. The column labeled **W** contains the value of the test statistic. The test statistic, W, is greater than 0 and less than or equal to 1 ($0 < W \leq 1$). Values of W that are too small indicate that the data is not a sample from a normal distribution. The second column, labeled **Prob<W**, contains the probability value, which describes how likely the idea of normality is. Probability values (p-values) can range from 0 to 1 ($0 < p \leq 1$). Probability values very close to 0 indicate that the data is not a sample from a normal distribution, and produce the most doubt in the idea. For the Falcons data, you can conclude that the aerie heights are not normally distributed.

JMP performs the Shapiro-Wilk test if the sample size (n) is less than 2000. JMP performs the Kolmogorov-Smirnoff-Lillifors (KSL) test for larger sample sizes. Figure 6.4 shows the Shapiro-Wilk test results. In the results for the KSL test, the columns are labeled **D** and **Prob>D**.

The Parameter Estimates report shows details on the fitted normal distribution.

Type	Identifies the type of parameter. Statisticians refer to the center of the distribution (or mean, for the normal distribution) as the *location*. They refer to the spread of the distribution (or standard deviation, for the normal distribution) as the *dispersion*.
Parameter	Identifies the population mean (μ) and standard deviation (σ) of the distribution.
Estimate	Gives the estimated value of the parameter.
Lower 95% **Upper 95%**	Indicates confidence intervals, which are discussed in Chapter 7.

JMP Hint:

Position the mouse pointer near the **Prob<W** column and move it around in a very small circle. JMP displays a pop-up window, which includes text explaining the hypothesis test. To close the window, move your mouse pointer again.

Other Methods of Checking for Normality

In addition to the formal test for normality, there are other methods for checking for normality. These methods improve your understanding about the distribution of the sample values. These methods include looking at a histogram of the data, looking at a box plot, checking the values of skewness and kurtosis, looking at a normal quantile plot, and looking at a stem-and-leaf lot. The next five topics discuss these methods.

Histogram

Figure 6.4 shows a histogram of the aerie heights. The histogram does not have the general bell shape of a normal distribution. Also, the histogram is not symmetric. The histogram shape indicates that the sample is not from a normal distribution.

As a result of fitting a normal distribution to the data, JMP added a normal curve to the histogram. The curve uses the sample average and sample standard deviation from the data. If the data were normal, the smooth red curve would more closely match the bars of the histogram. For the Falcons data, the curve helps show that the sample is not from a normal distribution.

When JMP adds a normal curve, the formula for the curve appears just below the histogram. In Figure 6.4, this appears as a short red line, followed by Normal(6.87879,4.79181). The Parameter Estimates report contains details on the curve.

JMP Hint:

As described in Chapter 4, you can double-click on a statistic in the Parameter Estimates report and change the number of decimal places that are displayed. This does not change the formula for the curve. You cannot change the formula's appearance.

Box Plot

Figure 6.4 shows an outlier box plot of the aerie heights. Chapter 4 discussed the box plot as a way to explore the data. Box plots are also useful when checking for normality. Because a normal distribution has the mean equal to the median, box plots for a normal distribution show the median line (center of the box) at about the same place as the mean (center of the diamond).

Figure 6.5 shows the histogram and outlier box plot from Figure 6.4, and displays another histogram and outlier box plot. The histogram and outlier box plot on the right is from a normal distribution, and has the mean very close to the median. For the Falcons data on the left, the center of the diamond (the mean) is much higher than the middle line of the box (the median). Figure 6.5 shows the difference in histograms for data from a normal distribution and for data from a non-normal distribution, the Falcons data. Reviewing the box plots reinforces the results from the formal test of normality that rejected the idea of normality.

Figure 6.5 Histograms and Box Plots for Non-Normal and Normal Data

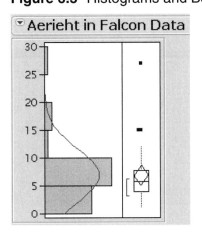 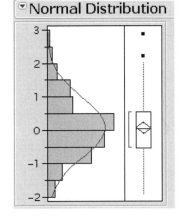

The histogram and box plot for the **Falcons** data in Figure 6.5 highlight three outliers. From Chapter 4, we know that outliers are worth investigating.

Skewness and Kurtosis

Recall that for a normal distribution, the skewness is 0. Also, as calculated in JMP, the kurtosis for a normal distribution is 0. To see the skewness and kurtosis in JMP:

1. Click the title of the **Distribution** window to make it the active window.

2. Click the hot spot for **Aerieht** and select **Display Options→More Moments**.

Figure 6.6 displays the **Moments** report. For the **Falcons** data, neither the skewness nor the kurtosis is close to 0. This reinforces the results from the formal test of normality that rejected the idea of normality.

Figure 6.6 Adding More Moments to the Falcons Data

Moments	
Mean	6.8787879
Std Dev	4.7918067
Std Err Mean	0.8341465
upper 95% Mean	8.5778886
lower 95% Mean	5.1796871
N	33
Sum Wgt	33
Sum	227
Variance	22.961411
Skewness	2.6517822
Kurtosis	9.2763068
CV	69.660625
N Missing	0

Normal Quantile Plot

A normal quantile plot of the data shows both the sample data and a line for a normal distribution. Because of the way the plot is constructed, the normal distribution appears as a straight line, instead of as the bell-shaped curve seen in the histogram. If the sample data is from a normal distribution, then the points for the sample data are very close to the normal distribution line. To add a normal quantile plot to the Distributions report in JMP:

1. Click the title of the Distribution window to make it the active window.

2. Click the hot spot for Aerieht and select **Normal Quantile Plot**.

Figure 6.7 displays the plot.

Figure 6.7 Adding a Normal Quantile Plot to the Falcons Data

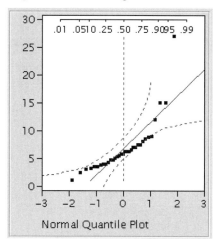

The black dots in Figure 6.7 are the data points for the Falcons data. The solid red line represents a normal distribution. The dotted red lines display confidence bounds for the normal distribution. If the Falcons data were normal, then the black dots would be close to the solid red line, and almost all of the black dots would be within the dotted red lines. For the Falcons data, many of the data points are outside the dotted red lines, and a few points are close to the solid red line. Once again, this reinforces the conclusion that the data is not a sample from a normal distribution.

The normal quantile plot in Figure 6.7 shows that there are three or four data points that are separated from most of the data points. From Chapter 4, we know that these are potential outlier points that should be investigated.

Figure 6.8 shows a normal quantile plot for data from a normal distribution. The black dots—the data points—are all fairly close to the solid red line that represents the normal distribution. The data points are all within the dotted red lines that are the confidence bounds. Compare the plots in Figures 6.7 and 6.8 to better understand the differences in a normal quantile plot for data that is from a normal distribution, and a normal quantile plot for data that is not from a normal distribution.

Figure 6.8 Normal Quantile Plot for Data from a Normal Distribution

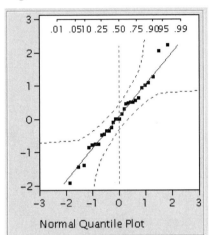

The dotted vertical green line in the normal quantile plot is a reference line that shows the center of the normal distribution. This is also the median. For the data in Figure 6.8, about half of the data points are on either side of the green line.

Figure 6.9 shows several patterns that can occur in normal quantile plots, and gives the interpretations for these patterns. Compare the patterns in Figure 6.9 to the normal quantile plot in Figure 6.7. The closest match is the pattern for a distribution that is skewed to the right. (Remember that the positive skewness measure also indicates that the data is skewed to the right.)

Figure 6.9 How to Interpret Patterns in Normal Quantile Plots

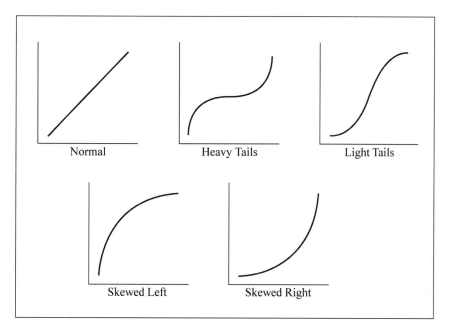

Using Stem-and-Leaf Plots

Chapter 4 discussed the stem-and-leaf plot as a way to explore data, and provided the JMP steps to generate the plot. Stem-and-leaf plots are also useful for visually checking data for normality. If the data is normal, then there will be a single bell-shaped curve of data. Figure 6.10 shows the stem-and-leaf plot for the Falcons data.

Figure 6.10 Adding a Stem-and-Leaf Plot to the Falcons Data

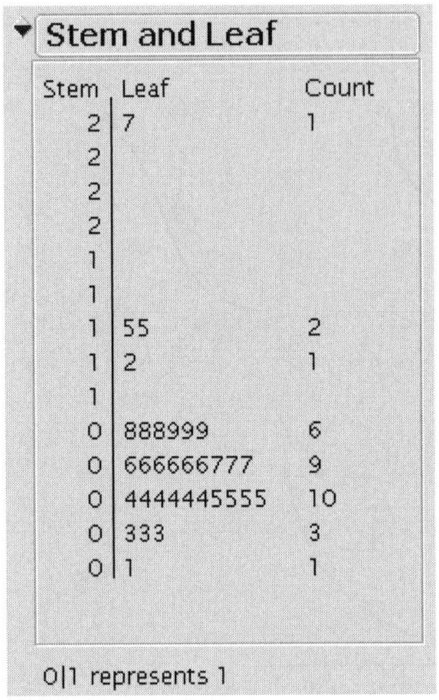

```
▼ Stem and Leaf

  Stem   Leaf             Count
     2   7                   1
     2
     2
     2
     1
     1
     1   55                  2
     1   2                   1
     1
     0   888999             6
     0   666666777          9
     0   4444445555        10
     0   333                3
     0   1                  1


  0|1 represents 1
```

Most of the data forms a single group that is roughly bell-shaped. Depending on how you look at the data, there are three or four outlier points. These are the data points for the aerie heights of 12, 15, 15, and 27 meters.

The histogram, outlier box plot, normal quantile plot, and stem-and-leaf plot all show outlier points that should be investigated. Perhaps these outlier points represent an unusual situation: for example, prairie falcons might have been using a nest built by another type of bird. If your data has outlier points, you should carefully investigate them to avoid incorrectly concluding that the data isn't a sample from a normal distribution. Suppose we do an investigation, and we find that the three highest points appear to be eagle nests. The next section shows how to recheck the data for normality.

Rechecking the Falcons Data

The full Falcons data table has four potential outlier points. Suppose you investigate and find that the three highest aerie heights are actually eagle nests that have been adopted by prairie falcons. You want to omit these data points from the check for normality. In JMP, this involves creating a subset of the data, using **Distribution** for the aerie height, and adding the additional reports and plots to check for normality. In JMP:

1. Click the title of the Distribution window to make it the active window.

2. Click the lasso 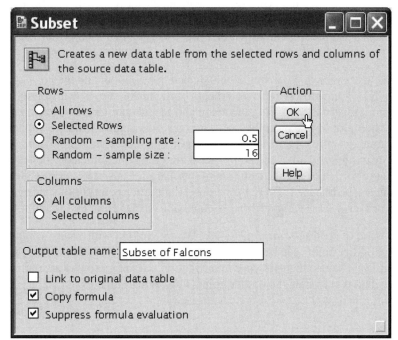 tool on the toolbar. Click and drag a circle around the three outlier points in the box plot. The points will highlight in the Distribution window and in the data table.

3. Click the title of the Falcons data table to make it the active window.

4. Click **Rows→Row Selection→Invert Row Selection**. All of the rows <u>except</u> the three outlier points are now highlighted.

5. Click **Tables→Subset**. The automatic choices are what you need, and they are shown in Figure 6.11.

Figure 6.11 Subset Window

6. Click **OK**.

7. Click the title of the Subset of Falcons data table to make it the active window.

8. In the JMP Starter window, click **Basic→Distribution**.

9. Click **Aerieht→Y, Columns**.

10. Click **OK**.

11. In the Distribution window, click the hot spot for Aerieht and select **Fit Distribution→Normal**.

12. Click the hot spot for Fitted Normal and select **Goodness of Fit**.

13. Click the hot spot for Aerieht and select:

   a. **Display Options→More Moments**.

   b. **Normal Quantile Plot**.

   c. **Stem and Leaf**.

Figure 6.12 shows the results with the Quantiles, Parameter Estimates, and Stem and Leaf reports hidden. **Prob<W** is now much closer to 1, with a value of **0.8228**. The formal test of normality leads you to conclude that this subset of the original Falcons data is a sample from a normal distribution. The other methods of checking for normality support this conclusion.

The histogram shows a single bell-shaped distribution, and the normal curve overlaying the histogram closely follows the bars of the histogram. The histogram is also mostly symmetric. In the box plot, the mean and median are much closer to each other than in the box plot for the original data. The skewness and kurtosis are both close to 0. In the normal quantile plot, most of the data points are near the solid red line for the normal distribution, and all of the points are within the dotted line confidence bounds. Although Figure 6.12 does not show the stem-and-leaf plot, it shows a single group of data that is roughly bell-shaped. There is one potential outlier point for the aerie height of 12 meters. However, we have already investigated this outlier point and found it to be valid.

A word of caution is important here. When working with your own data, do not assume that outlier points can be deleted from the data. If you find potential outlier points, you must investigate them. If your investigation does not uncover a valid reason for omitting the data points, then the outlier points must remain in the data.

Figure 6.12 Subset of Falcons Data

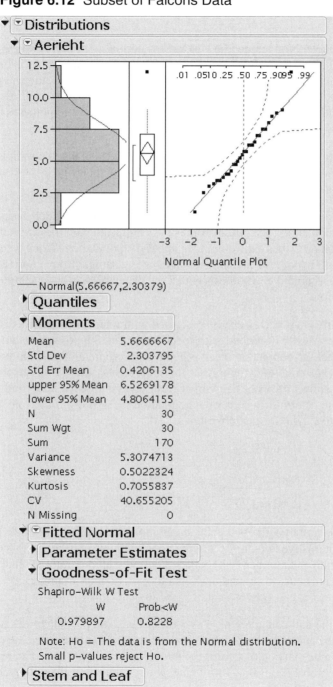

— Normal(5.66667,2.30379)

▶ **Quantiles**

▼ **Moments**

Mean	5.6666667
Std Dev	2.303795
Std Err Mean	0.4206135
upper 95% Mean	6.5269178
lower 95% Mean	4.8064155
N	30
Sum Wgt	30
Sum	170
Variance	5.3074713
Skewness	0.5022324
Kurtosis	0.7055837
CV	40.655205
N Missing	0

▼ ⏷ **Fitted Normal**

▶ **Parameter Estimates**

▼ **Goodness-of-Fit Test**

Shapiro–Wilk W Test

W	Prob<W
0.979897	0.8228

Note: Ho = The data is from the Normal distribution. Small p–values reject Ho.

▶ **Stem and Leaf**

Building a Hypothesis Test

Earlier in this chapter, you learned how to test for normality to decide whether your data is from a normal distribution. The process used for testing for normality is one example of a statistical method used in many types of analysis. This is also known as *performing a hypothesis test*, usually abbreviated to *hypothesis testing*. This section describes the general method of hypothesis testing. Later chapters discuss the hypotheses that are tested, in relation to this general method.

Recall the statistical test for normality: you start with the idea that the sample is from a normal distribution, and then you verify whether the data table agrees or disagrees with the idea. This concept is basic to hypothesis testing.

In building a hypothesis test, you work with the *null hypothesis*, which describes one idea about the population. The null hypothesis is contrasted with the *alternative hypothesis*, which describes a different idea about the population. When testing for normality, the null hypothesis is that the data table is a sample from a normal distribution. The alternative hypothesis is that the data table is a not a sample from a normal distribution.

Null and alternative hypotheses can be described with words. In statistics texts and journals, they are usually described with special notation. Suppose you want to test to determine whether the population mean is equal to a certain number. You want to know whether the average price of hamburger is the same as last year's average price of $3.29 per pound. You collect prices of hamburger from several grocery stores and you want to use this sample to determine whether the population mean is different from $3.29. The null and alternative hypotheses are written as:

$$H_o: \mu = 3.29$$

and

$$H_a: \mu \neq 3.29$$

H_o represents the null hypothesis that the population mean (μ) equals $3.29, and H_a represents the alternative hypothesis that the population mean (μ) does not equal $3.29. Combined, the null and alternative hypotheses describe all possibilities. In this example, the possibilities are equal to (=) and not equal to ($\neq$). In other examples, the possibilities might be less than (<) and greater than or equal to ($\geq$).

Once you have the null and alternative hypotheses, you use the data to calculate a statistic to test the null hypothesis. Then, you compare the calculated value of this *test statistic* to the value that could occur if the null hypothesis were true. The result of this comparison is a probability value, or *p*-value, which tells you if the null hypothesis should be believed. The *p*-value is the probability that the value of your test statistic could have occurred if the null hypothesis were true. Figure 6.13 shows the general process for hypothesis testing.

Figure 6.13 Performing a Hypothesis Test

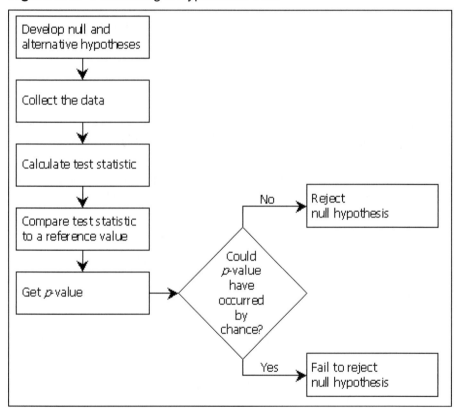

A *p*-value close to 0 indicates that the value of the test statistic could not reasonably have occurred by chance. You reject the null hypothesis and conclude that the null hypothesis is not true. However, if the *p*-value indicates that the value of the test statistic could have occurred by chance, you fail to reject the null hypothesis. You never accept the null hypothesis. Instead, you conclude that you do not have enough evidence to reject it. Unless you measure an entire population, you never have enough evidence to conclude that the population is exactly as described by the null hypothesis. For example, you could not conclude that the true mean price of hamburger is $3.29 per pound, unless you obtained prices from every place that sold hamburger.

For the example of testing for normality, you test the null hypothesis that the data is from a normal distribution. You calculate a test statistic that summarizes the shape of the distribution. Then, you compare the test statistic with a reference value, and you get a *p*-value. Based on this result, you can reject the null hypothesis that the data is normally distributed. Or, you can fail to reject the null hypothesis and proceed with the assumption that the data is normally distributed.

The next section explains how to decide whether a *p*-value indicates that a difference is larger than what would be expected by chance. It also discusses the concept of practical significance.

Statistical and Practical Significance

When you perform a statistical test and get a *p*-value, you usually want to know whether the result is significant. In other words, is the value of the test statistic larger than what you would expect to find by chance? To answer this question, you need to understand statistical significance and practical significance.

Statistical Significance

Statistical significance is based on *p*-values. Typically, you decide, in advance, what level of significance to use for the test. Choosing the significance level is a way of limiting the chance of being wrong. What chance are you willing to take that you are wrong in your conclusions?

For example, a significance level of 5% means that if you collected 100 samples and performed 100 hypothesis tests, you would make the wrong conclusion about 5 times (5/100=0.05). In the previous sentence, "wrong" has the meaning of concluding that the alternative hypothesis is true when it is not. For the hamburger example, "wrong" means concluding that the population mean is different from $3.29 when it is not. Statisticians call this definition of "wrong" the *Type I error*. By choosing a significance level when you perform a hypothesis test, you control the probability of making a Type I error.

When you choose a significance level, you define the reference probability. For a significance level of 10%, the reference probability is 0.10, which is the significance level expressed in decimals. The reference probability is called the α-level (pronounced "alpha level") for the statistical test.

When you perform a statistical test, if the *p*-value is less than the reference probability (the α-level), you conclude that the result is statistically significant. Suppose you decide to perform a statistical test at the 10% significance level, which means that the α-level is 0.10. If the *p*-value is less than 0.10, you conclude that the result is statistically significant at the 10% significance level. If the *p*-value is more than 0.10, you conclude that the result is not statistically significant at the 10% significance level.

As a more concrete example, suppose you perform a statistical test at the 10% significance level, and the *p*-value is 0.002. You limited the risk of making a Type I error to 10%, giving you an α-level of 0.10. Your test statistic value could occur only about 2 times in 1000 by chance, if the null hypothesis were true. Because the *p*-value of 0.002 is less than the α-level of 0.10, you reject the null hypothesis. The test is statistically significant at the 10% level.

Choosing a Significance Level

The choice of the significance level (or α-level) depends on the risk you are willing to take of making a Type I error. Three significance levels are commonly used: 0.10, 0.05, and 0.01. These are often referred to as moderately significant, significant, and highly significant, respectively.

Your situation should help you determine the level of significance you choose. If you are challenging an established principle, then your null hypothesis is that this established principle is true. In this case, you want to be very careful not to reject the null hypothesis if it is true. You should choose a very small α-level, for example 0.01 or even 0.001. If, however, you have a situation where the consequences of rejecting the null hypothesis are not so severe, then an α-level of 0.05 or 0.10 might be more appropriate.

More on *p*-values

As described in this book, hypothesis testing involves rejecting or failing to reject a null hypothesis at a predetermined α-level. You make a decision about the truth of the null hypothesis. But, in some cases, you might want to use the *p*-value only as a summary measure that describes the evidence against the null hypothesis. This situation occurs most often when conducting basic, exploratory research. The *p*-value describes the evidence against the null hypothesis. The smaller a *p*-value is, the more you doubt the null hypothesis. A *p*-value of 0.003 provides strong evidence against the null hypothesis, whereas a *p*-value of 0.36 provides less evidence.

Another Type of Error

In addition to the Type I error, there is another kind of error called the *Type II error*. A Type II error occurs when you fail to reject the null hypothesis when it is false. You can control this type of error when you choose the sample size for your study. The Type II error is not discussed in this book because design of experiments is not discussed. If you are planning an experiment (where you choose the sample size), consult with a statistician to ensure that the Type II error is controlled.

The following table shows the relationships between the true underlying situation (which you will never know unless you measure the entire population) and your conclusions. When you conclude that there is not enough evidence to reject the null hypothesis, and this matches the unknown underlying situation, you make a correct decision. When you reject the null hypothesis, and this matches the unknown underlying situation, you make a correct conclusion. When you reject the null hypothesis, and this does not match the unknown underlying situation, you make a Type I error. When you fail to reject the null hypothesis, and this does not match the unknown underlying situation, you make a Type II error.

	Unknown Underlying Situation	
Your Conclusion	Null Hypothesis True	Alternative Hypothesis True
Fail to Reject the Null Hypothesis	Correct	Type II error
Reject the Null Hypothesis	Type I error	Correct

Practical Significance

Practical significance is based on common sense. Sometimes, a *p*-value indicates statistical significance where the difference is not practically significant. This situation can occur with large data tables, or when there is a small amount of variation in the data.

Other times, a *p*-value indicates non-significant differences where the difference is important from a practical standpoint. This situation can occur with small data tables, or when there is a large amount of variation in the data.

You need to base your final conclusion on both statistical significance and common sense. Think about the size of difference that would lead you to spend time or money. Then, when looking at the statistical results, look at both the *p*-value and the size of the difference.

Example

Suppose you gave a proficiency test to employees who were divided into one of two groups: those who just completed a training program (trainees), and those who have been on the job for a while (experienced employees). Possible scores on the test could range from 0 to 100. You want to find out if the mean scores are different, and you want to use the result to decide whether to change the training program. You perform a hypothesis test at the 5% significance level and obtain a p-value of 0.025. From a statistical standpoint, you can conclude that the two groups are significantly different.

What if the average scores for the two groups are very similar? If the average score for trainees is 83.5, and the average score for experienced employees is 85.2, is the difference practically significant? Should you spend time and money to change the training program based on this small difference? Common sense says no. Finding statistical significance without practical significance is likely to occur with large sample sizes or small variances. If your sample contains several hundred employees in each group, or if the variation within each group is small, you are likely to find statistical significance without practical significance.

Continuing with this example, suppose your proficiency test has a different outcome. You obtain a p-value of 0.125, which indicates that the two groups are not significantly different from a statistical standpoint (at the 5% significance level). However, the average score for the trainees is 63.8, and the average score for the experienced employees is 78.4. Common sense says that you need to think about making some changes in the training program. Finding practical significance without statistical significance can occur with small sample sizes or large variation in each group. Your sample could contain only a few employees in each group, or there could be a lot of variability in each group. In these cases, you are likely to find practical significance without statistical significance.

The important thing to remember about practical and statistical significance is that you should not take action based on p-values alone. Sample sizes, variability in the data, and incorrect assumptions about your data can all produce p-values that indicate one action, where common sense indicates another action. To help avoid this situation, consult a statistician when you design your study. A statistician can help you plan a study so that your sample size is large enough to detect a practically significant difference, but not so large that it would detect a practically insignificant difference. In this way, you control both Type I and Type II errors.

Summaries

Key Ideas

- Populations and samples are both collections of values, but a population contains the entire group of interest, and a sample contains a subset of the population.

- A sample is a simple random sample if the process that is used to collect the sample ensures that any one sample is as likely to be selected as any other sample.

- Summary measures for a population are called parameters, and summary measures for a sample are called statistics. Different statistical notation is used for each.

- The normal distribution is a theoretical distribution with important properties. A normal distribution has a bell-shaped curve that is smooth and symmetric. For a normal distribution, the mean=mode=median.

- The Empirical Rule gives a quick way to summarize data from a normal distribution. The Empirical Rule says:

  □ About 68% of the values are within one standard deviation of the mean.

  □ About 95% of the values are within two standard deviations of the mean.

  □ More than 99% of the values are within three standard deviations of the mean.

- A formal statistical test is used to test for normality.

- Informal methods of checking for normality include:

  □ viewing a histogram to check the shape of the data and to compare the shape with a normal curve

  □ viewing an outlier box plot to compare the mean and median

  □ checking if skewness and kurtosis are close to 0

        ☐   comparing the data with a normal distribution in the normal quantile plot

        ☐   using a stem-and-leaf plot to check the shape of the data

- If you find potential outlier points when checking for normality, investigate them. Do not assume that outlier points can be deleted.

- Hypothesis testing involves choosing a null hypothesis and alternative hypothesis, calculating a test statistic from the data, obtaining the *p*-value, and comparing the *p*-value to an α-level.

- By choosing the α-level for the hypothesis test, you control the probability of making a Type I error, which is the probability of rejecting the null hypothesis when it is true.

JMP Steps

To test for normality:

1. Make sure the data table that you want to analyze is the active JMP window.

2. In the JMP Starter window, click **Basic→Distribution**.

3. Click the variables that you want to analyze and then **Y, Columns**.

4. Click **OK**.

5. In the Distribution window, click the hot spot for the variable and select **Fit Distribution→Normal**.

6. Click the hot spot for Fitted Normal and select **Goodness of Fit**.

To see plots and statistics to check for normality:

The previous steps automatically show the histogram with a normal curve and the outlier box plot. These plots are informal tools in testing for normality. For other informal tools:

1. Click the hot spot for the variable in the Distributions report.

2. Click **Display Options→More Moments** to see skewness and kurtosis.

3. Click **Normal Quantile Plot** to see the normal quantile plot and to compare the data to a normal distribution.

4. Click **Stem and Leaf** to see the stem-and-leaf plot and to compare the shape of the data with a normal distribution.

To create a subset of data that excludes potential outliers:

1. Select the outlier points, either in the data table, report, or graph. The lasso tool is useful for selecting outlier points in graphs.

2. Click the title of the data table window to make it the active window.

3. Click **Rows→Row Selection→Invert Row Selection**. This highlights all of the rows <u>except</u> the outlier points.

4. Click **Tables→Subset**. Accept the automatic choices in the **Subset** window, and click **OK**.

Exercises

1. Using the Companies data in the Sample Data Directory (under the Business and Demographic heading), test for normality of **Profits**. Use the statistical test and additional methods from this chapter. Discuss your results.

2. Using the Car Physical Data data table in the Sample Data Directory (under the Exploratory Modeling heading), test for normality of **Weight**. Use the statistical test and additional methods from this chapter. Discuss your results.

3. Using the Diet data in the Sample Data Directory (under the Medical Studies heading), test for normality of **Quack's Weight Change**. Use the statistical test and additional methods from this chapter. Discuss your results.

4. Using the Polycity data in the Sample Data Directory (under the Business and Demographic heading), test for normality of **Ozone**. Use the statistical test and additional methods from this chapter. Discuss your results.

5. Using the Lipid data in the Sample Data Directory (under the Medical Studies heading), test for normality of **Cholesterol**. Use the statistical test and additional methods from this chapter. Discuss your results.

6. Using the Lipid data, test for normality of **Coffee Intake**. Use the statistical test and additional methods from this chapter. Discuss your results.

7. For your own data, use the features discussed in this chapter to test variables for normality. Summarize the data and explain any insights from your results.

Chapter 7

Estimating the Mean

Like Chapter 6, this chapter focuses more on statistical concepts than on using JMP. This chapter shows how to use JMP to find a confidence interval for the mean. Confidence intervals are based on statistical concepts that are illustrated with simulated data. Major topics in this chapter are:

- estimating the mean with a single number
- exploring the effect of sample size when estimating the mean
- exploring the effect of population variance when estimating the mean
- understanding the distribution of sample averages
- building confidence intervals for the mean

JMP creates confidence intervals for continuous variables only. However, the general concepts discussed in this chapter apply to all types of variables.

Using One Number to Estimate the Mean

To estimate the mean of a normally distributed population, use the arithmetic average of a random sample that is taken from the population. Non-normal distributions also use the average of a random sample to estimate the mean. If your data is not normally distributed, you might want to consult with a statistician because another statistic might be better.

The sample average gives a *point estimate* of the population mean. The sample average gives one number, or point, to estimate the mean. The sample size and the population variance both affect the precision of this point estimate. Generally, larger samples produce more precise estimates, or produce estimates closer to the true unknown population mean. In general, samples from a population with a small variance produce more precise estimates than samples from a population with a large variance. Sample size and the population variance interact. Large samples from a population with a small variance are likely to produce the most precise estimates. The next two sections describe these ideas.

Effect of Sample Size

Suppose you want to estimate the average monthly starting salary of recently graduated male software quality engineers in the United States. You cannot collect the salaries of every recent graduate in the United States, so you take a random sample of salaries and use the sample values to calculate the average monthly starting salary. This average is an estimate of the population mean. How close do you think the sample average is to the population mean? One way to answer this question is to take many samples and then compute the average for each sample. This collection of sample averages will cluster around the population mean. If you knew what the population mean actually was, you could examine the collection to see how closely the sample averages are clustered around the mean.

In this salary example, suppose you could take 200 samples. How would the averages for the different samples vary? The rest of this section explores the effect of different sample sizes on the sample averages. This section uses simulation, which is the process of using the computer to generate data, and then exploring the data to understand concepts.

Suppose you know that the true population mean is $4850 per month, and that the true population standard deviation is $625. Now, suppose you sample 100 values from the population and you find the average for this sample. Then, you repeat this process 199 more times, for a total of 200 samples. From each sample, you get a sample average that estimates the population mean.

To demonstrate what would happen, we simulated this example in JMP. The simulation created 200 sample averages. Figure 7.1 shows the results of using the **Distribution** platform to plot the sample averages.

Figure 7.1 Distribution of 200 Samples with n=100, μ=4850, and σ=625

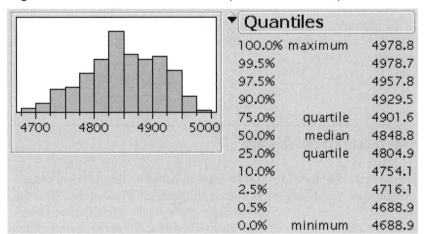

Quantiles		
100.0% maximum		4978.8
99.5%		4978.7
97.5%		4957.8
90.0%		4929.5
75.0%	quartile	4901.6
50.0%	median	4848.8
25.0%	quartile	4804.9
10.0%		4754.1
2.5%		4716.1
0.5%		4688.9
0.0%	minimum	4688.9

Figure 7.1 shows a histogram of the 200 sample averages, where each average is based on a sample that contains 100 values. Most of the sample averages are close to the true population mean of $4850. The **Quantiles** report shows the 2.5% and 97.5% values to be 4716 and 4958, rounded to the nearest dollar. Thus, about 95% of the values are between $4716 and $4958.

Reducing the Sample Size

What happens if you reduce the sample size to 50 values? For each sample, you calculate the average of 50 values. Then, you create a histogram that summarizes the averages from the 200 samples.

What happens if you reduce the sample size even further, so that each sample contains only 10 values? What happens if you reduce the sample size to 5 values?

Figure 7.2 shows the results of reducing the sample size. All of the histograms have the same scale to make comparing them easier.

Figure 7.2 Effect of Reducing Sample Size

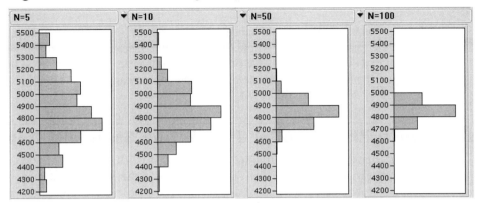

The averages for the larger sample sizes are more closely grouped around the true population mean of $4850. The range of values for the larger sample sizes is smaller than it is for the smaller sample sizes. The following table lists the 2.5% and 97.5% values from the **Quantiles** reports for these samples. This range encompasses about 95% of the averages.

Sample Size	Range that includes 95% of Averages (2.5%–97.5%)
100	4716-4958
50	4665-5056
10	4435-5194
5	4371-5434

The population with the smallest sample size of 5 values has the widest range that includes 95% of the averages. This matches the results in Figure 7.2, where the histogram for N=5 has the widest range of values.

This example shows how larger sample sizes produce more precise estimates. An estimate from a larger sample size is more likely to be closer to the true population mean.

Effect of Population Variability

This section continues with the salary example and explores how population variability affects the estimates from a sample. Recall that one measure of population variability is the standard deviation—σ. As the population standard deviation decreases, the sample average is a more precise estimate of the population mean.

Estimation with a Smaller Population Standard Deviation

Suppose that the true population standard deviation is $300, instead of $625. Note that you cannot change the population standard deviation the way you can change the sample size. The true population standard deviation is fixed, so you are now collecting samples from a different distribution of the population with a true population mean of $4850, and a true population standard deviation of $300. Suppose you collect 200 samples of size 10 from a population with a true standard deviation of 300. What happens to the histogram of sample averages?

What if the true population standard deviation is even smaller, say, $150? Now the samples are from another distribution of the population with a true population standard deviation of $150. What happens if the true population standard deviation is even smaller, say, $75?

Figure 7.3 shows the results for smaller population standard deviations. All of the histograms have the same scale to make comparing them easier.

Figure 7.3 Effect of Smaller Population Standard Deviations

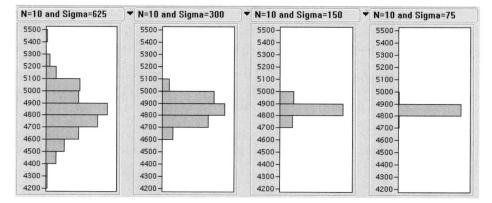

The averages for the populations with smaller standard deviations are more closely grouped around the true population mean of $4850. The range of values for the smaller standard deviations is smaller than it is for the larger standard deviations.

The following table lists the 2.5% and 97.5% values from the Quantiles reports for these samples. This range encompasses about 95% of the values.

Population Standard Deviation	Range that includes 95% of Averages (2.5%–97.5%)
625	4435-5194
300	4651-5043
150	4745-4957
75	4807-4899

The population with the largest standard deviation of 625 has the widest range that includes 95% of the averages. This matches the results in Figure 7.3, where the histogram for Sigma=625 has the widest range of values.

This example shows how samples from populations with smaller standard deviations produce more precise estimates. An estimate from a population with a smaller standard deviation is more likely to be closer to the true population mean.

The Distribution of Sample Averages

Figures 7.2 and 7.3 show how the sample size and the population standard deviation affect the estimate of the population mean. Look again at all of the histograms in Figures 7.2 and 7.3. Just as individual values in a sample have a distribution, so do the sample averages. This section discusses the distribution of sample averages.

The Central Limit Theorem

The histogram in Figure 7.1 is roughly bell-shaped. Normal distributions are bell-shaped. Combining these two facts, you conclude that sample averages are approximately normally distributed.

You might think that this initial conclusion is correct only because the samples are from a normal distribution (because salaries can conceivably be from a normal distribution). The fact is that your initial conclusion is correct, even for populations that cannot conceivably be from a normal distribution. As an example, consider another type of distribution—the exponential distribution. One common use for this type of distribution is to estimate the time to failure. For example, think about laptop computers, which typically have a 3-hour battery. Suppose you measure the time to failure for the battery for 100 laptops. Figure 7.4 shows a histogram of this sample.

Figure 7.4 Simulated Laptop Time to Failure (Exponential Distribution)

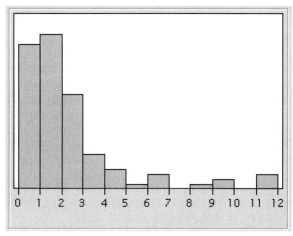

Now, suppose you measure the time to failure for the battery in 30 laptops, and repeat this process 200 times. (Note that this simplifies the experiment; in a real experiment, you would need to control the types of laptops, the types of batteries, and so on. However, for this example, assume that the experiment has been run correctly.) Figure 7.5 shows a histogram of the averages.

Figure 7.5 Distribution of Averages for 200 Exponential Distributions

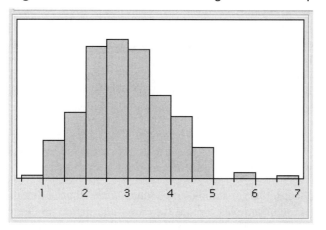

The distribution is roughly bell-shaped. This leads you to initially conclude that the sample averages are approximately normally distributed. The fact that sample averages from non-normal distributions are approximately normally distributed is one of the most important foundations of statistical theory.

The Central Limit Theorem is a formal mathematical theorem that supports your initial conclusion. Essentially, the Central Limit Theorem says:

> **if** you have a simple random sample of n observations from a population with mean μ and standard deviation σ
>
> **and if** n is large
>
> **then** the sample average $\overline{X}$ is approximately normally distributed with mean μ and standard deviation $\sigma/\sqrt{n}$

Two important practical implications of the Central Limit Theorem are:

- Even if the sample values are not normally distributed, the sample average is approximately normally distributed.

- Because the sample average is normally distributed, you can use the Empirical Rule to summarize the distribution of sample averages.

How Big Is Large?

The description of the Central Limit Theorem says "and if *n* is large." How big is large? The answer depends on how non-normal the population is. For moderately non-normal populations, sample averages based on as few as 5 observations (*n*=5) tend to be approximately normally distributed. But, if the population is highly skewed or has heavy tails (for example, it contains a lot of extremely large or extremely small values), then a much larger sample size is needed for the sample average to be approximately normally distributed. For practical purposes, samples with more than 5 observations are usually collected.

One reason for collecting larger samples is because larger sample sizes produce more precise estimates of the population mean. See Figure 7.2 for an illustration.

A second reason for collecting larger samples is to increase the chance that the sample is a representative sample. Small samples, even if they are random, are less likely to be representative of the entire population. For example, an opinion poll that is a random sample of 150 people might not be as representative of the entire population as an opinion poll that is a random sample of 1000 people. (Note that stratified random sampling, mentioned in Chapter 6, can enable you to take a smaller sample. Taking larger random samples might not always be the best way to sample.)

The Standard Error of the Mean

The Central Limit Theorem says that sample averages are approximately normally distributed. The mean of the normal distribution of sample averages is μ, which is also the population mean. The standard deviation of the distribution of sample averages is $\sigma/\sqrt{n}$, where σ is the standard deviation of the population. The standard deviation of the distribution of sample averages is called the *standard error of the mean*.

The Empirical Rule and the Central Limit Theorem

One of the practical implications of the Central Limit Theorem is that you can use the Empirical Rule to summarize the distribution of sample averages. In other words:

- About 68% of the sample averages are between $\mu - \sigma/\sqrt{n}$ and $\mu + \sigma/\sqrt{n}$.

- About 95% of the sample averages are between $\mu - 2\sigma/\sqrt{n}$ and $\mu + 2\sigma/\sqrt{n}$.

- More than 99% of the sample averages are between $\mu - 3\sigma/\sqrt{n}$ and $\mu + 3\sigma/\sqrt{n}$.

From now on, this book uses "between $\mu \pm 2\,\sigma/\sqrt{n}$" to mean "between $\mu - 2\,\sigma/\sqrt{n}$ and $\mu + 2\,\sigma/\sqrt{n}$."

The following table uses the second statement of the Empirical Rule to calculate the range of values that includes 95% of the sample averages. The last column of the table shows the 2.5% and 97.5% percentiles for the monthly salary data (which includes 95% of the averages). With different data, the range for the data would change. Because the Empirical Rule is based on the population mean, the population standard deviation, and the sample size, the range for the Empirical Rule stays the same. For this data, the ranges for the actual data are close to the ranges for the Empirical Rule: sometimes the ranges are higher and sometimes lower, but generally the ranges are close.

Sample Size	Population Standard Deviation	Range for 95% of values from Empirical Rule	Range that includes 95% of values (2.5%–97.5%)
100	625	4725-4975	4716-4958
50	625	4673-5027	4665-5056
5	625	4291-5409	4371-5434
10	625	4455-5245	4435-5194
10	300	4660-5040	4651-5043
10	150	4755-4945	4745-4957
10	75	4803-4897	4807-4899

With many sample averages, you can get a good estimate of the population mean by looking at the distribution of sample averages. You can use the distribution of sample averages to determine how close your estimate should be to the true population mean. However, typically, you have only one sample average. This one sample average gives a point estimate of the population mean, but a point estimate might not be close to the true population mean (as you have seen in the previous examples in this chapter). What if you want to get an estimate with upper and lower limits around it? To do this, form a confidence interval for the mean. The next section describes how.

Getting Confidence Intervals for the Mean

A *confidence interval* for the mean gives an *interval estimate* for the population mean. This interval estimate places upper and lower limits around a point estimate for the mean. The examples in this chapter show how the sample average estimates the population mean, and how the sample size and population standard deviation affect the precision of the estimate. The chapter also shows how the Central Limit Theorem and the Empirical Rule can be used to summarize the distribution of sample averages. A confidence interval uses all of these ideas.

A 95% confidence interval is an interval that is very likely to contain the true population mean (μ). Specifically, if you collect a large number of samples and then calculate a confidence interval for each sample, 95% of the confidence intervals would contain the true population mean (μ), and 5% would not. Unfortunately, with only one sample, you don't know whether the confidence interval you calculate is in the 95%, or in the 5%. However, you can consider your interval to be one of many intervals. And, any one of these many intervals has a 95% chance of containing the true population mean. Thus, the term "confidence interval" indicates your degree of belief, or confidence, that the interval contains the true population mean (μ). The term "confidence interval" is often abbreviated as CI.

Recall the 95% bound on estimates suggested by the Central Limit Theorem and the Empirical Rule. A conceptual bound to use in a 95% confidence interval can be determined with the formula $\pm 2\,\sigma/\sqrt{n}$ because this is the bound that contains 95% of the distribution of sample averages. However, in most real-life applications, the population standard deviation (σ) is unknown. A natural substitution is to use the sample standard deviation (s) to replace the population standard deviation (σ) in the formula. After you make this replacement, the conceptual bound formula is $\pm 2\,s/\sqrt{n}$. However, if you replace σ with s in the formula, the number 2 in the formula is not correct.

The normal distribution is completely defined by the population mean (μ) and the population standard deviation (σ). If you replace σ with s, the use of the normal distribution (and, thus, the Empirical Rule) is not exactly correct. A *t* distribution should be used instead. A *t* distribution is very similar to the normal distribution and allows you to adjust for different sample sizes. Thus, the conceptual bound formula becomes $\pm t\,s/\sqrt{n}$. The value of *t* (or the *t*-value) is based on the sample size and on the level of confidence you choose. The formula for a confidence interval for the mean is:

$$\overline{X} \pm t_{df,\,1-\alpha/2}\frac{s}{\sqrt{n}}$$

where:

$\overline{X}$	is the sample average.
$t_{df,\,1-\alpha/2}$	is the *t*-value for a given *df* and α. The *df* are one less than the sample size (*df=n-1*) and are called the *degrees of freedom* for the *t*-value. As *n* gets large, the *t*-value approaches the value for a normal distribution. The confidence level for the interval is 1-α. For a 95% confidence level, α=0.05. Calculating a 95% confidence interval for a data set with 12 observations requires $t_{11,0.975}$ (which is 2.201). When finding the *t*-value, divide α by 2 before subtracting it from 1.
s	is the sample standard deviation.
n	is the sample size.

You can use **Distribution** to get a confidence interval for the mean.

The data in Table 7.1 consists of interest rates for mortgages from several banks. Because mortgage rates differ based on discount points, the size of the loan, the length and type of loan, and whether an origination fee is charged, the data consists of interest rates for the same kind of loan. Specifically, the interest rates in the data set are for a 30-year fixed-rate loan for $295,000, with no points and a 1% origination fee. Also, because interest rates change quickly (sometimes even daily), all of the information was collected on the same day. The actual bank names are not used.

Table 7.1 Mortgage Data

Mortgage Rates				
5.750	5.750	5.875	5.750	5.750
5.750	5.750	5.625	5.875	5.500
5.500	5.625	5.750	5.625	5.625
5.750	5.750	5.750	5.750	5.750
5.500	5.875	5.750	5.750	5.500
5.750	5.625	5.875	5.500	5.625

This data is available in the **Mortgage** data table in the sample data for the book.

To see the confidence interval in JMP:

1. Open the **Mortgage** data table.

2. In the **JMP Starter** window, click **Basic→Distribution**.

3. Click **Rates→Y, Columns**.

4. Click **OK**.

Figure 7.6 shows the Moments report.

Figure 7.6 Confidence Interval for Mortgage Data

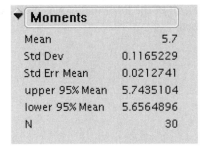

Moments	
Mean	5.7
Std Dev	0.1165229
Std Err Mean	0.0212741
upper 95% Mean	5.7435104
lower 95% Mean	5.6564896
N	30

Confidence intervals are often shown enclosed in parentheses with the lower and upper confidence limits separated by a comma—for example, (5.656,5.744). For this data, you can conclude with 95% confidence that the mean mortgage rate for all mortgage rates for this type of loan is between 5.656% and 5.744%.

Changing the Confidence Level

The most common confidence level is 95%. As presented in the Chapter 6 discussion on choosing a significance level, your situation determines the confidence level you choose.

Using the Falcons data from Chapter 6, suppose you want a 90% confidence interval on the aerie height. You want to use the subset of data that has the three outlier points omitted. In Chapter 6, Figure 6.12 shows the results in the Distributions report for this data. The 95% confidence interval for aerie height is (4.806,6.527). The JMP steps for changing the confidence level are:

1. Open the Subset of Falcons data table to make it the active window.

2. In the JMP Starter window, click **Basic→Distribution**.

3. Click **Aerieht→Y, Columns**.

4. Click **OK**.

5. In the Distribution window, click the hot spot for Aerieht and select **Confidence Interval**.

6. In the Confidence Intervals window, enter **0.90** in the field for **1-alpha**. Compare your window with Figure 7.7.

7. Click **OK**.

Figure 7.7 Confidence Intervals Window

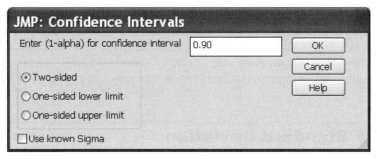

JMP prints a new report in the Distribution window, shown in Figure 7.8.

Figure 7.8 Confidence Intervals Report for Subset of Falcons Data

Parameter	Estimate	Lower CI	Upper CI	1-Alpha
Mean	5.666667	4.951991	6.381342	0.900
Std Dev	2.303795	1.901768	2.948177	

Confidence Intervals

The 90% confidence interval for the mean aerie height is (4.952,6.381). Compare this with the 95% confidence interval of (4.806,6.527). When you decrease the confidence level from 95% to 90%, the confidence interval is wider.

The Confidence Intervals report shows several details.

Parameter   Identifies the parameter as the mean or standard deviation.

Estimate   Gives the estimated value of the parameter.

Lower CI   Lists the lower and upper limits of the confidence interval.
Upper CI

1-Alpha   Gives the confidence level for the confidence interval listed in the previous two columns.

Using One-Sided Confidence Intervals

JMP automatically creates two-sided confidence intervals. Sometimes, a one-sided confidence interval might make more sense. Remember the laptop data from earlier in this chapter? A one-sided upper limit makes more sense with this data. You already know the lower limit—it's 0. This lower limit is reached when the laptop fails on its first use. To change from the automatic two-sided limits to a one-sided limit, select which kind of confidence interval you want in the Confidence Intervals window (see Figure 7.7).

Estimating the Standard Deviation

The standard deviation gives a point estimate of the width of the distribution for the data. Just as confidence intervals for the mean are useful for placing limits on this point estimate, confidence intervals are also useful for the standard deviation. Figure 7.8 shows a confidence interval for the standard deviation. You can conclude with 90% confidence that the true population standard deviation of the aerie height is between 1.902 meters and 2.948 meters.

JMP creates a confidence interval for the mean automatically. When you use the Confidence Intervals window, JMP also creates a confidence interval for the standard deviation. If you need a 95% confidence interval for the standard deviation, enter **0.95** in the **1–alpha** field. JMP creates the same confidence interval for the mean that appears in the Moments report, and creates a 95% confidence interval for the standard deviation.

Summaries

Key Ideas

- Larger sample sizes produce more precise estimates of the population mean than smaller sample sizes.

- Samples from populations with small standard deviations produce more precise estimates of the population mean than samples from populations with large standard deviations.

- The Central Limit Theorem says that for large samples, the sample average is approximately normally distributed, even if the sample values are not normally distributed.

- Confidence intervals for the mean when the population standard deviation is unknown use the following formula:

$$\overline{X} \pm t_{df,\,1-\alpha/2}\frac{s}{\sqrt{n}}$$

where $\overline{X}$ is the sample average, n is the sample size, and s is the sample standard deviation. The value of $t_{df,\,1-\alpha/2}$ is a t-value that is based on the sample size and the confidence level. The degrees of freedom (df) are one less than the sample size ($df=n-1$), and $1-\alpha$ is the confidence level for the confidence interval. For a 95% confidence interval for a data set with 12 observations, the t needed is $t_{11,0.975}$.

JMP Steps

JMP **Distribution** automatically creates 95% confidence intervals for the mean. To change the confidence level or to get a confidence interval for the standard deviation:

1. In the Distribution window, click the hot spot for the variable and select **Confidence Interval**.

2. In the Confidence Intervals window, enter a confidence level in the field for **1-alpha**.

3. Click **OK**.

Exercises

1. JMP provides a way for you to explore the Central Limit Theorem. Click the link for **Central Limit Theorem** in the Sample Data Directory (under the Examples for Teaching heading). JMP opens a data table with 5 columns and 0 rows. Click **Rows→Add Rows**, enter **30**, and click **OK**. JMP uses a formula and fills the rows and columns with values (Chapter 8 shows you how to create formulas.) The column headings identify the sample size represented by the values in the column. These variables are from an extremely non-normal distribution. Use the JMP **Distribution** features to create histograms and test for normality for each column. Apply **Uniform Scaling** to compare the results for different sample sizes. At what sample size can you proceed using the assumption of normality?

2. For your own data, use the features discussed in this chapter to build a confidence interval for the mean. Explain any insights from your results.

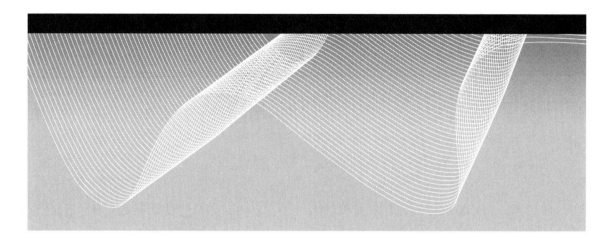

Part **3**

Comparing Groups

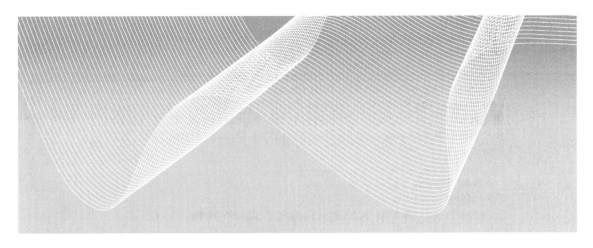

Chapter **8**

Comparing Two Groups

Do male accountants earn more money than female accountants? Do people who are given a new shampoo use more shampoo than people who are given an old shampoo? Do cows that are fed a grain supplement and hay gain more weight than cows that are fed only hay? Are students' grades on an achievement test higher after they complete a special course on how to take tests? Do employees who follow a regular exercise program for a year have a lower resting pulse rate than they had when they started the program?

All of these questions involve comparing two groups of data. In some cases, the groups are independent (male and female accountants), and in other cases, the groups are paired (test results before and after the special course). This chapter discusses comparing two groups and gives analysis methods for all types of data. The variable that classifies the data into two groups should be nominal. The response variable can be ordinal or continuous, and must be numeric. Specific topics are:

- deciding if you have independent or paired groups

- summarizing data from two independent groups

- summarizing data from paired groups

- building a statistical test of hypothesis to compare the two groups

- deciding which statistical test to use

- performing tests for independent groups
- performing tests for paired groups

For the various tests, this chapter shows how to use JMP to do the test and how to interpret the test results.

Deciding between Independent and Paired Groups

When comparing two groups, you want to know if the means for the two groups are different. The first step is to decide if you have independent or paired groups.

Independent Groups

Independent groups of data contain measurements for two unrelated samples of items. Suppose you have random samples of the salaries for male and female accountants. The salary measurements for men and women form two distinct, but unrelated groups. The goal of analysis is to compare the average salaries for men and women and decide if the difference between the average salaries is greater than what could happen by chance. As another example, suppose a researcher selects a random sample of children, some who use a fluoride toothpaste, and some who do not. There is no relationship between the children who use fluoride toothpaste and the children who do not. A dentist counts the number of cavities for each child. The goal of analysis is to compare the average number of cavities for children who use fluoride toothpaste and for children who do not.

Paired Groups

Paired groups of data contain measurements for one sample of items, but there are two measurements for each item. A common example of paired groups is before-and-after measurements, where the goal of analysis is to decide if the average change from before to after is greater than what could happen by chance. For example, a doctor weighs 30 people before they begin a program to quit smoking and weighs them again 6 months after they have completed the program. The goal of analysis is to decide if the average weight change is greater than what could happen by chance.

Summarizing Data from Two Independent Groups

This section explains how to summarize data from two independent groups. These summarization methods provide additional understanding of the statistical results.

Using Distribution to Summarize Independent Groups

Table 8.1 shows the percentages of body fat for several men and women. These people participated in unsupervised aerobic exercise or weight training (or both) about three times per week for a year. They were measured once at the end of the year. Chapter 2 introduced this data.

Table 8.1 Body Fat Data

Group	Body Fat Percentage				
Male	13.3	8	20	12	12
	19	18	31	16	24
	20	22	21		
Female	22	16	21.7	21	30
	26	12	23.2	28	23

This data is available in the Bodyfat data table in the sample data for this book.

To summarize the data in JMP:

1. Open the Bodyfat data table.

2. In the JMP Starter window, click **Basic→Distribution**.

3. Click **Body Fat** and **Gender** and then **Y, Columns**.

4. Click **OK**.

Figure 8.1 shows the histograms. Interacting with the histograms helps you to explore the data. By clicking on the histogram bars for **Male** and **Female**, you can see how the distribution changes for the two genders. Clicking on a bar does not change the statistics in the reports below the histogram. For example, Figure 8.1 shows the **Gender** and **Body Fat** histograms with **Male** selected.

Figure 8.1 Histograms with Male Selected

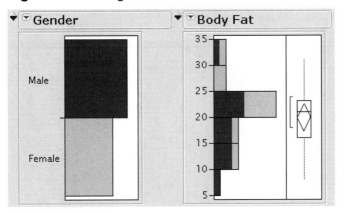

You can use all of the **Distribution** tools described in Chapters 4 and 6 for summarizing two independent groups.

Using a By Column in Distribution

While the results in Figure 8.1 are interesting, they summarize the data as a single group. You want to see the graphs and descriptive statistics for males and females separately. In JMP:

1. Open the Bodyfat data table.

2. In the JMP Starter window, click **Basic→Distribution**.

3. Click **Body Fat→Y, Columns**.

4. Click **Gender→By**.

5. Click **OK**.

6. In the Distribution window, find the hot spot for one of the two reports.

7. Click **Uniform Scaling**.

8. Hold down the CTRL key, click on a report's hot spot, and select **Display Options→Horizontal Layout**.

Figure 8.2 shows the results.

Figure 8.2 Distribution with Gender as a By Variable

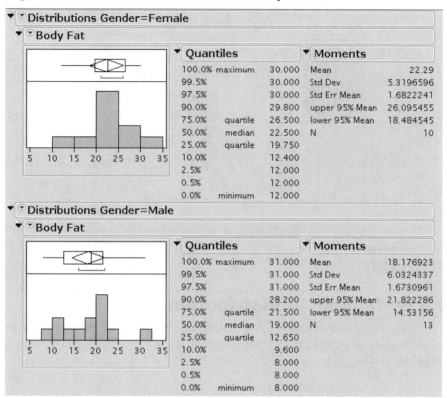

Figure 8.2 shows descriptive statistics for each gender. For example, the average percentage of body fat for women is 22.29. The average percentage of body fat for men is 18.18. Figure 8.2 shows separate histograms and box plots for each group. Because of uniform scaling, you can easily compare the histograms. More females than males have body fat percentages above 20. From this summary, you might initially conclude that the averages for the two groups are different. You don't know whether this difference is greater than what could happen by chance. Finding out whether the difference is due to chance or is real requires a statistical test, discussed in "Building Hypothesis Tests to Compare Two Groups" later in this chapter.

> **JMP Hints:**
>
> Using **Uniform Scaling** is important. Without it, JMP scales each graph for the data in each group. Comparing the graphs with different scales might be difficult.
>
> Holding down the CTRL key and clicking a hot spot is an easy way to apply your selection to all similar JMP reports. This feature works with all JMP reports.
>
> Clicking the Distributions hot spot and selecting **Stack** is an alternative to holding down the CTRL key, clicking on a report's hot spot, and selecting **Display Options→Horizontal Layout**.

You can use all of the **Distribution** tools described in Chapters 4 and 6 when you use a **By** variable.

Summarizing Data from Paired Groups

With paired groups, the first step is to find the paired-differences for each observation in the sample. The second step is to summarize the differences.

Finding the Differences between Paired Groups

Sometimes, the difference between the two measurements for an observation is already calculated. For example, you might be analyzing data from a cattle-feeding program, and the data gives the weight change of each steer. If you already have the difference in weight of each steer, you can skip the rest of this section.

Other times, only the before-and-after data is available. Before you can summarize the data, you need to find the differences. Instead of finding the differences with a calculator, you can compute them in JMP.

Table 8.2 shows data from an introductory statistics class, STA6207[1]. The table shows scores from two exams for the 20 students in the class. Both exams covered the same material. Each student has a pair of scores, one score for each exam. The professor wants to find out if the exams appear to be equally difficult. If they are, the average difference between exam scores should be small.

---

[1] Data is from Dr. Ramon Littell, University of Florida. Used with permission.

Table 8.2 Exam Data

Student	Exam 1 Score	Exam 2 Score
1	93	98
2	88	74
3	89	67
4	88	92
5	67	83
6	89	90
7	83	74
8	94	97
9	89	96
10	55	81
11	88	83
12	91	94
13	85	89
14	70	78
15	90	96
16	90	93
17	94	81
18	67	81
19	87	93
20	83	91

This data is available in the STA6207 data table in the sample data for the book.

To compute the score differences in JMP:

1. Open the STA6207 data table.

2. Click **Cols→New Column**.

3. Enter **Score Difference** as the column name in the New Column window. Figure 8.3 shows the New Column window.

Figure 8.3 New Column Window

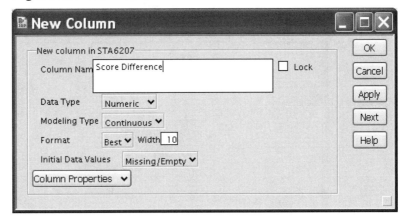

Continuing in JMP:

4. Click the menu for **Column Properties→Formula**.

5. The formula window displays with the title Score Difference, as shown in the following window.

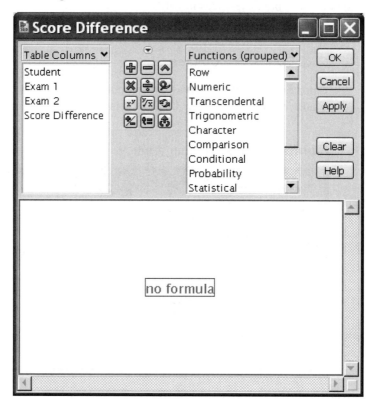

Continuing in JMP:

6. In the Score Difference window:

   a. Click **Exam 2**.

   b. Click the minus ⊟ key from the keypad area.

   c. Click **Exam 1**.

   d. Use Figure 8.4 to compare with your window.

Figure 8.4 Formula for Score Difference

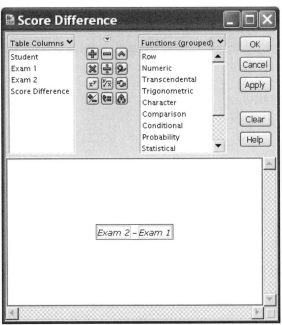

Continuing in JMP:

7. Click **OK**.

8. The New Column window now shows that the **Score Difference** column uses a formula, as seen in the following window.

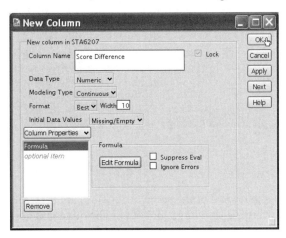

9. Click **OK** in the New Column window.

	Student	Exam 1	Exam 2	Score Difference
1	1	93	98	5
2	2	88	74	-14
3	3	89	67	-22
4	4	88	92	4
5	5	67	83	16

JMP adds the new variable to the data table, and uses the formula to compute the score differences for each row. The previous display shows a portion of the data table with the new **Score Difference** column.

Using Distribution to Summarize Differences for Paired Groups

After creating the differences, you can summarize them using **Distribution**. In JMP, select **Score Difference** as your **Y, Columns** choice. Figure 8.5 shows the results using **Horizontal Layout**. The average difference between exam scores is 2.55.

Figure 8.5 Distribution Results for Score Difference using Horizontal Layout

Quantiles			Moments	
100.0%	maximum	26.00	Mean	2.55
99.5%		26.00	Std Dev	10.971134
97.5%		26.00	Std Err Mean	2.4532202
90.0%		15.80	upper 95% Mean	7.6846489
75.0%	quartile	7.75	lower 95% Mean	-2.584649
50.0%	median	4.00	N	20
25.0%	quartile	-3.50		
10.0%		-13.90		
2.5%		-22.00		
0.5%		-22.00		
0.0%	minimum	-22.00		

The histogram shows that most of the score differences are between 0 and 10. However, some of the score differences are large, in both the positive and negative directions. You might think that the average difference in exam scores is not statistically significant. However, you cannot be certain from simply looking at the data.

Building Hypothesis Tests to Compare Two Groups

So far, this chapter has discussed how to summarize differences between two groups. Suppose you want to know how important the differences are, and if the differences are large enough to be significant. In statistical terms, you want to perform a hypothesis test. This section discusses hypothesis testing when comparing two groups. (See Chapter 6 for the general idea of hypothesis testing.)

In building a test of hypothesis, you work with two hypotheses. In the case of comparing two independent groups, the null hypothesis is that the two means for the independent groups are the same, and the alternative hypothesis is that the two means are different. In this case, the notation is:

$$H_o: \mu_A = \mu_B$$

and:

$$H_a: \mu_A \neq \mu_B$$

where H_o indicates the null hypothesis, H_a indicates the alternative hypothesis, and μ_A and μ_B are the population means for independent groups A and B.

When comparing paired groups, the null hypothesis is that the mean difference is 0, and the alternative hypothesis is that the mean difference is different from 0. In this case, the notation is:

$$H_o: \mu_D = 0$$

and:

$$H_a: \mu_D \neq 0$$

where μ_D indicates the mean difference.

In statistical tests that compare two groups, the hypotheses are tested by calculating a test statistic from the data and comparing its value to a reference value that would be the result if the null hypothesis were true. The test statistic is compared to different reference values that are based on the sample size. In part, this is because smaller differences can be detected with larger sample sizes. As a result, if you used the same set of reference values for large and small sample sizes, you would be more likely to make incorrect decisions.

This concept is similar to the concept of confidence intervals, in which different *t*-values are used (discussed in Chapter 7). With confidence intervals, the *t*-value is based on the degrees of freedom, which were determined by the sample size. Similarly, when comparing two independent groups, the degrees of freedom for a reference value are based on the sample sizes of the two groups. Specifically, the degrees of freedom are equal to N-2, where N is the total sample size for the two groups.

Deciding Which Statistical Test to Use

Because you test different hypotheses for independent and paired groups, you use different tests. In addition, there are parametric and nonparametric tests for each type of group. When deciding which statistical test to use, first, decide if you have independent groups or paired groups. Then, decide if you should use a parametric or a nonparametric test. This second decision is based on whether the assumptions for the parametric test seem reasonable. The rest of this chapter describes the test to use in each of the four situations. Table 8.3 summarizes the tests.

Table 8.3 Statistical Tests for Comparing Two Groups

Type of Test	Groups	
	Independent	**Paired**
Parametric	Two-sample *t*-test	Paired-difference *t*-test
Nonparametric	Wilcoxon Rank Sum test	Wilcoxon Signed Rank test

Understanding Significance

For each of the four tests in Table 8.3, there are two possible results: the *p*-value is less than the predetermined reference probability, or it is not.

Groups Significantly Different

If the *p*-value is less than the reference probability, the result is statistically significant, and you reject the null hypothesis. For independent groups, you conclude that averages for the two groups are significantly different. For paired groups, you conclude that the average difference is significantly different from 0.

Groups Not Significantly Different

If the *p*-value is greater than the reference probability, the result is not statistically significant, and you fail to reject the null hypothesis. For independent groups, you conclude that averages for the two groups are not significantly different. For paired groups, you conclude that the average difference is not significantly different from 0.

Do not conclude that the means for the two groups are the same or that the mean difference is 0. You do not have enough evidence to make either of these conclusions. You do not know that the averages are the same; the results of the test indicate only that the averages are not significantly different from one another. Similarly, for paired groups, you do not have enough evidence to conclude that the difference is 0. The results of the test indicate only that the average difference is not significantly different from 0.

In statistical hypothesis testing, do not accept the null hypothesis; instead, either reject or fail to reject the null hypothesis. For a more detailed discussion of hypothesis testing, see Chapter 6.

Performing the Two-Sample *t*-test

The two-sample *t*-test is a parametric test that compares two independent groups.

Assumptions and Hypothesis Test

The null hypothesis is that the means for the two independent groups are equal and the alternative hypothesis is that they are not. There are three assumptions for the two-sample *t*-test:

- observations are independent
- observations in each group are a random sample from a population with a normal distribution
- variances for the two independent groups are equal

Because of the second assumption, the two-sample *t*-test applies to continuous variables only.

The steps for performing the two-sample *t*-test are:

1. Create a JMP data table.

2. Check the data table for errors.

3. Choose the significance level for the test.

4. Check the assumptions for the test.

5. Perform the test.

6. Make conclusions from the test results.

The rest of this chapter uses these steps for all analyses.

Checking Data and Assumptions, and Choosing a Significance Level

For the body fat data, suppose you have checked the data and found no errors.

You decide to use a 5% significance level.

The assumption that these are independent observations is reasonable because each person's body fat measurement is unrelated to every other person's body fat measurement. For the assumption of normality, you can test for normality of each group (see Chapter 6) and find that this assumption is reasonable. The assumption of equal variances seems reasonable based on the similarity of the standard deviations of the two groups. From Figure 8.2, the standard deviation is 5.32 for females and 6.03 for males. The next topic shows how to use JMP to test this assumption of equal variances.

Testing for Equal Variances with JMP

To test the assumption of equal variances in JMP:

1. Open the Bodyfat data table.

2. In the JMP Starter window, click **Basic→Oneway**.

3. Click **Body Fat→Y, Response**.

4. Click **Gender→X, Grouping**.

5. Click **OK**. JMP creates a graph as shown in the following display.

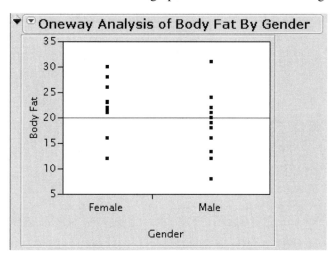

6. Click the hot spot for the Oneway Analysis of Body Fat By Gender report.

7. Click **UnEqual Variances**.

Figure 8.6 shows the results. The top graph shows the data points for each group. Testing for unequal variances adds standard deviation lines (the blue lines) to the top graph. With some enhancements, this graph helps you better visualize the differences between the two independent groups. Later in the chapter, "Enhancing the Two-Sample Graph" discusses how to enhance this graph with JMP features.

Figure 8.6 Test Results for Unequal Variances

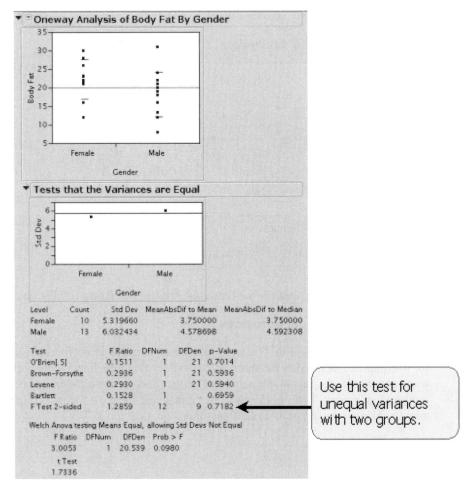

Understanding Results

The graph in the Tests that the Variances are Equal report in Figure 8.6 shows the standard deviations for the two groups. The center line shows the pooled standard deviation (s_p). See "Technical Details: Pooled and Unpooled" for details on pooled standard deviation.

Immediately below the graph is a table that summarizes the data in the graph. For our purposes, the relevant columns are:

Level	Identifies the groups. In the body fat data, these are **Female** and **Male**.
Count	Lists the number of observations in each group.
Std Dev	Gives the standard deviation of each group.

The next table has the heading of **Test** for the first column. This table contains several tests. The last test is relevant for testing equal variances for two groups. The columns in the table are:

Test	Identifies the test. The last row is the two-sided **F Test**.
F Ratio	Statistics for the test. For the two-sided F test, the statistic is the ratio of the larger variance to the smaller variance.
DFNum **DFDen**	Degrees of freedom. **DFNum** is the degrees of freedom for the numerator, which is n_1-1, where n_1 is the size of the group with the larger variance (**Males** in the Bodyfat data). **DFDen** is the degrees of freedom for the denominator, which is n_2-1, where n_2 is the size of the group with the smaller variance (**Females** in the Bodyfat data).
***p*-value**	Significance probability for the test of unequal variances. Typically, values less than 0.05 lead you to conclude that the variances for the two groups are not equal.

The *p*-value of **0.7182** for the body fat data leads you to proceed based on the assumption that the variances for the two groups are equal.

Figure 8.6 shows other tests for equal variances and a Welch Anova report table. These other tests are more appropriate when comparing more than two groups. Chapter 9 discusses these tests.

JMP Hints:

Position the mouse pointer near the **p-Value** column and move it in a very small circle. JMP displays a pop-up window that explains the value. To close the pop-up window, move your mouse pointer again. JMP displays pop-up windows for all *p*-values.

If you want to know more about the statistics or tests in the report, click the ? tool and click on the report table. JMP displays a detailed help window for the report table. You might need to scroll down to see the specifics on a given statistic or test.

Testing to Compare Two Means with JMP

You have now checked the data table for errors, chosen a significance level, and tested the assumptions for the analysis. You are ready to compare the means.

JMP automatically performs a *t*-test for unequal variances and a *t*-test for equal variances. JMP calls these tests the *unpooled t-test* and the *pooled t-test*, respectively For the body fat data, you assume equal variances. However, to illustrate these two tests, this topic performs both tests and discusses the differences.

In JMP:

1. Click the hot spot for the Oneway Analysis of Body Fat By Gender report as shown in the following display.

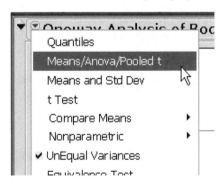

2. Select **Means/Anova/Pooled t**. This generates the pooled *t*-test that assumes equal variances.

3. Click the hot spot again and select **t Test**. This generates the unpooled *t*-test that assumes unequal variances.

4. Click **Display Options→All Graphs**. This hides the graph at the top of the report.

5. Click to hide the following reports: Summary of Fit, Analysis of Variance, Means for Oneway Anova, and Tests that the Variances are Equal. This changes the window to show the two t Test reports and hides all other reports.

Figure 8.7 shows the results.

Figure 8.7 Pooled and Unpooled t Test Report Tables for Bodyfat Data

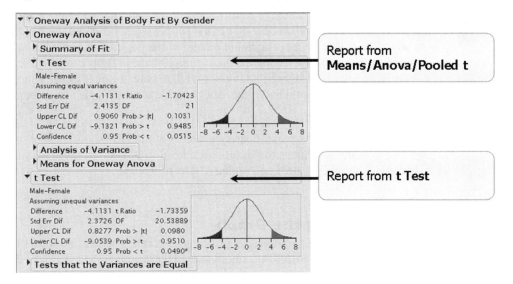

There are two reports titled **t Test**. The top report, for equal variances, is the result of selecting **Means/Anova/Pooled t**. The bottom report, for unequal variances, is the result of selecting **t Test**. Both reports have the same information.

To compare two independent groups, look at the line labeled **Prob > |t|**. This line gives the *p*-value for testing that the means for the two groups are different. For the equal variances report, the value is $p=0.1031$. Because you can assume equal variances for the body fat data, use this report. The *p*-value is greater than 0.05. This indicates that the body fat averages for men and women are not significantly different at the 5% significance level.

For the unequal variances report, the value is $p=0.0980$. This also indicates that the body fat averages for men and women are not significantly different at the 5% significance level. For the equal and unequal variances reports, the driver for the difference in *p*-values is the calculation for the standard deviations. See "Technical Details: Pooled and Unpooled" for formulas.

Other studies show that the body fat averages for men and women are significantly different. Why don't you find a significant difference in this set of data? One possible reason is the small sample size. Only a few people were measured; perhaps a larger data set would have given a more accurate picture of the population. Another possible reason is uncontrolled factors affecting the data. Although these people were exercising regularly during the year, their activities and diet were not monitored. These factors, as well as other factors could have had enough influence on the data to obscure differences that do indeed exist.

The two groups would be significantly different at the 15% significance level. Now you see why you always choose the significance level first; your criterion for statistical significance should not be based on the results of the test.

Understanding the Graph

Each t Test report table in Figure 8.7 displays a graph. The red line shows the value of **Difference**, which is **-4.1131** for both tests. The two blue-shaded areas relate to the *p*-values. Each shaded area represents *p*/2, where *p* is the *p*-value. In statistical terms, the area under the curve in each tail is *p*/2. The shading for the two areas highlights the direction of the difference. The darker blue area is associated with the side of the distribution that shows the direction of the difference, and the lighter blue area is associated with the other side. See "Technical Details: t Test Graph" for more examples.

Understanding the Report Table

The list describes the information in each t Test report table:

Difference   Estimates the difference between the two group's means. This is the average of the second group, subtracted from the average of the first group. (JMP decides which group is first and second based on the data, but you can change the order as discussed in "Ordering Values" in Chapter 3.)

For the Bodyfat data, JMP subtracts the **Female** average from the **Male** average (18.18–22.29=-4.1131). The hidden Means for Oneway Anova report table shows the averages used to calculate **Difference**.

The first line in the report table also shows how **Difference** is calculated. Figure 8.7 shows **Male-Female**, which tells you that JMP subtracts the average for females from the average for males.

Std Err Dif   Standard error of the **Difference**. This is the first key distinction between the equal and unequal variances tests. Because the standard deviation is involved in calculating the standard error, and the two tests calculate the standard deviation as pooled and unpooled, the values of the standard error differ.

Upper CL Dif   Upper and lower confidence limits for the difference, using the
Lower CL Dif   confidence level listed on the next row of the report table. Because the confidence intervals use the standard errors, the confidence intervals differ for the equal and unequal variances report tables.

Confidence   Confidence level for the confidence intervals. JMP sets this at 0.95, but you can change it. See "Changing the Alpha Level for Confidence Intervals."

t Ratio   Value of the *t*-statistic. This is **Difference** divided by its standard error. For the body fat data and equal variances, this is:

-4.1131/2.4135=-1.70423

Because the standard errors differ for the equal and unequal variances tests, the **t Ratio** also differs.

Generally, values of the **t Ratio** over 2 (or less than -2) give significant differences between the two groups at the 95% confidence level.

DF   Degrees of freedom for the test. This is the second key distinction between the equal and unequal variances tests. For the equal variances test, the degrees of freedom are calculated by adding the sample sizes for each group, and then subtracting 2 (21=10+13-2). For the unequal variances test, the degrees of freedom uses a different calculation.

Prob > |t| Gives the *p*-values associated with the test. The first
Prob > t   *p*-value is for a two-sided test, which tests the alternative
Prob < t   hypothesis that the means for the two independent groups are different. The other two *p*-values are for one-sided tests. See "Technical Details: One-Sided Hypothesis Tests" for more detail.

To perform the test at the 5% significance level, you conclude that the two groups are significantly different if the *p*-value is less than 0.05. To perform the test at the 10% significance level, you conclude that the two groups are significantly different if the *p*-value is less than 0.10. Conclusions for tests at other significance levels are made in a similar manner.

JMP uses a special format for displaying *p*-values. Look again at Figure 8.7. In the t Test report table for unequal variances, look at the value for **Prob < t**. JMP shows **0.0490***. The asterisk indicates significance at the 95% confidence level.

Technical Details: Pooled and Unpooled

Here are the formulas for how JMP calculates the *t*-statistic for the pooled and unpooled tests. For the equal variances (pooled) test, JMP calculates:

$$t = \frac{\overline{X}_1 - \overline{X}_2}{s_p \sqrt{1/n_1 + 1/n_2}}$$

where $\overline{X}_1$ and $\overline{X}_2$ are the averages for the two groups. And:

$$s_p^2 = \frac{(n_1 - 1)s_1^2 + (n_2 - 1)s_2^2}{n_1 + n_2 - 2}$$

where n_1 and n_2 are sample sizes for the two groups, and s_1 and s_2 are the standard deviations for the two groups.

For the unequal variances (unpooled) test, JMP calculates:

$$t' = \frac{\overline{X}_1 - \overline{X}_2}{\sqrt{s_1^2 / n_1 + s_2^2 / n_2}}$$

where n_1, n_2, s_1, and s_2 are as defined the same as above.

Technical Details: t Test Graph

JMP shows a graph in both t Test report tables, one for equal variances and one for unequal variances. Figure 8.7 shows a graph with a negative difference that is not significant. Here's an example of a graph with a positive difference that is significant.

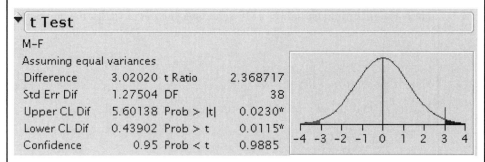

The difference is **3.02**, indicated by the red line on the right side of the graph. Each of the blue-shaded areas represents $p/2 = 0.023/2 = 0.0115$.

When the difference is highly significant, the graph does not show any blue-shaded area. Here's an example of a graph with a negative difference that is highly significant.

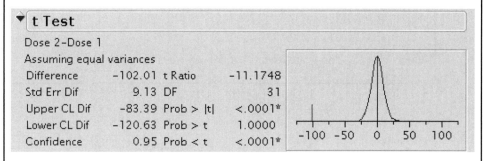

The difference is **-102.01**, indicated by the red line on the left side of the graph. The *p*-value is less than 0.0001, which is nearly impossible to show on the graph. As a result, the graph does not include blue-shaded areas.

Technical Details: One-Sided Hypothesis Tests

JMP shows the two-sided test and both one-sided tests. To understand the direction of the one-sided tests, look at the first line of the report table. In Figure 8.7 for example, **Male-Female** is in the first line. This means that **Prob > t** tests the following hypotheses:

$$H_o: \mu_M \leq \mu_F \quad \text{and} \quad H_a: \mu_M > \mu_F$$

The **>** sign for the alternative hypothesis matches the **>** sign in **Prob > t**. Also, notice that **Male** or (**M**) appears on both the left side of the hypotheses and on the left side of the difference in the first line.

Similarly, **Prob < t** tests the following hypotheses:

$$H_o: \mu_M \geq \mu_F \quad \text{and} \quad H_a: \mu_M < \mu_F$$

The **<** sign for the alternative hypothesis matches the **<** sign in **Prob < t**. **Male** or (**M**) appears on both the left side of the hypotheses and on the left side of the difference in the first line.

Changing the Alpha Level for Confidence Intervals

JMP performs the two-sample *t*-test at the 95% confidence level. In statistical terms, JMP performs the two-sample *t*-test at the 5% alpha level. You can change the alpha level for the confidence intervals, but not for the *t*-tests. In JMP:

1. Click the hot spot for the Oneway Analysis of Body Fat By Gender report.

2. Click **Set α level→.01**.

This changes the alpha level for confidence intervals in both t Test reports. Figure 8.8 shows the results without the graphs.

Figure 8.8 Alpha Levels and Confidence Intervals

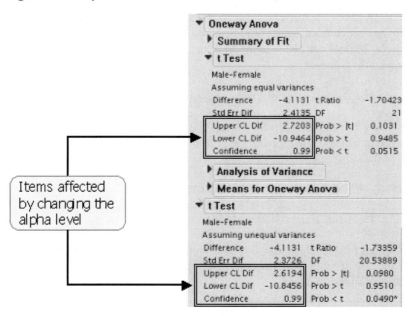

Compare Figures 8.7 and 8.8. **Confidence** is **0.95** in Figure 8.7 and **0.99** in Figure 8.8, corresponding to setting the alpha level to 0.05 (the automatic choice) and 0.01. As a result of changing the alpha level, the confidence intervals change. **Upper CL Dif** and **Lower CL Dif are** different in Figures 8.7 and 8.8. All the other statistics remain the same.

Be careful! Changing the alpha level for the two-sample *t*-test affects only the confidence interval. JMP always performs the statistical test at the 5% alpha level.

Performing the Wilcoxon Rank Sum Test

The Wilcoxon Rank Sum test is a nonparametric test for comparing two independent groups. It is a nonparametric analogue to the two-sample *t*-test, and is sometimes referred to as the Mann-Whitney *U* test. The null hypothesis is that the two means are the same. The only assumption for this test is that the observations are independent. JMP performs this test on continuous, ordinal, and nominal variables, but gives a warning message when the response variable is not continuous.

To illustrate the Wilcoxon Rank Sum test, consider an experiment to analyze the content of the gastric juices of two groups of patients.[†] The patients are divided into two groups: patients with peptic ulcers, and normal or control patients without peptic ulcers. The goal of the analysis is to determine if the mean lysozyme levels for the two groups are significantly different at the 5% significance level. (Lysozyme is an enzyme that can destroy the cell walls of some kinds of bacteria.) Table 8.4 shows the data.

Table 8.4 Gastric Data

Group	Lysozyme Levels										
Ulcers	0.2	10.9	1.1	16.2	3.3	20.7	4.8	40.0	5.3	60.0	
	10.4	0.4	12.4	2.1	18.9	4.5	25.4	5.0	50.0	9.8	
	0.3	11.3	2.0	17.6	3.8	24.0	4.9	42.2	7.5		
Normal	0.2	5.7	0.7	8.7	1.5	10.3	2.4	16.5	3.6	20.7	
	5.4	0.4	7.5	1.5	9.1	2.0	16.1	2.8	20.0	4.8	
	0.3	5.8	1.2	8.8	1.9	15.6	2.5	16.7	4.8	33.0	

This data is available in the **Gastric** data table in the sample data for the book.

The first four steps of analysis are complete.

1. Create a JMP data table.

2. Check the data table for errors. **Distribution** was used to check for errors (see the exercise at the end of the chapter). Although outlier points appear in the box plots, the authors of the original data did not find any underlying reason for these outlier points. Assume that the data is free of errors.

3. Choose the significance level for the test. Choose a 5% significance level, which requires a p-value less than 0.05 to conclude that the groups are significantly different.

4. Check the assumptions for the test. The only assumption for this test is that the observations are independent. This seems reasonable, because each observation is a different person. The lysozyme level in one person is not dependent on the lysozyme level in another person. (This fact ignores the possibility that two people could be causing stress—or ulcers—in each other!)

[†] Data is from K. Myer et al., "Lysozyme activity in ulderative alimentary disease," *American Journal of Medicine* 5 (1948): 482-495. Used with permission.

5. Perform the test. See "Using JMP for the Wilcoxon Rank Sum Test."

6. Make conclusions from the test results. See "Understanding Results."

Using JMP for the Wilcoxon Rank Sum Test

JMP performs parametric and nonparametric tests in the same analysis platform. The nonparametric test is usually an additional analysis option for a parametric test. To perform the Wilcoxon Rank Sum test in JMP:

1. Open the **Gastric** data table.

2. In the JMP Starter window, click **Basic→Oneway**.

3. Click **Lysozyme→Y, Response**.

4. Click **Group→X, Grouping**.

5. Click **OK**.

6. Click the hot spot for the Oneway Analysis of Lysozyme By Group report.

7. Click **Nonparametric→Wilcoxon Test**.

8. Click the hot spot again and select **Display Options→All Graphs** to hide the graph.

Figure 8.9 shows the results.

Figure 8.9 Wilcoxon Rank Sum Test for Gastric Data

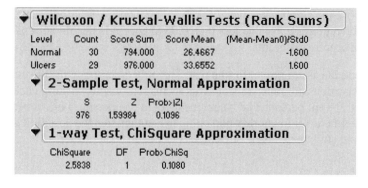

The fifth step of analysis is now completed. Next, make conclusions from the test results.

Understanding Results

Figure 8.9 shows the results of the Wilcoxon Rank Sum test. First, answer the research question: Are the mean lysozyme levels significantly different for patients without ulcers and patients with ulcers?

Finding the *p*-value

In Figure 8.9, look under the heading **2-Sample Test, Normal Approximation**. Look at the number under **Prob>|Z|**. For the gastric data, this value is **0.1096**, which is greater than the significance level of 0.05. You conclude that the mean lysozyme levels for the patients without ulcers and for the patients with ulcers are not significantly different at the 5% significance level.

In general, to interpret JMP results, look at the *p*-value under **Prob>|Z|**. If this *p*-value is less than the significance level, you conclude that the means for the two groups are significantly different. If this *p*-value is greater than the significance level, you conclude that the means are not significantly different. Do not conclude that the means are the same. (See the discussion earlier in this chapter.)

Understanding Other Items in the Report

This list describes the information in Figure 8.9:

Level	Variable that defines the groups.
Count	Number of observations in each group.
Score Sum	Sum of the Wilcoxon scores for each group. To get the scores, JMP ranks the variable from lowest to highest, assigning the lowest value a 1, and the highest value *n*, where *n* is the sample size. JMP sums the scores for each group to get the score sum.
Score Mean	Average score for each group, calculated as (**Score Sum**)/**Count**.

(Mean-Mean0)/Std0	Standardized score for each group. It uses the expected mean and expected standard deviation under the assumption that the means for the two groups are the same.
S	Test statistic for the two-sample test.
Z	Normal approximation to **S**.

Figure 8.9 also shows an approximate Chi Square test. Chapter 9 discusses this test, which is more appropriate when comparing more than two groups.

Enhancing the Two-Sample Graph

JMP tests provide a definite statistical answer to the question of whether groups are different. The automatic graph that JMP creates shows a simple visual summary of the data. JMP calls this basic graph the "Continuous by Nominal/Ordinal plot." This section describes several features that can increase your understanding of the data by enhancing the basic graph.

Figure 8.6 shows the basic graph for the Bodyfat data. The dots represent the data points for each group. The blue lines for each group represent plus or minus one standard deviation. JMP adds these blue lines when performing the test for unequal variances. The solid horizontal line across the entire graph represents the overall mean of the data. This graph is useful, but the plus or minus one standard deviation lines (the small blue lines) can be hard to see, especially with a lot of data points.

The steps enhance the graph in several ways. All of the features are available from **Display Options** in the hot spot menu. You can select them one at a time, or you can use a shortcut:

1. Hold down the ALT key and click the **Display Options** hot spot for the Oneway Analysis of Body Fat By Gender window.

2. Select the check boxes for: **All Graphs, Box Plots**, **Points Jittered**, and **Histograms. Histograms** is in the last column in the Select Options window (see Figure 8.10).

3. Deselect the check boxes for **Std Dev Lines** and **Mean Diamonds**.

4. Click **OK**.

Figure 8.10 displays the Select Options window with the options selected. The third column and the beginning of the fourth column list **Display Options**. The other options in the Select Options window match other selections in the hot spot menu.

Figure 8.10 Select Options Window for Oneway Analysis

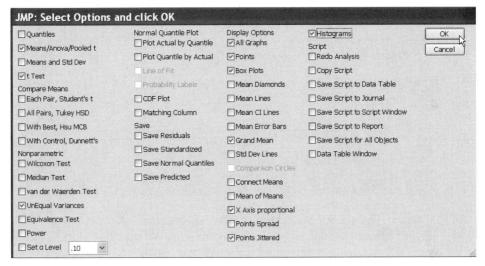

JMP Hint:

Hold down the ALT key and click on hot spots when you expect to make more than a few choices in the hot spot menu. This feature works for every hot spot discussed in the book.

Figure 8.11 shows the results of the enhanced graph.

Figure 8.11 Enhanced Two-Sample Graph for Bodyfat Data

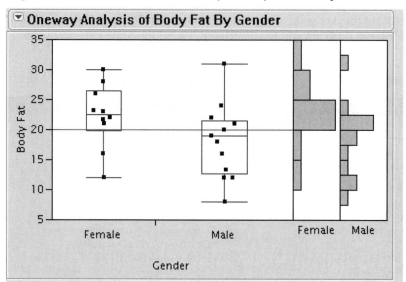

Compare Figures 8.6 and 8.11 to see the enhancements. Also, compare the basic plot in Figure 8.6 with the enhanced plot in Figure 8.11. With the box plots, it's easier to see the potential difference in means for the males and females. It's easier to see the impact of the spread of the data. **Points Jittered** reveals points that were previously hidden because they were too close in value to display distinctly. Like the box plots, the histograms highlight the potential difference in means for the two groups. Hiding the standard deviation lines helps highlight the data. Start with the options in Figure 8.10 for your own data. Then, explore by selecting and deselecting options to see which ones work best for your situation.

The list describes the **Display Options** discussed in this chapter and shown in Figure 8.11. Chapter 9 discusses **Mean Diamonds** and **Comparison Circles**. All of the options work like a toggle switch. Selecting the check box turns on the option; deselecting the check box turns off the option.

All Graphs	Displays the two-sample graph when selected. When deselected, hides the graph.
Points	Displays the data points. JMP automatically displays the data points.
Box Plots	Displays a box plot for each group. The box plot and its whiskers are red.
Mean Lines	Adds a green line that shows the mean for each of the two groups.
Mean CI Lines	Adds two green lines that show a confidence interval for each of the two groups. Changing the alpha level (with **Set α level**) also changes these lines.
Mean Error Bars	Displays blue bars that show the mean plus or minus one standard error.
Grand Mean	Displays a black line that shows the overall mean of the data. JMP automatically displays the overall mean.
Std Dev Lines	Displays two dashed blue lines for each group. The upper line shows the mean plus a standard deviation; the lower line shows the mean minus a standard deviation. JMP adds these lines when performing the test for unequal variances.
Connect Means	Adds a blue line that connects the means for the two groups.
Mean of Means	Average of the two means for the two groups.
X Axis proportional	Spaces the groups on the *x*-axis in proportion to their sample size. This is very useful with groups that do not have similar sample sizes. JMP automatically spaces groups.

Points Spread	Spreads the data points across the width of the spacing for the group (proportional or not). **Points Jittered** is generally more helpful.
Points Jittered	Adds a random horizontal adjustment to the data points to show all of the points in the data. Jittering does not impact the *y*-values (the responses).
Histograms	Adds histograms for each group to the right of the plot.

Performing the Paired-Difference *t*-test

The paired-difference *t*-test is a parametric test for comparing paired groups.

Assumptions

The two assumptions for the paired-difference *t*-test are:

- each pair of measurements is independent of other pairs of measurements

- differences are from a normal distribution

Because the test analyzes the differences between paired observations, it is appropriate for continuous variables.

To illustrate this test, consider an experiment in liquid chromatography.[1] A chemist was investigating synthetic fuels produced from coal, and wanted to measure the naphthalene values by using two different liquid chromatography methods. Each of the 10 fuel samples was divided into two units: one unit was measured using standard liquid chromatography, and the other unit was measured using high-pressure liquid chromatography. The goal of analysis is to test whether the mean difference between the two methods is different from 0 at the 5% significance level. The chemist is willing to accept a 1-in-20 chance of saying that the mean difference is significantly different from 0, when in fact it is not. Table 8.5 shows the data.

---

[1] Data is from C. K. Bayne and I. B. Rubin, *Practical Experimental Designs and Optimization Methods for Chemists* (New York: VCH Publishers, 1986). Used with permission.

Table 8.5 Liquid Chromatography Data

Sample	High-Pressure	Standard
1	12.1	14.7
2	10.9	14.0
3	13.1	12.9
4	14.5	16.2
5	9.6	10.2
6	11.2	12.4
7	9.8	12.0
8	13.7	14.8
9	12.0	11.8
10	9.1	9.7

This data is available in the Chemistry data table in the sample data for the book.

Applying the six steps of analysis:

1. Create a JMP data table.

2. Check the data table for errors. Use **Distribution** to check for errors (see the exercise at the end of the chapter). Based on the results, assume that the data is free of errors.

3. Choose the significance level for the test. Choose a 5% significance level, which requires a *p*-value less than 0.05 to conclude that the groups are significantly different.

4. Check the assumptions for the test. The first assumption is independent pairs of measurements. The assumption seems reasonable because there are 10 different samples that are divided into two units. The second assumption is that the differences are from a normal distribution. We created a new variable, named **Difference** (**Standard** subtracted from **High Pressure**) and used **Distribution** to check for normality. Although there are only a few data points, the assumption seems reasonable (see the exercise at the end of the chapter.)

What if the second assumption was not reasonable? With only 10 samples, you do not have a very complete picture of the distribution. Think of weighing 10 people, and then deciding whether the weights are normally distributed based only on the weights of these 10 people. Sometimes you have additional knowledge about the population that enables you to use tests that require a normally distributed population. For example, you might know that the weights are generally normally distributed and you can use that information. However, this approach should be used with caution. Use it only when you have substantial additional knowledge about the population. Otherwise, if you are concerned about the assumption of normality, or if a test for normality indicates that your data is not a sample from a normally distributed population, consider performing a Wilcoxon Signed Rank test, which is discussed later in this chapter.

5. Perform the test. Refer to "Building Hypothesis Tests to Compare Two Groups" earlier in this chapter. For paired groups, the null hypothesis is that the mean difference (μ_D) is zero. The alternative hypothesis is that the mean difference (μ_D) is different from 0.

   JMP provides two ways to test these hypotheses. In some cases, you have only the difference between the pairs. See "Using Distribution to Test Paired Differences" for this case. In other cases, you have the raw data with the values for each pair. See "Using Matched Pairs to Test Paired Differences" for this case.

6. Make conclusions from the test results. See the section "Finding the *p*-value" for each test.

Using Distribution to Test Paired Differences

For the Chemistry data, we created a **Difference** variable to check our assumptions. Suppose that there is only the **Difference** variable. Use the following JMP steps to perform the hypothesis test:

1. Open the Chemistry with Diff data table. (This data table is available in the sample data for the book.)

2. In the JMP Starter window, click **Basic→Distribution**.

3. Click **Difference→Y, Columns**.

4. Click **OK**.

5. Click the hot spot for the Difference report.

6. Select **Test Mean**.

7. In the **Test Mean** window, accept the automatic choice of 0 for the hypothesized mean.

8. Click **OK**.

Figure 8.12 shows the **Test Mean=value** report.

Figure 8.12 Test Mean=value Report for Chemistry with Diff Data

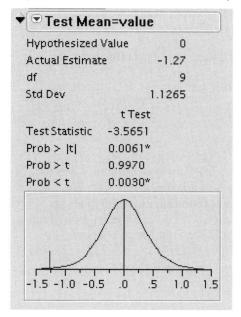

Finding the *p*-value

Look to the right of the heading **Prob > |t|** in Figure 8.12. The value is **0.0061**, which is less than the significance level of 0.05. You conclude that the mean difference in naphthalene values from the two methods is significantly different from 0.

In general, to interpret JMP results, look at the *p*-value that appears to the right of the **Prob > |t|** heading. If the *p*-value is less than the predetermined significance level, then you can conclude that the mean difference between the paired groups is significantly different from 0. If the *p*-value is greater than the significance level, then you can conclude that the mean difference is not significantly different from 0. Do not conclude that the mean difference is 0 (see the discussion earlier in this chapter).

Understanding Other Items in the Report

The list describes other items in Figure 8.12.

Hypothesized Value	Value for the hypothesized mean. For a paired-difference *t*-test, this is 0. This value corresponds to the automatic choice of 0 in the **Test Mean** window.
Actual Estimate	Average of the **Difference** variable.
df	Degrees of freedom, which is calculated as *n*-1, where *n* is the number of pairs.
Std Dev	Standard deviation of the **Difference** variable.
Test Statistic	Test statistic for the *t*-test. It is calculated as:

$$t = \frac{\overline{X} - \mu_0}{s/\sqrt{n}}$$

where $\overline{X}$ is the average difference, *s* is the standard deviation, and *n* is the sample size. For testing paired groups, μ_0 is 0 (testing the null hypothesis of no difference between groups). You can specify a different value by entering it in the **Test Mean** window.

Prob < t **Prob > t**	Gives *p*-values for one-sided *t*-tests.

Understanding the Graph

Figure 8.12 also shows a graph. You interpret this graph the same way you interpret the graph for the independent groups. See "Understanding the Graph" and "Technical Details: t Test Graph" earlier in the chapter.

Using Matched Pairs to Test Paired Differences

So far, this section has discussed how to test paired differences using a **Difference** variable. This is important because sometimes you receive data and you don't have the original pairs of information. When you do have the original pairs, JMP provides another way to test paired differences. In JMP:

1. Open the **Chemistry** data table.

2. In the JMP Starter window, click **Basic→Matched Pairs**.

3. Click **Standard→Y, Paired Response**.

4. Click **High Pressure→Y, Paired Response**.

5. Click **OK**.

Figure 8.13 shows the Matched Pairs report.

Figure 8.13 Matched Pairs Report for Chemistry Data

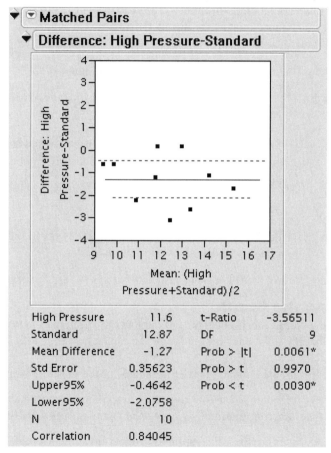

Finding the *p*-value

Look to the right of the heading **Prob > |t|** in Figure 8.13. The value is **0.0061**, which is less than the significance level of 0.05. This has the same result as the analysis of the single **Difference** variable. You conclude that the mean difference in naphthalene values from the two methods is significantly different from 0.

You interpret the *p*-value for this test the exact same way as described for the Test Mean=value report.

Understanding Other Items in the Report

Compare the results in Figures 8.12 and 8.13. The statistics reported in both reports are the same, although some are labeled differently. The **Actual Estimate** in Figure 8.12 estimates the average difference, just as the **Mean Difference** in Figure 8.13 does. The **Test Statistic** in Figure 8.12 gives the *t*-ratio, just as the **t-Ratio** in Figure 8.13 does.

The list describes items that are in Figure 8.13, but are not in Figure 8.12.

High Pressure Standard	Average for each group. In general, JMP displays the variable name as the heading.
Std Error	Standard error of the difference. It is calculated as $s/\sqrt{n}$, where s is the standard deviation of the difference and n is the sample size.
N	Sample size.
Correlation	Pearson correlation coefficient for the two variables. Chapter 10 discusses correlation.

Understanding the Graph

Figure 8.13 shows the paired *t*-test plot. The plot depicts the differences between the pairs and highlights whether the difference is significant. To understand the plot:

- The dots represent the data points of differences for the matched pairs.

- The solid red horizontal line across the entire graph represents the average difference. The report in Figure 8.13 shows the value as **Mean Difference**.

- The red dotted lines are the 95% confidence interval for the average difference. The report in Figure 8.13 shows the values as **Upper95%** and **Lower95%**.

If the 95% confidence interval includes 0, then the average difference between the matched pairs is not significantly different from 0. In contrast, if the 95% confidence interval does not include 0, then the difference is significant.

> **JMP Hint:**
>
> The order of selection matters for **Matched Pairs**. JMP subtracts the first variable selected from the second variable selected.

To explain the JMP hint, **Difference** is calculated as **Standard** subtracted from **High Pressure** in the Chemistry data. In **Matched Pairs**, **Standard** was selected first. If **Standard** was selected second, JMP would calculate **Difference** as **High Pressure** subtracted from **Standard**. Regardless of which of the variable pairs you choose first, the statistical results are exactly the same. The only change is that the signs for the difference (**Actual Estimate**) and the *t*-statistic (**Test Statistic**) are reversed.

Performing the Wilcoxon Signed Rank Test

The Wilcoxon Signed Rank test is a nonparametric analogue to the paired-difference *t*-test. The Wilcoxon Signed Rank test assumes that each pair of measurements is independent of other pairs of measurements. This test can be used with ordinal and continuous variables. This topic uses the **Chemistry** data as an example.

Apply the six steps of analysis to the **Chemistry** data:

1. Create a JMP data table.

2. Check the data table for errors. We checked and found no errors.

3. Choose the significance level for the test. We chose a 5% significance level.

4. Check the assumptions for the test. We checked the assumption of independent pairs of measurements (see the earlier discussion for the paired-difference *t*-test).

5. Perform the test. As with the parametric test, JMP provides two ways to test the hypothesis, depending on whether you have only the differences between pairs or whether you have the raw data.

6. Make conclusions from the test results.

Using Distribution for the Wilcoxon Signed Rank Test

Suppose that you have only the differences between pairs. Use the following JMP steps to perform a hypothesis test:

1. Open the Chemistry with Diff data table.

2. In the JMP Starter window, click **Basic→Distribution**.

3. Click **Difference→Y, Columns**.

4. Click **OK**.

5. Click the hot spot for the Difference report.

6. Click **Test Mean**.

7. In the Test Mean window, accept the automatic choice of 0 for the hypothesized mean. Also, select the check box for **Wilcoxon Signed Rank**.

8. Click **OK**.

Except for selecting the check box in step 7, these are the same steps as for the paired-difference *t*-test. Figure 8.14 shows the text report. The steps also create the t Test graph, which is interpreted the same way as discussed earlier.

Figure 8.14 Wilcoxon Signed Rank Test from Distribution

Test Mean=value		
Hypothesized Value	0	
Actual Estimate	-1.27	
df	9	
Std Dev	1.1265	
	t Test	Signed-Rank
Test Statistic	-3.5651	-24.5000
Prob > |t|	0.0061*	0.0078*
Prob > t	0.9970	0.9961
Prob < t	0.0030*	0.0039*

Figure 8.14 repeats all the information from Figure 8.12. Figure 8.14 adds a **Signed-Rank** column with details for the Wilcoxon Signed Rank test.

Finding the *p*-value

Look in the second column to the right of the heading **Prob > |t|** in Figure 8.14. The value is **0.0078**, which is less than the significance level of 0.05. You conclude that the mean difference in naphthalene values from the two methods is significantly different from 0.

In general, you interpret the *p*-values for the Wilcoxon Signed Rank test the exact same way as described for the paired-difference *t*-test.

Understanding Other Items in the Report

Compare the results in Figures 8.12 and 8.14. The statistics reported in both reports are the same. See the explanation of items for Figure 8.12 for details on these statistics. You interpret the three *p*-values for the Wilcoxon Signed Rank test just as you do for the other tests. The only item in Figure 8.14 that does not appear in Figure 8.12 is the value of the Wilcoxon Signed Rank test statistic. For the Chemistry data, this is **-24.5**. In general, this statistic appears immediately below the heading **Signed-Rank**.

Using Matched Pairs for the Wilcoxon Signed Rank Test

Suppose that you have the original matched pairs data. Use the following JMP steps to perform the hypothesis test:

1. Open the Chemistry data table.

2. In the JMP Starter window, click **Basic→Matched Pairs**.

3. Click **Standard→Y, Paired Response**.

4. Click **High Pressure→Y, Paired Response**.

5. Click **OK**.

6. Click the hot spot for the Matched Pairs report.

7. Select **Wilcoxon Signed Rank**.

Except for steps 6 and 7, these are the same steps for using **Matched Pairs** to perform the paired-difference *t*-test. These steps generate the same results shown in Figure 8.13, and add a report for the **Wilcoxon Sign-Rank** test. Figure 8.15 shows this report.

Figure 8.15 Wilcoxon Signed Rank Report

Wilcoxon Sign-Rank	
	High Pressure-Standard
Test Statistic	-24.500
Prob > |z|	0.008
Prob > z	0.996
Prob < z	0.004

Finding the *p*-value

Look to the right of the heading **Prob > |z|** in Figure 8.15. The value is **0.008**, which is less than the significance level of 0.05. You conclude that the mean difference in naphthalene values from the two methods is significantly different from 0.

In general, you interpret the *p*-values for the Wilcoxon Signed Rank test the exact same way as described for the paired-difference *t*-test.

JMP Hints:

Double-click on the column of statistics and change the number of decimal places to four. The number of decimal places for the *p*-values shown by the Distribution and Matched Pairs reports will then be the same. Do not change the format of the column to **p-value**. JMP formats the whole column the same way, so the **Signed-Rank** statistic would then use the **p-value** format. This would cause confusion.

Matched Pairs accepts ordinal variables. JMP displays a warning window, but you can click **Continue** and create the analysis. In contrast, JMP requires a continuous difference variable to perform the Wilcoxon Signed Rank test in **Distribution**.

Understanding Other Items in the Report

The steps for Figure 8.15 generate the same JMP reports as are generated in Figure 8.13. See the explanation of items for Figure 8.13 for details. The only addition is the Wilcoxon Sign-Rank report, which contains the test statistic and the *p*-values. You interpret these values just as you interpret the Wilcoxon Signed Rank results from **Distribution**.

Summaries

Key Ideas

- Independent groups contain measurements for two different and unrelated groups in the population. Paired groups contain paired measurements for each item.

- To summarize data for independent groups, summarize each group separately. To summarize data for paired groups, create a **Difference** variable and use it to summarize.

- To choose a statistical test, first, decide if the data is from independent or paired groups. Then, decide whether to use a parametric or a nonparametric test. The second decision is based on whether the assumptions for a parametric test seem reasonable. Tests for the four cases are:

	Groups	
Type of Test	**Independent**	**Paired**
Parametric	Two-sample *t*-test	Paired-difference *t*-test
Nonparametric	Wilcoxon Rank Sum test	Wilcoxon Signed Rank test

- Regardless of the statistical test you choose, the steps of analysis are:
  1. Create a JMP data table.

  2. Check the data table for errors.

  3. Choose the significance level for the test.

  4. Check the assumptions for the test.

  5. Perform the test.

  6. Make conclusions from the test results.

- Regardless of the statistical test, to make conclusions, compare the p-value for the test with the predetermined significance level.

  □ If the *p*-value is less than the significance level, then you reject the null hypothesis and conclude that the groups are significantly different. JMP helps by displaying an asterisk next to *p*-values that are less than the 0.05 significance level.

  □ If the *p*-value is greater than the significance level, then you do not reject the null hypothesis. You conclude that the groups are not significantly different. (Remember, do not conclude that the groups are the same!)

- Test for normality using **Distribution** as described in Chapter 5. For independent groups, check each group separately. For paired groups, check the **Difference** variable.

- When comparing two independent groups, test for equal variances using **Basic→Oneway** from the JMP Starter window. Then, click **UnEqual Variances**. Use the two-sided *F*-test (**F Test 2-sided**) to test for unequal variances.

- When comparing two independent groups, the JMP analysis option depends on the outcome of the unequal variances test. In either case, click **Basic→Oneway** in the JMP Starter window. Then, for unequal variances, use the **t Test** analysis option. For equal variances, use the **Means/Anova/Pooled t** analysis option.

- When comparing paired groups, JMP provides analysis options that use the original pairs in **Matched Pairs**. When only the **Difference** variable is available, JMP provides analysis options in **Distribution**.

- For some tests, JMP creates a confidence interval. If the confidence interval includes 0, then the test will not be significant. If the confidence interval does not include 0, then the test will be significant.

- Use the appropriate JMP graphs to help visualize the difference.

JMP Steps

For summarizing data from two groups

- To summarize data from two independent groups, use **Distribution** with a **By** variable. Useful analysis options are **Uniform Scaling** (to create the same scale for both histograms) and **Horizontal Layout** (easier for viewing and printing).

- To summarize data from paired groups, use **Distribution** on the **Difference** variable.

- To create a **Difference** variable:
  1. Click **Cols→New Column**.

  2. Name the new column (difference, for example).

  3. Click the menu for **Column Properties** and select **Formula**.

  4. In the formula window, click the first variable name, then the minus (⊟) key, and then the second variable name. Click **OK**.

  5. Click **OK** to close the New Column window.

For analysis step 4, checking assumptions

- To check the assumption of independent observations, you need to think about your data and whether this assumption is reasonable. This is not a step where using JMP will answer this question.

- To check the assumption of normality, use **Distribution** as described in Chapter 6. For independent groups, check each group separately. For paired groups, check the **Difference** variable.

- To test for equal variances for the two-sample *t*-test:
  1. In the JMP Starter window, click **Basic→Oneway**.

  2. Click the response variable and then **Y, Response**. Click the variable that identifies the groups and then **X, Grouping**. Click **OK**.

  3. Click the hot spot for the Oneway Analysis of *Y* By *X* report. Then, click **UnEqual Variances**.

For analysis step 5, perform the test

- To perform the two-sample *t*-test to compare two independent groups, click **Basic→Oneway**. Click the response variable and grouping variable as described in testing for equal variances. Then, click the hot spot for the Oneway Analysis of *Y* By *X* report:

  For unequal variances, select the **t Test** analysis option.

  For equal variances, select the **Means/Anova/Pooled t** analysis option.

- To perform the nonparametric Wilcoxon Rank Sum test to compare two independent groups, click **Basic→Oneway**. Click the response variable and grouping variable as described in testing for equal variances. Then, click the hot spot for the Oneway Analysis of *Y* By *X* report. Click **Nonparametric→Wilcoxon Test**.

- To perform the paired-difference *t*-test on a **Difference** variable, use **Distribution** on the **Difference** variable. Click the hot spot for the Difference report and select **Test Mean**. Accept the automatic choice of 0 for the hypothesized mean. Click **OK**.

- **To perform the paired-difference *t*-test** with the original pairs:
  1. In the JMP Starter window, click **Basic→Matched Pairs**.
  2. Click both of the paired variables and then **Y, Paired Response**.
  3. Click **OK**.

- To perform the Wilcoxon Signed Rank test on a **Difference** variable, use **Distribution** as described in the paired-difference *t*-test. In the Test Mean window, select the check box for **Wilcoxon Signed Rank**. Click **OK**.

- To perform the Wilcoxon Signed Rank test with the original pairs, follow the steps for the paired-difference *t*-test with the original pairs. Click the hot spot for the Matched Pairs report, and select **Wilcoxon Signed Rank**.

Enhancements

- To change the alpha level for confidence intervals for independent groups, follow the steps for the two-sample *t*-test. Click the hot spot for the Oneway Analysis of *Y* By *X* report. Click **Set α level** and select a level. Remember, this affects the confidence intervals, but does not change the significance level for the test.

- To enhance the two-sample graph, follow the steps for the two-sample *t*-test. This creates the graph.

  □ Click the hot spot for the **Oneway Analysis of** *Y* **By** *X* report, select **Display Options**, and select the options individually. Or, hold down the ALT key and click the **Display Options** hot spot to see a window where you can select all of the options at once.

- Useful analysis options for adding features are:

  □ **Box Plots**, which adds box plots for each group to the plot of data points

  □ **Points Jittered**, which makes the data points easier to see, especially if there are a lot of data points

  □ **Histograms**, which adds histograms for each group to the right of the plot of data points

- Useful analysis options for hiding features are:

  □ **All Graphs**, which hides the graph

  □ **Std Dev Lines**, which can be hard to see

- Useful analysis options that JMP automatically chooses are:

  □ **Points**, which displays the data

  □ **Grand Mean**, which shows the overall mean of the data

  □ **X Axis proportional**, which spaces the groups on the *x*-axis in proportion to their sample size

Exercises

1. Click **Help→Tutorials** in the JMP menu bar. Complete the **Two Means** and **Paired Means** tutorials.

2. For the STA6207 data in this chapter, perform the appropriate nonparametric test. Discuss your conclusions and compare them with the parametric results in this chapter.

3. Summarize the two groups in the Gastric data in this chapter. Test each group for normality. As appropriate, perform parametric tests on this data. Discuss your conclusions.

4. Use the **Matched Pairs** approach for the Chemistry data in this chapter. Use **Distribution** to test for normality. Discuss your conclusions and compare them with the **Distribution** approach in the chapter.

5. Open the Bodyfat data and click **Basic→Two-Sample t-Test** in the JMP Starter window. With this selection, JMP always performs the *t*-test for unequal variances. Although this selection is a quick way to create results, the *t*-test that assumes unequal variances might not be the correct test. Compare your results with the results in the chapter.

6. Use the Therm data in the Sample Data Directory (under the Medical Studies heading). The research question is whether there is a significant difference between the two thermometers. Does this data contain paired or independent groups? Depending on the answer, use JMP to summarize the data. Perform the steps for analysis, define the null and alternative hypotheses, and test the assumptions. Use a 5% alpha level. Discuss your conclusions, and answer the research question.

7. Use the Nonparametrics data in the Sample Data Directory (under the Examples for Teaching heading). The research question is whether there is a significant difference between the two doses. Does this data contain paired or independent groups? Depending on the answer, use JMP to summarize the data. Perform the steps for analysis, define the null and alternative hypotheses, and test the assumptions. Use a 5% alpha level. Discuss your conclusions, and answer the research question.

8. Use the Baby Sleep data in the Sample Data Directory (under the Examples for Teaching heading). The research question is whether there is a significant difference between the time babies are awake and asleep. Does this data contain paired or independent groups? Depending on the answer, use JMP to summarize the data. Perform the steps for analysis, define the null and alternative hypotheses, and test the assumptions. Use a 10% alpha level. Discuss your conclusions, and answer the research question.

9. Use the **Companies** data in the **Sample Data Directory** (under the **Business and Demographic** heading). The research question is whether the mean profit per employee (**profit/emp**) is different for pharmaceutical and computer companies. Does this data contain paired or independent groups? Depending on the answer, use JMP to summarize the data. Perform the steps for analysis, define the null and alternative hypotheses, and test the assumptions. Use a 5% alpha level. Discuss your conclusions, and answer the research question.

10. Use the **Bptime** data in the **Sample Data Directory** (under the **Examples for Teaching** heading). The research question is whether there is a significant difference between the morning and afternoon readings. Does this data contain paired or independent groups? Depending on the answer, use JMP to summarize the data. Perform the steps for analysis, define the null and alternative hypotheses, and test the assumptions. Use a 5% alpha level. Discuss your conclusions, and answer the research question.

11. Use the **Cars 1993** data in the **Sample Data Directory** (under the **Exploratory Modeling** heading). The research question is whether there is a significant difference between the highway mileage for cars from domestic and foreign manufacturers (**Domestic Manufacturer**). Does this data contain paired or independent groups? Depending on the answer, use JMP to summarize the data. Perform the steps for analysis, define the null and alternative hypotheses, and test the assumptions. Use a 5% alpha level. Discuss your conclusions, and answer the research question.

12. Use the **Lipid** data in the **Sample Data Directory** (under the **Medical Studies** heading). The research question is whether there is a significant difference in cholesterol (**Cholesterol**) for men and women. Does this data contain paired or independent groups? Depending on the answer, use JMP to summarize the data. Perform the steps for analysis, define the null and alternative hypotheses, and test the assumptions. Use a 5% alpha level. Discuss your conclusions, and answer the research question.

Special Topic: Paired Data in a Single Column

What if you receive paired data that has all the results in a single column? First, don't panic. You don't need to re-enter the data. Instead, you can use JMP to reformat the data for you. Suppose you receive the Chemistry data formatted as shown in Figure 8S.1:

Figure 8S.1 Chemistry Data with Results in a Single Column

Sample	Method	Naphthalene
1	High Pressure	12.1
1	Standard	14.7
2	High Pressure	10.9
2	Standard	14
3	High Pressure	13.1
3	Standard	12.9
4	High Pressure	14.5
4	Standard	16.2
5	High Pressure	9.6
5	Standard	10.2
6	High Pressure	11.2
6	Standard	12.4
7	High Pressure	9.8
7	Standard	12
8	High Pressure	13.7
8	Standard	14.8
9	High Pressure	12
9	Standard	11.8
10	High Pressure	9.1
10	Standard	9.7

You need to split the single column of naphthalene values into two columns, one for each of the methods. In JMP, click **Tables→Split**. Then, complete the window as shown in Figure 8S.2:

Figure 8S.2 Split Window

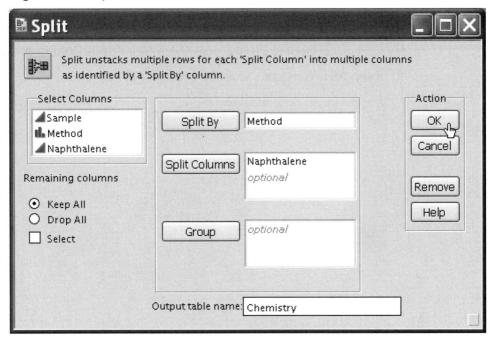

Clicking **OK** in Figure 8S.2 creates the data table shown in Figure 8S.3, which is the same as the Chemistry data table.

Figure 8S.3 Results from Splitting

Sample	High Pressure	Standard
1	12.1	14.7
2	10.9	14
3	13.1	12.9
4	14.5	16.2
5	9.6	10.2
6	11.2	12.4
7	9.8	12
8	13.7	14.8
9	12	11.8
10	9.1	9.7

See the JMP documentation for more on splitting. As a brief summary of steps, select:

- The column that contains the names of the pairs for **Split By**
- The column that contains the numeric results for **Split Columns**
- **Keep All** to carry other variables over to the new data table
- A name for the new data table

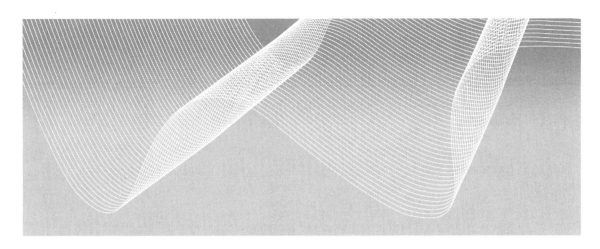

Chapter 9

Comparing More Than Two Groups

Suppose you are a greenhouse manager and you want to compare the effects of 6 fertilizers on the growth of geraniums. You have 30 plants, and you randomly assigned 5 plants to each of the 6 fertilizer groups. You carefully controlled other factors: you used the same type of soil for all 30 plants, you made sure that they all received the same number of hours of light each day, and you applied the fertilizers on the same day and in the same amounts to all 30 plants. At the end of this designed experiment, you measured the height of each plant. Now, you want to compare the 6 fertilizer groups in terms of plant height. This chapter discusses the analysis of this type of situation. Specific topics are:

- summarizing data from more than two groups

- building a test of hypothesis for data in several groups

- performing a one-way analysis of variance

- performing a Kruskal-Wallis test

- exploring group differences with multiple comparison procedures

The methods that are discussed are appropriate for situations where each group consists of measurements of different items. The methods are not appropriate when "groups" consist of measurements of the same item at different times; for example, if you were to measure the same 15 plants at 2, 4, and 6 weeks after applying fertilizer. (This would be a repeated measures design. See "Further Reading" for references.)

Depending on the method, it can be used with ordinal or continuous variables. JMP requires a numeric variable for the response, but it can be continuous, ordinal, or nominal. JMP accepts a numeric or character variable for classifying data into groups, and it can be ordinal or nominal.

Summarizing Data from Multiple Groups

This section discusses the methods that are used to summarize groups. These methods do not replace formal statistical tests, but they do give you a better understanding of the data and can help you understand the results from formal statistical tests.

Before you can summarize data, you need data in a JMP data table. Then, you check the data table for errors before you make any decisions. For a small data table, you can print the data and compare the printout with the data that you collected. For a larger data table, you can use the methods discussed in Chapter 4. You can use the same JMP steps to check for errors and to summarize the data. The steps are straightforward and simple.

Suppose you have data from an investigation of teachers' salaries for different subject areas. You want to know whether the teachers' salaries are significantly different for different subject areas. Table 9.1 shows the data.[1]

_____

[1] Data is from Dr. Ramon Littell, University of Florida. Used with permission.

Table 9.1 Teacher Salaries

Subject Area	Annual Salary					
Special Education	35584	41400	42360	31319	57880	39697
	43128	42222	39676	41899	45773	53813
	51096	44625	35762	35083	52616	31114
	36844					
Mathematics	27814	25470	34432	45480	25358	29360
	29610	25000	29363	25091	55600	31624
	47770	31908	33000	26355	39201	45733
	32000	37120	62655	36733	28521	28709
	26674	48836	25096	27038	27197	51655
	25125	27829	28935	31124	37323	32960
	26428	39908	34692	23663	32188	45268
	33957	34055	53282	43890	26000	27107
	31615	24032	56070	24530	40174	24305
	35560	35955				
Language	26162	23963	27403	30180	32134	29594
	33472	28535	34609	49100	44207	47902
	26705	44888	29969	27599	28662	38948
	27664	29612	47316	27556	35465	33042
	38250	30171	32022	33884	36980	30230
	33618	29485	31006	48411	33058	49881
	42485	26966	27878	27607	30665	34001
Music	21827	35787	30043	27847	24150	29954
	21635	46691	24895	22515	27827	24712
	46001	25666	27178	41161	23092	24720
	44444	28004	32040	26417	41220	22148
	38914	28770				
Science	44324	43075	30000	24532	34930	25276
	39784	32576	40330	59910	47475	
Social Science	42210	36133	49683	31993	38728	46969
	59704					

This data is available in the Salary data table in the sample data for the book.

To summarize the data in JMP:

1. Open the Salary data table.

2. In the JMP Starter window, click **Basic→Distribution**.

3. Click **Annual Salary** and **Subject Area** and then **Y, Columns**.

4. Click **OK**.

Figure 9.1 shows the results, with the **Mathematics** subject area selected. The Quantiles report is hidden.

Figure 9.1 Distribution Results for Salary Data with Mathematics Selected

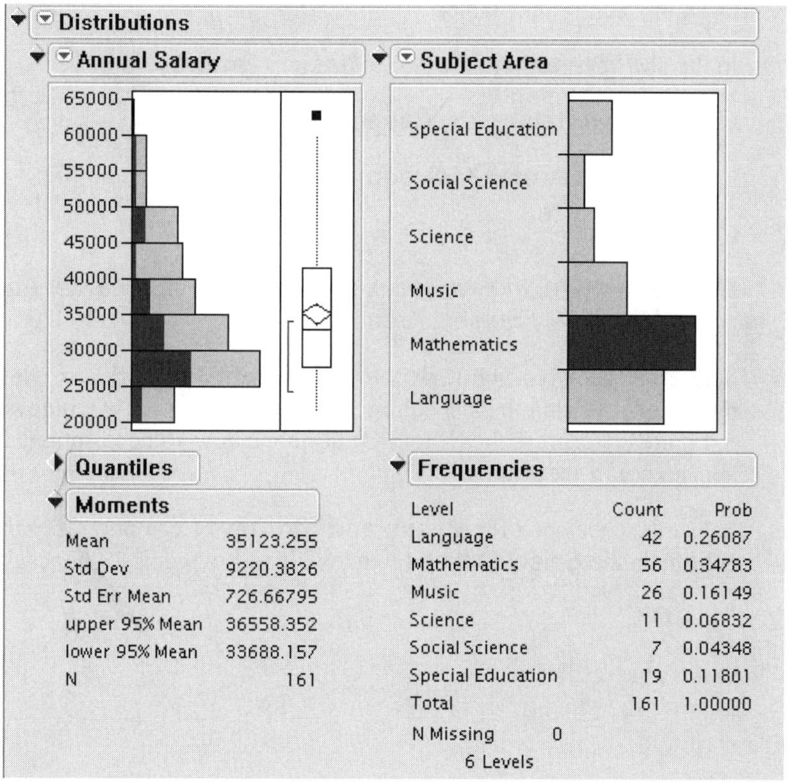

First, check the data for errors. Notice the outlier point at the top of the box plot for Annual Salary. If you click on the outlier point and check it in the data table and in Table 9.1, you find that this is a valid value. This is observation 41, for a Mathematics teacher earning $62,655.

Figure 9.1 shows that over half of the data is from **Mathematics** and **Language** teachers. You can also see this in Table 9.1, but the graph highlights the issue. The Annual Salary report provides an overall summary, instead of grouping the data by subject area.

To summarize the salaries by subject area, you can use **Distribution** with a **By** variable. See Chapter 8 and follow the steps for using a **By** column in the Bodyfat data. JMP provides another approach, which gives a more compact report. In JMP:

1. Open the Salary data table.

2. In the JMP Starter window, click **Basic→Oneway**.

3. Click **Annual Salary→Y, Response**.

4. Click **Subject Area→X, Grouping**.

5. Click **OK**.

6. Hold down the ALT key and click the hot spot for the Oneway Analysis of Annual Salary By Subject Area report.

7. Select the check boxes for: **Box Plots**, **Points Jittered**, and **Histograms**. (**Histograms** is in the last column in the Select Options window. In Chapter 8, Figure 8.10 shows the Select Options window.) These options control the appearance of the graphs.

8. Select the check box for **Means and Std Dev**. This option is in the first column in the Select Options window. It adds a report to the results.

9. Click **OK**.

Figure 9.2 shows the results.

Figure 9.2 Summarizing Subject Areas for Salary Data

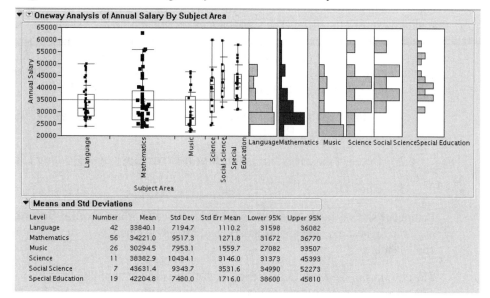

▼ ▽ **Oneway Analysis of Annual Salary By Subject Area**

▼ **Means and Std Deviations**

Level	Number	Mean	Std Dev	Std Err Mean	Lower 95%	Upper 95%
Language	42	33840.1	7194.7	1110.2	31598	36082
Mathematics	56	34221.0	9517.3	1271.8	31672	36770
Music	26	30294.5	7953.1	1559.7	27082	33507
Science	11	38382.9	10434.1	3146.0	31373	45393
Social Science	7	43631.4	9343.7	3531.6	34990	52273
Special Education	19	42204.8	7480.0	1716.0	38600	45810

Adding the appearance options in step 7 enhanced the automatic graphs of the data points. Step 8 added the **Means and Std Deviations** report.

The histograms to the right of the plot show the different distributions of salaries for the subject areas. Although there might be salary differences in the subject areas, you don't know whether the differences are greater than what could have happened by chance.

The box plots highlight the potential differences. The automatic choice of **X Axis proportional** adjusts the widths of the boxes depending on the sample size for each group. This highlights the small size for the **Science**, **Social Science**, and **Special Education** subject areas. Looking at the median (the center line of the box), you observe differences in the subject areas. But, you don't know whether the differences are greater than what could have happened by chance.

Also, looking at the box plots highlights potential outlier points in several subject areas. In checking the data for errors, you highlight the data points and compare them with the original data. You find that all of the data values are valid.

Adding the Means and Std Deviations report also added the blue lines to the plot. The horizontal blue lines connected by a vertical blue bar show the mean plus or minus one standard error of the mean. The stand-alone horizontal blue lines show the mean plus or minus one standard deviation. These stand-alone blue lines can be hard to see, especially when there are a lot of data points. Compare how much easier you can see the blue lines for the **Science** subject area (with only a few data points) than for the **Mathematics** subject area (with a lot of data points). To remove these lines in JMP:

1. Hold down the ALT key and click the hot spot for the Oneway Analysis of Annual Salary By Subject Area report.

2. Deselect the check boxes for: **Mean Error Bars** and **Std Dev Lines**.

3. Click **OK**.

Figure 9.2 shows simple descriptive statistics for each group. **Social Science** teachers have the highest average annual salary, and **Music** teachers have the lowest average annual salary.

The columns in the Means and Std Deviations report should be familiar because they also appear in the Moments report for the **Distribution** platform. Briefly, **Number** is the sample size for each group, **Mean** is the average, **Std Dev** is the standard deviation, **Std Err Mean** is the standard error of the mean ($s/\sqrt{n}$), and **Lower 95%** and **Upper 95%** form the 95% confidence interval for the mean.

JMP Hints:

Click the report's hot spot and select **Display Options→Set α level** to change the 95% confidence interval. Select 0.10 for a 90% confidence interval, 0.01 for a 99% confidence interval, or enter your own alpha level. JMP changes the headings for the confidence interval columns, and recalculates the confidence intervals.

Click the report's hot spot and select **Quantiles** to display a report that gives the values for the box plot. In addition to the 25th, 50th, and 75th percentiles, the Quantiles report shows the minimum, 10th, and 90th percentiles and the maximum for each group.

Reviewing the other statistics in the **Means and Std Deviations** report indicates that there might be differences among groups. To find out if these differences are greater than what would be expected by chance requires a statistical test.

Building Hypothesis Tests to Compare More Than Two Groups

So far, this chapter has discussed how to summarize groups. When you start a study, you want to know how important the differences between groups are, and if the differences are large enough to be statistically significant. In statistical terms, you want to perform a hypothesis test. This section discusses hypothesis testing when comparing multiple groups. (See Chapter 6 for the general idea of hypothesis testing.)

When you compare multiple groups, the null hypothesis is that the means for the groups are the same, and the alternative hypothesis is that the means are different. The salary example has six groups. In this case, the typical notation is:

$$H_o: \quad \mu_A = \mu_B = \mu_C = \mu_D = \mu_E = \mu_F$$

and:

$$H_a: \quad \text{at least two means are different}$$

where H_o indicates the null hypothesis, H_a indicates the alternative hypothesis, and μ_A, μ_B, μ_C, μ_D, μ_E, and μ_F are the population means for the six groups of teachers. The alternative hypothesis does not specify which means are different from one another, only that some differences exist in the means. The preceding notation shows the hypotheses for comparing six groups. For more groups or fewer groups, add or delete the appropriate number of means in the notation.

In statistical tests that compare several groups, the hypotheses are tested by partitioning the total variation in the data into variation due to differences between groups and variation due to error. The error variation does not refer to mistakes in the data. It refers to the natural variation within a group (and, possibly, to variation due to other factors that were not considered). This error variation is sometimes called the "within group" variation. The error variation represents the natural variation that would be expected by chance; if the variation between groups is large relative to the error variation, the means are likely to be different.

Because the hypothesis test analyzes the variation in the data, it is called an *analysis of variance* and is abbreviated as "ANOVA." The specific case of considering only the variation between groups and the variation due to error is called a *one-way ANOVA*. Figure 9.3 depicts how the total variation is partitioned into variation between groups and variation due to error.

Figure 9.3 How One-Way ANOVA Partitions Variation

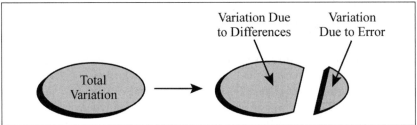

Using Parametric and Nonparametric Tests

In this book, the term "ANOVA" refers specifically to a parametric analysis of variance, which can be used if the assumptions are reasonable. If the assumptions are not reasonable, use the nonparametric Kruskal-Wallis test, which has fewer assumptions.

Balanced and Unbalanced Data

If all of the groups have the same sample size, the data is *balanced*. If the sample sizes are different, the data is *unbalanced*.

This distinction can be important for follow-up tests to an ANOVA, or for other types of experimental designs. However, for a one-way analysis of variance or a Kruskal-Wallis test, you don't need to know whether the data is balanced. JMP automatically handles balanced and unbalanced data correctly in this situation.

Understanding Significance

In either an ANOVA or a Kruskal-Wallis test, there are two possible results: the *p*-value is less than the predetermined reference probability, or it is not.

Groups Significantly Different

If the *p*-value is less than the reference probability, the result is statistically significant, and you reject the null hypothesis. You conclude that the means for the groups are significantly different. You don't know which means are different from one another, only that some differences exist in the means.

Your next step might be to use a *multiple comparison procedure* to further analyze the differences between groups. An alternative to a multiple comparison procedure is to perform some comparisons that you planned before you collected data. If you have certain comparisons that you know you want to make, consult a statistician for help in designing your study. (Although you can perform your own comparisons in JMP, this task uses options in the **Fit Model** platform that the book does not discuss. See "Further Reading" for references, and see the JMP documentation for help on the **Fit Model** platform.)

Groups Not Significantly Different

If the *p*-value is greater than the reference probability, the result is not statistically significant, and you fail to reject the null hypothesis. You conclude that the means for the groups are not significantly different. **Do not "accept the null hypothesis" and conclude that the groups are the same.** This distinction is very important. When testing for differences between groups, you do not have enough evidence to conclude that the groups are the same. A larger sample might have led you to conclude that the groups are different. Perhaps there are other factors that were not controlled, and these factors influenced the experiment enough to obscure the differences between groups. For more information, see the general discussion about building hypothesis tests in Chapter 6.

Performing a One-way Analysis of Variance

This section discusses the assumptions for a one-way analysis of variance, how to test the assumptions, how to use JMP, and how to interpret the results. The steps of analysis for comparing multiple groups are the same as the steps for comparing two groups:

1. Create a JMP data table.

2. Check the data table for errors.

3. Choose the significance level for the test.

4. Check the assumptions for the test.

5. Perform the test.

6. Make conclusions from the test results.

Steps 1 and 2 are complete. For step 3, compare the groups at the 10% significance level. For significance, the *p*-value needs to be less than the reference probability value of 0.10.

Assumptions

The assumptions for an analysis of variance are:

- Observations are independent. The measurement of one observation cannot affect the measurement of another observation

- Observations are a random sample from a population with a normal distribution. If there are differences between groups, there might be a different normal distribution for each group.

- Groups have equal variances.

Assuming normality requires that the measurement variable is continuous. If your measurement variable is ordinal, go to the section on the Kruskal-Wallis test later in this chapter.

Testing Assumptions

The assumption of independent observations is reasonable because the annual salary for one teacher is unrelated to the annual salary for another teacher.

The assumption of equal variances is reasonable. Look at the similarity of the standard deviations and the relatively similar heights of the box plots in Figure 9.2. The standard deviations vary, but it is difficult to determine whether the variability is due to true changes in the variances, or due to sample sizes. Look at the differences in sample sizes for the different subject areas. There are 7 observations for **Social Science** and 56 observations for **Mathematics**. The standard deviations for these subject areas are relatively similar. However, compare the standard deviations for **Social Science** and **Special Education**. It's more difficult to determine whether the difference in standard deviations (which is larger) is due to true changes in the variances, or due to less precise estimates of variances as a result of smaller sample sizes. For now, assume equal variances and perform an analysis of variance.

The assumption of normality is difficult to verify. Testing this assumption requires performing a test of normality for each group. For the subject areas that have a larger number of observations, this test could be meaningful. But, for the subject areas that have only a few observations, you don't have enough data to perform an adequate test. And, because you need to verify the assumption of normality for all of the groups, this is difficult. For now, assume normality and perform an analysis of variance.

In general, if you have additional information (such as other data) that indicates that the populations are normally distributed, and if your data is a representative sample of the population, you can usually proceed based on the idea that the assumption of normality is reasonable. In addition, the analysis of variance works well even for data from non-normal populations. However, if you are uncomfortable with proceeding, do not have other data or additional information about the distribution of measurements, or have large groups that don't seem to be samples from normally distributed populations, you can use the Kruskal-Wallis test.

Using JMP Oneway for ANOVA

JMP uses the same analysis platform for summarizing multiple groups and for performing hypothesis tests. If you still have the Oneway Analysis of Annual Salary By Subject Area report open from summarizing the data, start at step 6. Otherwise, in JMP:

1. Open the Salary data table.

2. In the JMP Starter window, click **Basic→Oneway**.

3. Click **Annual Salary→Y, Response**.

4. Click **Subject Area→X, Grouping**.

5. Click **OK**.

6. Click the hot spot for the Oneway Analysis of Annual Salary By Subject Area report and select **Means/Anova**.

7. Click to hide the Summary of Fit report.

Figure 9.4 shows the results. JMP adds mean diamonds to the basic graph and creates reports for the analysis. Figure 9.4 hides the Summary of Fit report. If you started at step 6, your window will show the Means and Std Deviations report, box plots, and histograms, which you can hide if you want to. The rest of this topic discusses the Analysis of Variance report and the Means for Oneway Anova report, and explains means diamonds.

Figure 9.4 Analysis of Variance for Salary Data

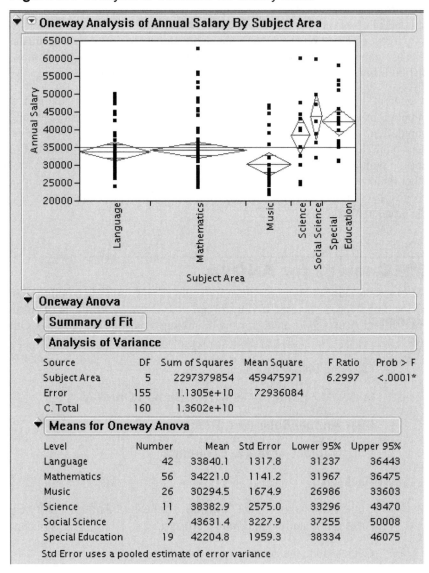

Oneway Analysis of Annual Salary By Subject Area

Oneway Anova

▶ **Summary of Fit**

▼ **Analysis of Variance**

Source	DF	Sum of Squares	Mean Square	F Ratio	Prob > F
Subject Area	5	2297379854	459475971	6.2997	<.0001*
Error	155	1.1305e+10	72936084		
C. Total	160	1.3602e+10			

▼ **Means for Oneway Anova**

Level	Number	Mean	Std Error	Lower 95%	Upper 95%
Language	42	33840.1	1317.8	31237	36443
Mathematics	56	34221.0	1141.2	31967	36475
Music	26	30294.5	1674.9	26986	33603
Science	11	38382.9	2575.0	33296	43470
Social Science	7	43631.4	3227.9	37255	50008
Special Education	19	42204.8	1959.3	38334	46075

Std Error uses a pooled estimate of error variance

Understanding Results

Figure 9.4 shows the details of the ANOVA. First, answer the research question: Are the mean salaries different for subject areas?

Finding the *p*-value

Look in the Analysis of Variance report and find the heading **Prob > F**. The number under this heading gives the *p*-value for comparing groups. Figure 9.4 shows a value of **<.0001**. Because 0.0001 is less than the reference probability of 0.10, you conclude that the mean salaries are significantly different across subject areas. (JMP highlights values less than 0.05 with an asterisk.)

In general, to perform the test at the 5% significance level, you conclude that the groups are significantly different if the *p*-value is less than 0.05. To perform the test at the 10% significance level, you conclude that the groups are significantly different if the *p*-value is less than 0.10. Conclusions for tests at other significance levels are made in a similar manner.

Understanding Other Items in the Report

The list describes items in the Analysis of Variance report:

Source   Lists the sources of variation in the data. For a one-way analysis of variance, the model is:

$$Y = X + \varepsilon$$

where **Y** is the response variable, **X** is the grouping variable, and ε is the error. For your data, **Source** shows the **X** variable you selected and **Error**.

DF   Degrees of freedom. For a one-way analysis of variance, the **DF** for **C. Total** (which stands for "corrected total") is the number of observations minus 1 (160=161–1). The **DF** for your **X** variable is one less than the number of groups. For the salary data, (5=6–1). The **DF** for **Error** is the difference between these two (155=160–5).

Sum of Squares	Measures the amount of variation that is attributed to a given source. The **Sum of Squares** for the **X** variable and **Error** add to the **C. Total Sum of Squares**.
	For the Salary data, JMP uses scientific notation to display the **Sum of Squares**, because the numbers are so large.
Mean Square	**Sum of Squares** divided by **DF**. JMP uses **Mean Square** to construct the statistical test for differences between groups.
F Ratio	Value of the test statistic. The **F Ratio** is the **Mean Square** for the **X** variable divided by the **Mean Square** for **Error**. Remember that an analysis of variance involves partitioning the variation, and testing to find out how much variation is due to differences between groups. Partitioning is done by the *F*-test, which involves calculating an *F*-value from the mean squares.

The list describes items in the Means for Oneway Anova report:

Level	Values for the **X** variable (the grouping variable). For the Salary data, this lists the **Subject Areas**.
Number	Number of observations in each group.
Mean	Average for each group.
Std Error	Standard error for each group. This uses a pooled standard deviation, not the simple standard deviation for each group. Compare the standard errors in Figures 9.2 and 9.4, and note that they are not the same. In Figure 9.4, the pooled estimate of error variance is the **Mean Square** for **Error**.

| Lower 95% | Lower and upper limits of a 95% confidence interval for the |
| Upper 95% | mean. This calculation uses **Std Error**. |

Click **Display Options→Set α level** to change the 95% confidence interval, as described for the Means and Std Deviations report. JMP changes the headings for the confidence interval columns, and recalculates the confidence intervals.

Understanding Means Diamonds

When you perform an ANOVA, JMP adds means diamonds to the basic graph. You can add means diamonds without performing an ANOVA with **Display Options→Mean Diamonds**.

Means diamonds are similar to box plots in that they both display aspects of the distribution of the data. Interpret means diamonds as follows:

- The line across the middle of the diamond is the mean for the group.

- The width of the diamond is related to the sample size of the group, if **X Axis proportional** is selected. (If you know that the group sizes vary, and all of the diamonds are the same width, review your display options to verify that **X Axis proportional** is indeed selected.)

- The top and bottom of the diamond are the ends of 95% confidence intervals for the mean. In calculating the confidence intervals, JMP assumes equal variances. You can change the confidence level by clicking **Display Options→Set α level**. This affects the means diamonds and the confidence intervals in the Means for Oneway Anova report.

- The lines across the top and bottom of the diamond are *overlap marks*. Use these overlap marks when groups have equal sample sizes (see "Summarizing with an Example").

With both box plots and means diamonds displayed, you can compare the centers of the box and diamond for each group. This gives a visual comparison of the median and the mean.

Analysis of Variance with Unequal Variances

Earlier, this chapter discussed the assumption of equal variances, and performed an ANOVA after looking at standard deviations and box plots. Some statisticians perform an ANOVA without testing for equal variances. Unless the variances in the groups are very different, or there are many groups, an ANOVA detects appropriate differences when all of the groups are about the same size.

JMP provides four tests for unequal variances, and provides an alternative to the usual ANOVA when the assumption of equal variances is not reasonable.

Testing for Equal Variances with JMP

For the Salary data, the sample sizes of the groups vary from 7 to 56. Suppose you want to test for equal variances at the 10% significance level, giving a reference probability of 0.10. To test the assumption of equal variances in JMP:

1. Open the Salary data table.

2. In the JMP Starter window, click **Basic→Oneway**.

3. Click **Recall** and JMP fills in your choices from the previous analysis in the JMP session. If you have exited and restarted JMP, then follow steps 1 through 5 for summarizing the data.

4. Click the hot spot for the Oneway Analysis of Annual Salary By Subject Area report.

5. Select **UnEqual Variances**.

Figure 9.5 shows the results of testing for unequal variances.

Figure 9.5 Tests for Unequal Variances for Salary Data

▼ **Tests that the Variances are Equal**

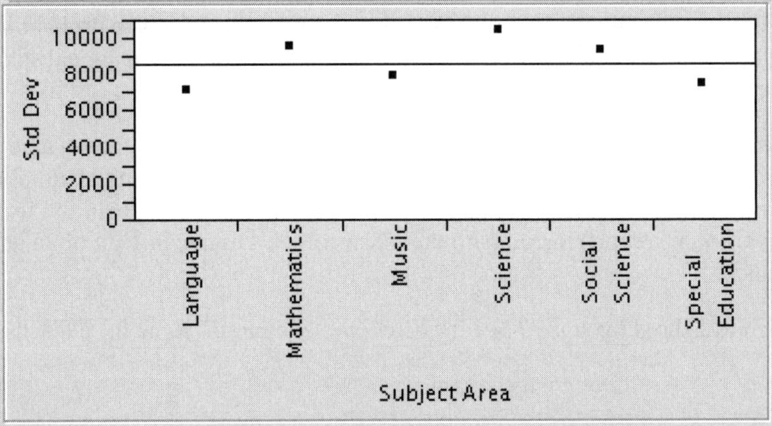

Level	Count	Std Dev	MeanAbsDif to Mean	MeanAbsDif to Median
Language	42	7194.69	5653.582	5382.405
Mathematics	56	9517.30	7453.402	7114.857
Music	26	7953.11	6453.976	5926.692
Science	11	10434.09	8109.190	8031.455
Social Science	7	9343.73	7274.776	7569.143
Special Education	19	7480.01	5649.463	5650.368

Test	F Ratio	DFNum	DFDen	Prob > F
O'Brien[.5]	0.9352	5	155	0.4599
Brown-Forsythe	0.7320	5	155	0.6005
Levene	0.9450	5	155	0.4537
Bartlett	1.0506	5	.	0.3858

Welch Anova testing Means Equal, allowing Std Devs Not Equal

F Ratio	DFNum	DFDen	Prob > F
6.5605	5	34.764	0.0002*

Finding the *p*-value

Find the heading **Prob > F** in Figure 9.5. The numbers under this heading give the *p*-values for four tests that the variances are equal. Compare the *p*-value to the reference probability. For all tests, the *p*-value is greater than the reference probability of 0.10. You conclude that there is not enough evidence that the variances in annual salaries for the six subject areas are significantly different.

In general, compare the *p*-value to the reference probability. If the *p*-value is greater than the reference probability, proceed with the ANOVA based on the assumption that the variances are equal. If the *p*-value is less than the reference probability, use the Welch Anova (in this report) to compare the means of the groups, instead of an analysis of variance.

Which test should you use? See the "Recommendations" topic for a discussion.

Understanding the Graph

The graph in Figure 9.5 shows the standard deviations for each group. The center line shows an estimate of the pooled standard deviation across all groups. JMP displays this estimate as **Root Mean Square Error** in the Summary of Fit table. For the Salary data, this is 8540.26.

JMP scales the graph to start at 0 on the vertical axis. As a result, it might be hard to see the differences in standard deviations across groups. As with other JMP graphs, you can double-click on the vertical axis and change the scale. For the Salary data, an axis scale from 6000 to 11000 helps visualize the differences in the standard deviations, as shown in the display below.

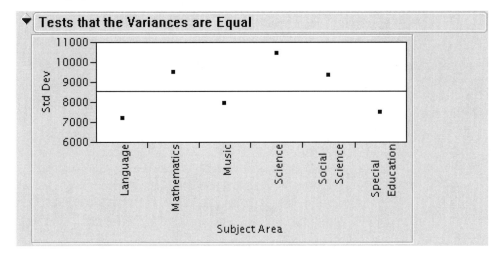

Understanding the Report Tables

In Figure 9.5, the first report table below the graph shows statistics for each subject area. The **Level** column identifies the group (subject area for this example), **Count** lists the number of observations in the group, and **Std Dev** gives the standard deviation of the group. The last two columns show statistics used by the different tests. The Levene and O'Brien tests use the mean absolute difference from the mean (**MeanAbsDif to Mean**). The Brown-Forsythe test uses the mean absolute difference from the median (**MeanAbsDif to Median**). The Bartlett test uses a statistic based on the group standard deviation.

In Figure 9.5, the second report table below the graph shows statistics for each test. This report table is similar to the report table for two groups, shown in Figure 8.6 in Chapter 8. Chapter 8 provides details on the columns in this report. When comparing multiple groups, the numerator degrees of freedom (**DFNum**) are $k–1$, where k is the number of groups. Also, the denominator degrees of freedom (**DFDen**) are generally $n–k$, where n is the total sample size. The Bartlett test uses a calculation that does not involve degrees of freedom for the denominator, so the column is blank.

Recommendations

Use the Levene and Brown-Forsythe tests. The Levene test is most widely used by statisticians, and is considered to be the standard test. Simulations have shown that the Brown-Forsythe test is good at detecting appropriate differences, while controlling the risk of declaring that variances are different when, in fact, they are not. For your data, check the p-values for these two tests. If either p-value is less than the reference probability, use the Welch Anova test, which is discussed next.

The O'Brien test is a modification of the Levene test.

Statisticians do not generally recommend the Bartlett test because it can be inaccurate when the distributions are non-normal.

Performing the Welch Anova Test

When you test for unequal variances, JMP provides an alternative test to the analysis of variance. Find the last report in Figure 9.5. The Welch Anova tests for differences in the means of the groups, while allowing for unequal variances across groups.

Find the heading **Prob > F** under the **Welch Anova** heading. The number under this heading gives the p-value for testing for differences in the means of the groups. For the Salary data, this is **0.0002**. (JMP highlights values less than 0.05 with an asterisk.) You conclude that the mean salaries are significantly different across subject areas. For the

Salary data, this is for example only—you already know that the assumption of equal variances is reasonable, and that you can apply the usual ANOVA test.

The **F Ratio** gives the value of the test statistic. **DFNum** gives the degrees of freedom for the numerator, which is the number of groups minus one. **DFDen** gives the degrees of freedom for the denominator, which has a more complicated formula. See the JMP Help or documentation for formulas.

Performing a Kruskal-Wallis Test

The Kruskal-Wallis test is a nonparametric analogue to the one-way analysis of variance. Use this test when the normality assumption is not reasonable for your data. If you do have normally distributed data, this test can be conservative and can fail to detect differences between groups. The steps of the analysis are the same as for an ANOVA.

You have already performed the first three steps of the analysis. As with the ANOVA, use a 10% significance level to test for differences between groups.

Assumptions

In practice, the Kruskal-Wallis test is used for ordinal or continuous variables. The null hypothesis is that the populations for the groups are the same.

The only assumption for this test is that the observations are independent.

For the Salary data, this assumption is reasonable because the salary for one teacher is independent of the salary for another teacher.

Using JMP Oneway for the Kruskal-Wallis Test

JMP uses the same platform for parametric and nonparametric tests to compare more than two groups. To perform a Kruskal-Wallis test with JMP:

1. Open the Salary data table.

2. In the JMP Starter window, click **Basic→Oneway**.

3. Click **Recall** and JMP fills in your choices from the previous analysis in the JMP session. If you have exited and restarted JMP, then follow steps 1 through 5 for summarizing the data.

4. Click the hot spot for the Oneway Analysis of Annual Salary By Subject Area report.

5. Select **Nonparametric→Wilcoxon**.

Figure 9.6 shows the results.

Figure 9.6 Kruskal-Wallis Test for Salary Data

Wilcoxon / Kruskal-Wallis Tests (Rank Sums)

Level	Count	Score Sum	Score Mean	(Mean-Mean0)/Std0
Language	42	3280.00	78.095	-0.468
Mathematics	56	4183.00	74.696	-1.251
Music	26	1391.00	53.500	-3.282
Science	11	1061.00	96.455	1.136
Social Science	7	857.000	122.429	2.400
Special Education	19	2269.00	119.421	3.822

1-way Test, ChiSquare Approximation

ChiSquare	DF	Prob>ChiSq
29.8739	5	<.0001*

JMP Hints:

When you perform the Kruskal-Wallis test, JMP adds blue standard deviation lines to the basic continuous-by-nominal/ordinal plot. Click **Display Options→Std Dev Lines** to remove these lines.

As you have worked with sample data in the exercises, you have observed data tables with saved scripts. This chapter has performed several analyses using the Salary data. Suppose you want to save those analyses and run them again in a later JMP session. Click the hot spot for the Oneway Analysis of Annual Salary By Subject Area report and select **Script→Save Script to Data Table**. JMP automatically saves the script with the name **Oneway** and shows it in the table panel. To run the analysis in a later JMP session, click the hot spot for the saved script and select **Run Script**.

JMP provides two other nonparametric tests from the **Nonparametric** choice in the hot spot menu. Position your mouse pointer over the name of the test to see a brief description. See the JMP Help or documentation for more details.

Understanding Results

First, answer the research question: Are the mean salaries different for subject areas?

Finding the *p*-value

Find the heading **Prob>ChiSq** in Figure 9.6. The number under this heading gives the *p*-value for comparing groups. Figure 9.6 shows a value of **<.0001**. (JMP highlights values less than 0.05 with an asterisk.) Because 0.0001 is less than the reference probability of 0.10, you conclude that the mean salaries are significantly different across subject areas.

In general, to interpret JMP results, look at the *p*-value under **Prob>ChiSq**. If the *p*-value is less than the significance level, you conclude that the means for the groups are significantly different. If the *p*-value is greater, you conclude that the means for the groups are not significantly different. Do not conclude that the means are the same.

Understanding Other Items in the Report

The 1-way Test table displays the statistic for the test (**ChiSquare**) and the degrees of freedom for the test (**DF**). The degrees of freedom are calculated by subtracting 1 from the number of groups. For the Salary data, this is 5=6–1.

Chapter 8 explains the Wilcoxon / Kruskal-Wallis Tests (Rank Sums) report. See "Using JMP for the Wilcoxon Rank Sum Test" in Chapter 8 for details.

JMP and Ordinal or Nominal Responses

The response variable for the Salary data is continuous. What if your response variable is nominal or ordinal? How can you perform the Kruskal-Wallis test?

JMP requires the response variable to be numeric. However, if you use the JMP Starter window and select **Oneway**, JMP allows the response variable to be continuous, ordinal, or nominal. For nominal or ordinal response variables, JMP displays a caution window to remind you that the response variable is not continuous. Click **Continue** and proceed with your analysis.

Caution: If you use the **Analyze→Fit Y by X** platform, JMP tries to determine the correct analysis for you. What JMP determines might not be what you want to do. With a nominal or ordinal response, and a nominal grouping variable, JMP performs a contingency table analysis instead of an ANOVA. See Chapter 12 for more details on this type of analysis. Also, if you use **Analyze→Fit Y by X**, the button for the grouping variable is **X, Factor** instead of **X, Grouping**. JMP renames the button to accommodate the multiple analyses available from **Analyze→Fit Y by X**.

If your response variable is not continuous, use the Kruskal-Wallis test instead of an ANOVA. An ANOVA assumes normality, which makes sense only for continuous variables.

Enhancing JMP Graphs

Figure 9.2 shows box plots and histograms for groups, which are helpful when summarizing data. Figure 9.4 shows means diamonds, which are created when you perform an analysis of variance. Both figures show the data points.

JMP creates a basic plot of the data points whenever you use the **Oneway** platform. This basic continuous-by-nominal/ordinal plot shows only the data points. Previous topics have described enhancements to the basic plot for summarizing and analyzing groups. This topic describes additional enhancements for reporting results. These enhancements can help highlight the differences between groups and augment the statistical reports. Suppose you want to:

- display box plots and means diamonds

- connect the group averages

- hide the data points

- keep the *x*-axis proportional to the group sample size

In JMP, assume that you have created the Oneway Analysis of Annual Salary By Subject Area report. To enhance the graph for reporting results:

1. Hold down the ALT key and click the **Display Options** hot spot for the Oneway Analysis of Annual Salary By Subject Area report.

2. Select the check boxes for: **Box Plots**, **Mean Diamonds**, and **Connect Means**.

3. Deselect the check box for **Points**.

4. Confirm that JMP's automatic choices are selected for: **All Graphs, Grand Mean**, and **X Axis proportional**.

5. Confirm that all other **Display Options** check boxes are deselected. (These options appear in the third and fourth columns of the Select Options window.)

6. Click **OK**.

Figure 9.7 shows the results.

Figure 9.7 JMP Plot Enhanced for Reporting Salary Data

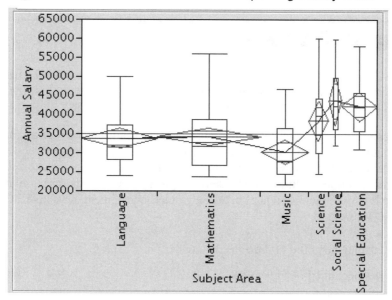

Multiple Comparison Procedures

When you conclude that the means are significantly different after performing an ANOVA, you don't know enough detail to take action. Which means differ from other means? At this point, you know only that some means differ from other means. Your next step is to use a multiple comparison procedure.

Most statisticians agree that multiple comparison procedures should be used only after a significant ANOVA test. Technically, this is called a "prior significant *F*-test," because the ANOVA performs an *F*-test.

To make things more complicated, statisticians disagree about which tests to use, and which tests are best. This chapter discusses JMP decisions, and discusses the tests available in JMP. You need to know that other tests are available in other software applications.

Chapter 6 compared choosing an alpha level to choosing the level of risk of making a wrong decision. To use multiple comparison procedures, you consider risk again. Specifically, you decide whether you want to control the risk of making a wrong decision (deciding that means are different when they are not) for all comparisons overall, or if you want to control the risk of making a wrong decision for each individual comparison.

To make this decision process a little clearer, think about the Salary data. There are 6 subject areas, so there are 15 combinations of 2 means to compare. Do you want to control the risk of making a wrong decision (deciding that the 2 means are different when they are not) for all 15 comparisons at once? If you do, you are controlling the risk for the experiment overall, or the *experimentwise error rate*. Some statisticians call this the "overall error rate." On the other hand, do you want to control the risk of making a wrong decision for each of the 15 comparisons? If you do, you are controlling the risk for each comparison, or the *comparisonwise error rate*.

Introducing Comparison Circles

JMP performs four statistical tests for multiple comparisons. For each test, JMP creates report tables and *comparison circles*. This topic explains comparison circles in general. The next topic discusses the reports and statistical tests.

Figure 9.8 shows comparison circles for one statistical test for the Salary data. For now, concentrate on the information from the circles, not which statistical test was used.

Figure 9.8 Comparison Circles for Salary Data

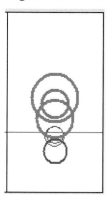

JMP displays a circle for each subject area in the Salary data. In Figure 9.8, the bottom circle is selected. In general, JMP displays a circle for each level of the grouping variable. As with many JMP features, circles are interactive.

Here's how to work with circles:

- The horizontal line is the grand mean, which is the overall average of the data. If the groups are similar to each other, then the circles will be close to the grand mean.

  For the Salary data, some circles are close to the grand mean, but other circles are not. This visual comparison supports the conclusions that the means are significantly different.

- The size of each circle is related to the variability within the group. Specifically, the diameter of the circle forms a 95% confidence interval for the mean of the group. Larger circles represent groups that have more variability.

  For the Salary data, some of the circles are much larger than other circles, corresponding to the differences in variability.

- Circles are ordered vertically, top to bottom, according to their group averages. The top circle has the highest average, and the bottom circle has the lowest average. The center of each circle corresponds to the group average.

- Clicking on a circle turns that circle to a bold red color, and highlights the name of the group in the basic plot. Groups that are not significantly different from the group you select are also red (but not bold red). Groups that are significantly different are gray.

Comparison circles can be used with unbalanced data (when groups are different sizes). In contrast, the overlap marks for means diamonds should be used only with balanced data.

For the Salary data, Figure 9.8 shows the bottom circle selected. The next two circles are red, so these groups are not significantly different from the selected group. The top three circles are gray, so these groups are significantly different from the selected group.

- Circles that are nested within other circles are not significantly different from each other. Figure 9.8 shows the second circle completely nested within the top circle. Regardless of the statistical test, these two groups will not be significantly different.

- Circles that do not overlap with another circle are significantly different from each other. Figure 9.8 shows the top and bottom circles not overlapping. These two circles (groups) will be significantly different.

- Circles that overlap with another circle might be significantly different. The easiest way to determine this is to click on the circles and view the results. JMP displays reports tables that describe the differences in more detail.

For technical readers, the circles have a mathematical basis, which the JMP documentation explains. Briefly, if the angle of overlap between two circles is less than 90 degrees, then the groups are significantly different. Because many of us have difficulty seeing the angle of overlap, using colors to show significance is very helpful.

JMP creates comparison circles for all tests. The next four topics discuss the four statistical tests that JMP provides, in the order that they appear in JMP menus. Each test prints a separate report.

Performing an Each Pair, Student's *t* Test

Assume that you have performed an ANOVA in JMP, and you have concluded that there are significant differences between the means. Specifically, you have run the JMP steps to create the Oneway Analysis report. Now, you want to compare each pair of means. Statisticians often refer to this as 'performing pairwise Student's *t* tests'. In JMP:

1. Click the hot spot for the Oneway Analysis of Annual Salary By Subject Area report.

2. Select **Compare Means→Each Pair, Student's t**.

Figure 9.9 displays the comparison circles, with **Social Science** (the top circle) selected. Figure 9.10 shows the text reports for this test.

Figure 9.9 Comparison Circles for Each Pair, Student's t Test

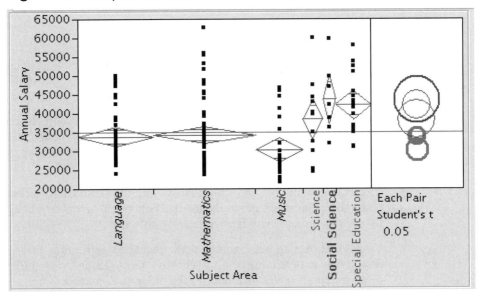

Figure 9.9 shows the JMP graph of points and mean diamonds. When you add comparison circles and click on a circle, JMP highlights the group you clicked with bold red text in this graph. JMP uses red text for other groups with red circles, and italic text for groups with gray circles. This color feature is especially helpful for data with many groups.

The Student's *t* test performs each comparison at the 95% confidence level (or 5% alpha level). The test does not adjust for the fact that you might be making many comparisons. In other words, the test controls the comparisonwise error rate, but not the experimentwise error rate. See "Technical Details: Overall Risk" for more discussion.

Deciding Which Means Differ

You can click the various comparison circles and get an understanding of which means differ from other means. When you click a circle, JMP highlights the group name in the plot.

Figure 9.10 Text Reports for Each Pair, Student's t Test

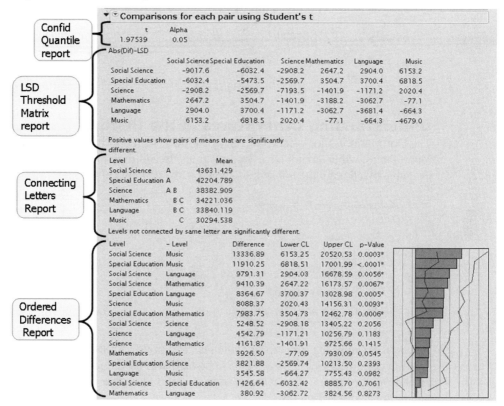

Confid Quantile report

LSD Threshold Matrix report

Connecting Letters Report

Ordered Differences Report

Comparisons for each pair using Student's t

t	Alpha
1.97539	0.05

Abs(Dif)-LSD

	Social Science	Special Education	Science	Mathematics	Language	Music
Social Science	-9017.6	-6032.4	-2908.2	2647.2	2904.0	6153.2
Special Education	-6032.4	-5473.5	-2569.7	3504.7	3700.4	6818.5
Science	-2908.2	-2569.7	-7193.5	-1401.9	-1171.2	2020.4
Mathematics	2647.2	3504.7	-1401.9	-3188.2	-3062.7	-77.1
Language	2904.0	3700.4	-1171.2	-3062.7	-3681.4	-664.3
Music	6153.2	6818.5	2020.4	-77.1	-664.3	-4679.0

Positive values show pairs of means that are significantly different.

Level		Mean
Social Science	A	43631.429
Special Education	A	42204.789
Science	A B	38382.909
Mathematics	B C	34221.036
Language	B C	33840.119
Music	C	30294.538

Levels not connected by same letter are significantly different.

Level	– Level	Difference	Lower CL	Upper CL	p-Value
Social Science	Music	13336.89	6153.25	20520.53	0.0003*
Special Education	Music	11910.25	6818.51	17001.99	<.0001*
Social Science	Language	9791.31	2904.03	16678.59	0.0056*
Social Science	Mathematics	9410.39	2647.22	16173.57	0.0067*
Special Education	Language	8364.67	3700.37	13028.98	0.0005*
Science	Music	8088.37	2020.43	14156.31	0.0093*
Special Education	Mathematics	7983.75	3504.73	12462.78	0.0006*
Social Science	Science	5248.52	-2908.18	13405.22	0.2056
Science	Language	4542.79	-1171.21	10256.79	0.1183
Science	Mathematics	4161.87	-1401.91	9725.66	0.1415
Mathematics	Music	3926.50	-77.09	7930.09	0.0545
Special Education	Science	3821.88	-2569.74	10213.50	0.2393
Language	Music	3545.58	-664.27	7755.43	0.0982
Social Science	Special Education	1426.64	-6032.42	8885.70	0.7061
Mathematics	Language	380.92	-3062.72	3824.56	0.8273

The Connecting Letters report, which is the third block of information in Figure 9.10, is the easiest way to summarize differences. This report orders groups from highest group average to lowest group average. Groups that do not share a letter are significantly different from each other. For example, **Social Science** (with an **A**) is significantly different from **Music** (with a **C**). You conclude:

- The mean annual salary for **Social Science** and **Special Education** are significantly different from **Mathematics**, **Language**, and **Music**.

- The mean annual salary for **Science** is significantly different from **Music**.

- The mean annual salaries for other pairs of subject areas are not significantly different.

Books sometimes use connecting lines instead of connecting letters. For the Salary data, a connecting lines report would look like:

Social-Sci   Special-Ed   Science   Math   Language   Music

Understanding Other Items in the Report

The Comparisons for each pair using Student's t report in Figure 9.10 contains four report tables, which do not have separate titles. In addition, two other reports are available by clicking the hot spot as shown in the display below.

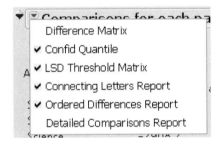

Figure 9.10 shows the first report, which is the Confid Quantile report, shorthand for "confidence quantiles." It shows the *t*-statistic that is used to compare groups, and the alpha level for the test. The contents of the Confid Quantile report change, depending on the multiple comparison test.

Figure 9.10 shows the second report, which is the LSD Threshold Matrix report. It starts with the **Abs(Dif)-LSD** heading. LSD stands for "least significant difference." Positive values indicate the means that are significantly different. Look at the value for **Mathematics** and **Social Science** (fourth row in the first column). The value is positive, indicating that the means for these two subject areas are significantly different. See "Technical Details: LSD" for more on how these values are calculated.

Figure 9.10 shows the third report, which is the Connecting Letters Report. The previous topic discussed this report. JMP shows the connecting letters vertically.

Figure 9.10 shows the fourth report, which is the Ordered Differences Report. It lists the pairs of differences, ordered from largest to smallest. The **Level–Level** heading identifies each pair. The line for each pair shows the difference between the two averages (**Difference**), a confidence interval for the difference (**Lower CL** and **Upper CL**), and the *p*-value of the *t*-test to compare the two groups (**p-Value**).

When the confidence interval in the Ordered Differences Report includes 0, the means for the two groups are not significantly different. When the confidence interval does not include 0, the means for the two groups are significantly different. Look at the report in Figure 9.10. All of the rows up to the **Special Education—Mathematics** comparison have confidence intervals that do not include 0. These rows correspond to pairs of means that have different letters in the Corresponding Letters Report. Similarly, starting with the **Social Science—Science** row and down, all of the confidence intervals do include 0, and correspond to pairs of means that share letters in the Corresponding Letters Report.

The Ordered Differences Report shows a bar chart of the differences. The blue lines show the confidence intervals for the differences. This is one of the very few JMP graphs in this book that is not interactive. You cannot click in the bar chart to change anything.

Technical Details: LSD

The LSD Threshold Matrix report shows the **Abs(Dif)-LSD**, as described in the heading. The **Abs(Dif)** is the absolute value of the difference between the two group averages. What is **LSD**, or the least significant difference? JMP calculates this as:

$$ts\sqrt{1/n_1 + 1/n_2}$$

where t is from the Confid Quantile report, s is **Root Mean Square Error** from the Summary of Fit report for the ANOVA, and n_1 and n_2 are the sample sizes for the two groups.

The diagonal of the matrix shows the least significant difference (LSD), because the absolute value of the difference is 0 (the diagonal compares each group with itself). When all groups have the same sample size, the values on the diagonal are the same.

JMP provides options to display two other reports in the hot spot for the Comparisons for each pair using Student's t report.

The Difference Matrix lists the differences between the means. Because these same differences are shown in the Ordered Differences Report, JMP hides the report.

Finally, the Detailed Comparisons Report provides a separate two-sample *t*-test report for each of the group comparisons. This report is the same as the report for comparing two groups (see Chapter 8 for details). The Ordered Differences Report shows the *p*-values from these tests.

Technical Details: Overall Risk

When you perform multiple comparison tests that control the comparisonwise error rate, you control the risk of making a wrong decision about each comparison. Here, "wrong" means concluding that groups are significantly different when they are not.

Controlling the comparisonwise error rate at 0.05 might give you a false sense of security. The more comparisonwise tests you perform, the higher your overall risk of making a wrong decision.

The Salary data has 15 two-way comparisons for the six groups. The overall risk of making a wrong decision is:

$$1 - (0.95)^{15} = 0.537$$

This means that there is about a 54% chance of incorrectly concluding that two means are different for the Salary data when the Student's *t* test is used. Most statisticians agree that this overall risk is too high to be acceptable.

In general, this overall risk is:

$$1 - (0.95)^{m}$$

where *m* is the number of pairwise comparisons to be performed. These formulas assume you perform each test at the 95% confidence level, which controls the comparisonwise error rate at 0.05. You can apply this formula to your own data to help you understand the overall risk of making a wrong decision.

The Bonferroni approach and the Tukey-Kramer HSD test are two solutions for controlling the experimentwise error rate.

Using the Bonferroni Approach

To control the experimentwise error rate with the **Each Pair, Student's t** test, you can "Bonferroni the alpha level." This means that you decrease the alpha level for each test so that the overall risk of incorrectly concluding that the means are different is 5%. Basically, each test is performed using a very low alpha level. If you have many groups, the Bonferroni approach can be very conservative and can fail to detect significant differences between groups.

For the Salary data, you want to control the experimentwise error rate at 0.05. There are 15 two-way comparisons. Perform each test at:

$$\alpha = 0.05 \,/\, 15 = 0.0033$$

In JMP, assume that you have performed the analysis of variance. To use the Bonferroni approach:

1. Click the hot spot for the Oneway Analysis of Annual Salary By Subject Area report.

2. Select **Set α Level→Other**.

3. Enter **0.0033** in the Please Enter a Number window. (For your data, enter the appropriate number, which depends on the number of groups that you have.)

4. Click **OK**.

5. Click the hot spot for the Oneway Analysis of Annual Salary By Subject Area report.

6. Select **Compare Means→Each Pair, Student's t**.

Figure 9.11 shows a portion of the results. Specifically, it shows the comparison circles, the Confid Quantile report, and the Connecting Letters Report. In Figure 9.11, the comparison circle for **Social Science** is selected.

JMP Hints:

If you have already run the **Each Pair, Student's t** multiple comparison test, JMP dynamically changes the results after you change the alpha level.

Click the hot spot for the Comparisons for each pair using Student's t report to control the detailed reports that appear. Each of the multiple comparison procedures creates a separate report with its own hot spot.

Figure 9.11 Selected Reports Using Bonferroni Approach for Salary Data

Level		Mean
Social Science	A B	43631.429
Special Education	A	42204.789
Science	A B C	38382.909
Mathematics	B C	34221.036
Language	B C	33840.119
Music	C	30294.538

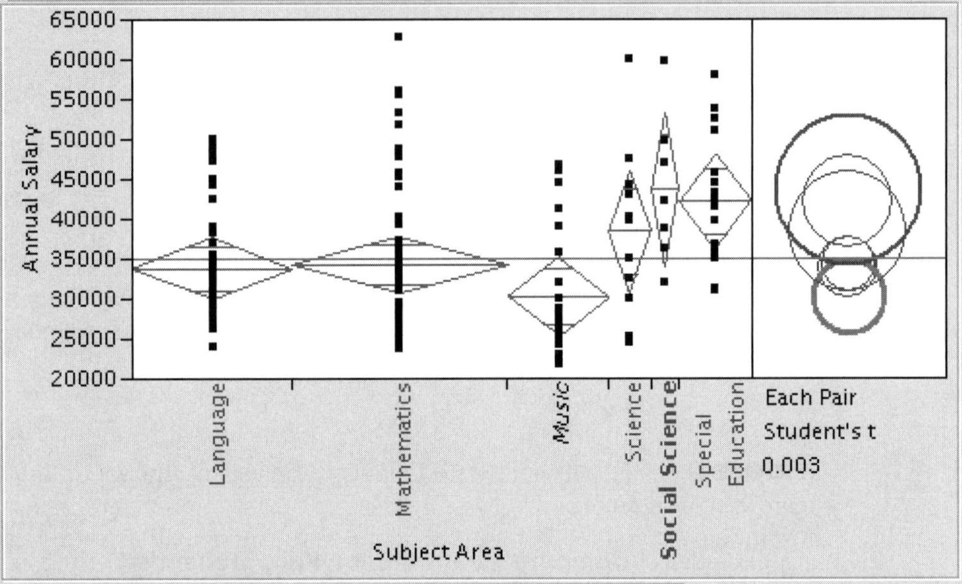

Levels not connected by same letter are significantly different.

Deciding Which Means Differ

Using the Connecting Letters Report, you conclude that:

- The mean annual salary for **Social Science** is significantly different from **Music**.

- The mean annual salary for **Special Education** is significantly different from **Mathematics**, **Language**, and **Music**.

- The mean annual salaries for other pairs of subject areas are not significantly different.

Compare the Bonferroni conclusions with the conclusions from the Student's *t* tests. When controlling the experimentwise error rate, you find fewer significant differences between groups. However, you decrease your risk of incorrectly concluding that means are different from each other.

Understanding Other Items in the Report

Figure 9.11 shows the comparison circles and the Confid Quantile report. Both of these show the alpha level. When working with your own data, always make sure that the alpha level is set to what you want.

Figure 9.11 shows the Connecting Letters Report.

Figure 9.11 does not show the other parts of the report.

This list summarizes the effects of changing the alpha level:

- The Difference Matrix report does not change.

- The LSD Threshold Matrix report changes, because changing the alpha level changes the *t*-statistic used to calculate the least significant difference (LSD).

- The Connecting Letters Report changes, because the tests use the new alpha level.

- The confidence intervals in the Ordered Differences Report change, because they use the new alpha level.

- The Detailed Comparisons Report changes. Each report uses the new alpha level for both the tests and the confidence intervals. This affects the *t*-statistic, *p*-values, and confidence intervals in these reports. Neither Figure 9.10 nor Figure 9.11 shows these reports.

Performing a Tukey-Kramer HSD Test

The Tukey-Kramer HSD (or "Honestly Significant Difference") test controls the experimentwise error rate. Many statisticians prefer this test to using the Bonferroni approach. Assume that you have performed an ANOVA in JMP, and concluded that there are significant differences between the means. Specifically, you have performed the JMP steps to create the Oneway Analysis of Annual Salary By Subject Area report. Now, you want to find out which means differ. In JMP:

1. Click the hot spot for the Oneway Analysis of Annual Salary By Subject Area report.

2. Select **Compare Means→All Pairs, Tukey HSD**.

3. Click the hot spot for the Comparisons for all pairs using Tukey-Kramer HSD report and deselect the reports: Difference Matrix, LSD Threshold Matrix, and Ordered Differences Report.

Caution: If you have previously changed the alpha level, the Tukey-Kramer HSD test uses the new alpha level, instead of the automatic choice of 0.05.

Figure 9.12 shows the comparison circle for **Music** (the bottom circle) selected, the Confid Quantile report, and the Connecting Letters Report.

Deciding Which Means Differ

Using the Connecting Letters Report, you conclude that:

- The mean annual salary for **Social Science** is significantly different from **Music**.

- The mean annual salary for **Special Education** is significantly different from **Mathematics**, **Language**, and **Music**.

- The mean annual salaries for other pairs of subject areas are not significantly different.

These results are the same as the Bonferroni approach results, which makes sense, because both approaches control the experimentwise error rate. For your data, you might get the exact same results from these two.

Figure 9.12 Selected Results for Tukey-Kramer HSD Test for Salary Data

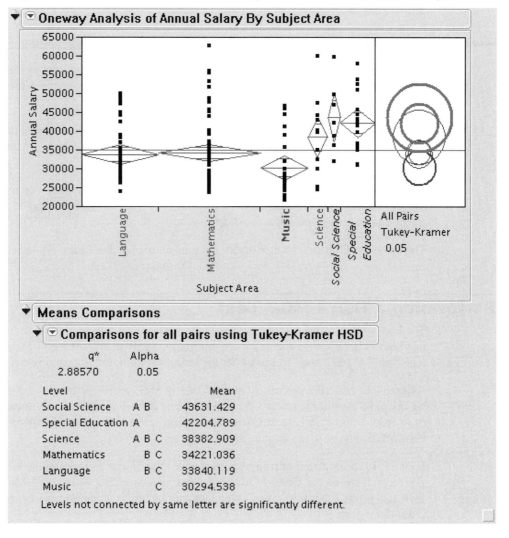

Comparisons for all pairs using Tukey-Kramer HSD

	q*	Alpha
	2.88570	0.05

Level		Mean
Social Science	A B	43631.429
Special Education	A	42204.789
Science	A B C	38382.909
Mathematics	B C	34221.036
Language	B C	33840.119
Music	C	30294.538

Levels not connected by same letter are significantly different.

Understanding Other Items in the Report

The Confid Quantile report in Figure 9.12 shows a *q* statistic. This replaces the *t*-statistic in the least significant difference calculations, and is used to test for differences between the means for the groups.

The hidden Difference Matrix report for this test has the same content as it does for the Student's *t* test. This report table shows the differences between means, which are the same, regardless of the test that is used.

You interpret the hidden LSD Threshold Matrix report the same way you do for the Student's *t* test. The calculations use *q* instead of *t*, but otherwise, they are the same as what is defined in "Technical Details: LSD."

You interpret the hidden Ordered Differences Report the same way you interpret the Student's *t* test. The calculations for the confidence interval use *q* instead of *t*. Also, the report does not show *p*-values for individual tests.

The Detailed Comparisons Report is not available for the Tukey-Kramer HSD test.

Performing a Hsu's MCB Test

The Hsu's MCB test determines whether the means of groups are less than the unknown maximum, or more than the unknown minimum. MCB stands for "multiple comparison with best," where "best" can be either the unknown minimum or unknown maximum.

Assume that you have performed an ANOVA in JMP, and concluded that there are significant differences between the groups. Click the hot spot for the Oneway Analysis of Annual Salary By Subject Area report, and select **Compare Means→With Best, Hsu MCB**. Figure 9.13 displays the text reports.

Figure 9.13 looks different from the results for the Student's *t* test and the Tukey-Kramer HSD test. It shows the Confid Quantile report and two LSD Threshold Matrix reports. JMP also prints a p-value report (which cannot be hidden) that appears below the Confid Quantile report.

JMP reports results from Hsu's MCB test as similarly as possible as the results from the other multiple comparison tests. However, with unequal sample sizes for groups, this test has a different statistic for each mean. The Confid Quantile report shows multiple values of the *d* statistic.

Figure 9.13 Text Reports from Hsu's MCB Test

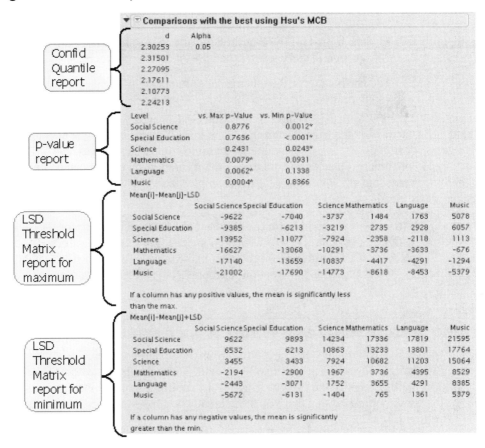

The first **LSD Threshold Matrix** report compares the means of the groups against the unknown maximum. Follow the instructions at the bottom of this report to conclude:

- The means for the **Mathematics**, **Language**, and **Music** groups are significantly less than the unknown maximum.

- The means for the other groups are not significantly different from the unknown maximum.

The second LSD Threshold Matrix report compares the means of the groups against the unknown minimum. Follow the instructions at the bottom of this report to conclude:

- The means for the **Social Science**, **Special Education**, and **Science** groups are significantly greater than the unknown minimum.

- The means for the other groups are not significantly different from the unknown minimum.

Figure 9.13 does not show comparison circles, even though JMP created them. With unequal sample sizes for groups, do not use comparison circles with Hsu's MCB test. JMP must use a single d value for creating comparison circles, and JMP picks the maximum value. As a result, clicking on comparison circles can be misleading or confusing when you have unequal sample sizes. Use the LSD Threshold Matrix reports instead.

JMP provides an option for the Difference Matrix in the hot spot for the Comparisons with the best using Hsu's MCB report. The Connecting Letters Report and the Ordered Differences Report do not make sense with this test, so JMP omits them. See the JMP Help or documentation for more details on Hsu's MCB test.

Using Dunnett's Test When Appropriate

Some experiments have a control group. For example, clinical trials to investigate the effectiveness of a new drug often include a placebo group, where the patients receive a look-alike pill. The placebo group is the control group. Dunnett's test is designed for this situation. Assuming that you have already performed an ANOVA in JMP:

1. Click the hot spot for the Oneway Analysis of Annual Salary By Subject Area report.

2. Select **Compare Means→With Control, Dunnett's**.

3. JMP displays a window in which you choose the control group. Figure 9.14 shows the window for the Salary data. For example purposes, select the **Mathematics** group. (See "JMP Hints.")

4. Click **OK**.

Figure 9.14 Window for Dunnett's Test

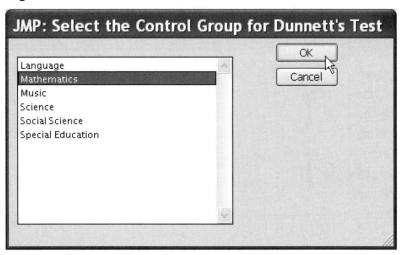

JMP adds comparison circles for Dunnett's test and prints a report. Figure 9.15 shows the results. The Confid Quantile, Difference Matrix, and LSD Threshold Matrix reports are either printed or are available in the hot spot for the Comparisons with a control Dunnett's Method report. With Dunnett's test, the Connecting Letters Report, Ordered Differences Report, and Detailed Comparisons Report don't make sense, so JMP omits them.

JMP Hints:

If you have selected a point in the data table, or a comparison circle in the plot, JMP assumes that your selection indicates the control group. To deselect a comparison circle, click in any blank area in the comparison circles plot. All circles will turn gray. Because the plot and the data table are linked, clicking also deselects any points in the data table.

Once you choose a control group for Dunnett's test, you cannot change your selection in the current analysis report. If you make a mistake, close the analysis window, and recreate the analysis.

Figure 9.15 Comparison Circles and Reports for Dunnett's Test
(Mathematics as Control Group)

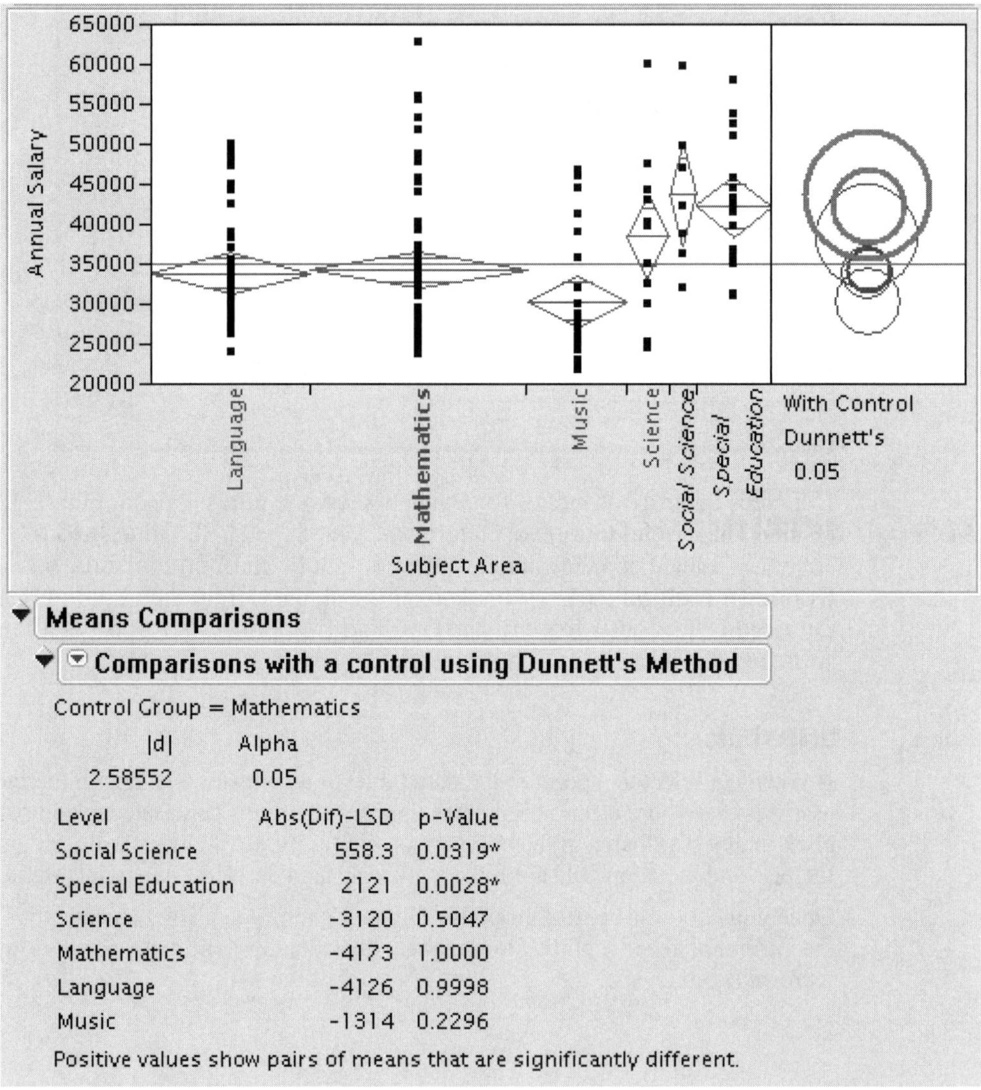

▼ Means Comparisons

▼ ▽ Comparisons with a control using Dunnett's Method

Control Group = Mathematics

|d|	Alpha
2.58552	0.05

Level	Abs(Dif)-LSD	p-Value
Social Science	558.3	0.0319ʷ
Special Education	2121	0.0028ʷ
Science	-3120	0.5047
Mathematics	-4173	1.0000
Language	-4126	0.9998
Music	-1314	0.2296

Positive values show pairs of means that are significantly different.

With **Mathematics** as the control group, Dunnett's test shows that this group is significantly different from **Social Science** and **Special Education**. For your data, use the instructions at the bottom of the report to help you make decisions.

Recommendations

First, use a multiple comparison test only after an analysis of variance is significant. If the ANOVA indicates that the means are not significantly different, then multiple comparison tests are not appropriate.

If you have a few pre-planned comparisons between groups, you can use the Student's *t* test and the Bonferroni approach for those comparisons. However, the temptation to look at other comparisons might be difficult to resist!

In the general situation where you want to compare all the means of the groups, use either the Tukey-Kramer HSD test or the Bonferroni approach. The Bonferroni approach is more conservative, and many statisticians prefer the Tukey-Kramer HSD test.

If you have the special case of a known control group, use Dunnett's test.

Summarizing with an Example

This section summarizes the steps for comparing multiple groups. This data has equally sized groups, so it is balanced.

Step 1. Create a JMP data table.

The data is from an experiment that compares muzzle velocities for different types of gunpowder. The muzzle velocity is measured for eight cartridges from each of the three types of gunpowder. Table 9.2 shows the data.

Table 9.2 Muzzle Velocities for Three Types of Gunpowder

Gunpowder	Muzzle Velocity			
Blasto	27.3	28.1	27.4	27.7
	28.0	28.1	27.4	27.1
Zoom	28.3	27.9	28.1	28.3
	27.9	27.6	28.5	27.9
Kingpow	28.4	28.9	28.3	27.9
	28.2	28.9	28.8	27.7

This data is available in the Bullets data table in the sample data for the book.

Step 2. Check the data table for errors.

Following similar steps as you did for the Salary data, use **Oneway** with **Velocity** as the **Y, Response** variable, and **Gunpowder** as the **X, Grouping** variable. Figure 9.16 shows the summary.

From the box plots, you initially conclude that **Kingpow** has a higher average velocity than the other two types of gunpowder, but you don't know whether this observed difference is statistically significant.

The plots don't reveal any outlier points or potential errors in entering the data. Proceed with the analysis.

Figure 9.16 Summarizing the Bullets Data

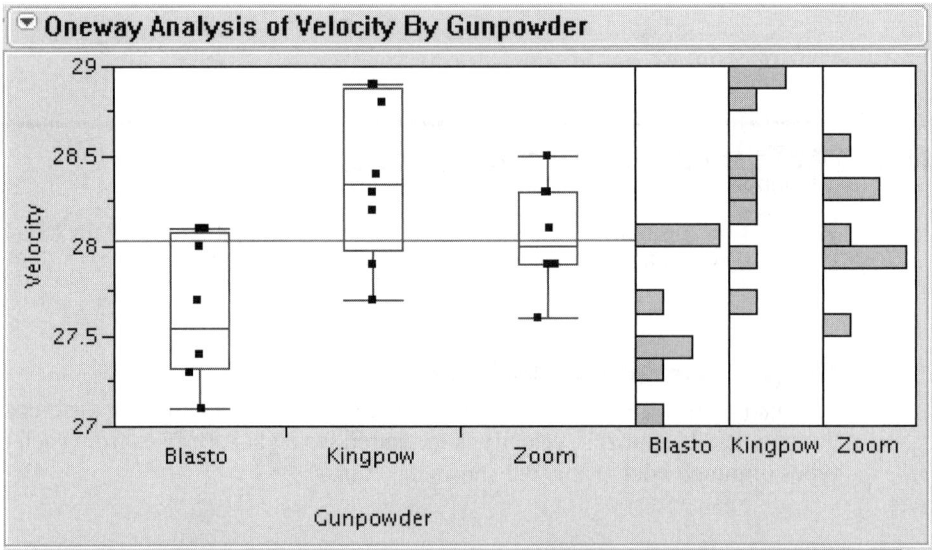

Means and Std Deviations

Level	Number	Mean	Std Dev	Std Err Mean	Lower 95%	Upper 95%
Blasto	8	27.6375	0.392565	0.13879	27.309	27.966
Kingpow	8	28.3875	0.454933	0.16084	28.007	28.768
Zoom	8	28.0625	0.292465	0.10340	27.818	28.307

Step 3. Choose the significance level for the test.

Test for differences between the three groups of gunpowder using the 5% significance level, so the reference value is 0.05.

Step 4. Check the assumptions for the test.

In considering the assumptions for an analysis of variance, the observations are independent. The standard deviations for the three groups are similar. With only eight observations, it is difficult to test for normality.

For completeness in this example, Figure 9.17 shows the text reports from testing for equal variances. Review the **Levene** and **Brown-Forsythe** tests, and proceed with the ANOVA on the assumption that the variances for the three groups are the same.

Figure 9.17 Testing for Equal Variances in Bullets Data

Level	Count	Std Dev	MeanAbsDif to Mean	MeanAbsDif to Median
Blasto	8	0.3925648	0.3375000	0.3375000
Kingpow	8	0.4549333	0.3625000	0.3625000
Zoom	8	0.2924649	0.2375000	0.2375000

Test	F Ratio	DFNum	DFDen	Prob > F
O'Brien[.5]	1.3636	2	21	0.2775
Brown-Forsythe	0.9005	2	21	0.4215
Levene	1.0316	2	21	0.3738
Bartlett	0.6255	2	.	0.5350

Welch Anova testing Means Equal, allowing Std Devs Not Equal

F Ratio	DFNum	DFDen	Prob > F
6.1796	2	13.51	0.0124*

Figure 9.18 shows the text reports from testing for normality for each group, using **Distribution** with a **By** variable of **Gunpowder**. See Chapter 6 for steps in testing for normality. Figure 9.18 removes the Moments and Quantiles reports, and hides the Parameter Estimates reports. Figure 9.18 uses the **Horizontal Layout** and **Uniform Scaling** options. Even though the sample sizes are small, the Goodness-of-Fit Tests indicate that you can assume normality and proceed with the ANOVA.

Figure 9.18 Testing for Normality in Bullets Data

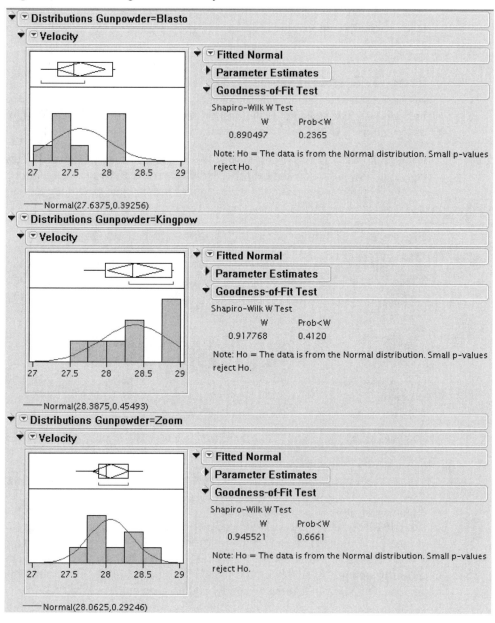

Step 5. Perform the test.

Use **Oneway** to perform an analysis of variance. For example purposes only, this topic also shows results for the Kruskal-Wallis test. Figure 9.19 shows the results.

Figure 9.19 ANOVA and Kruskal-Wallis Results for Bullets Data

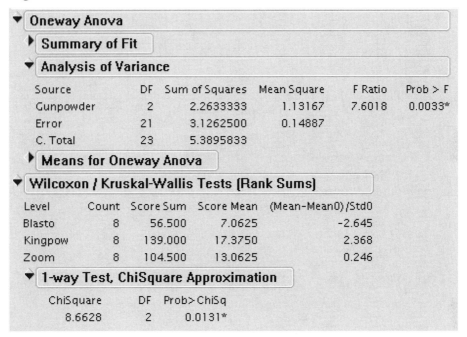

Step 6. Make conclusions from the test results.

The *p*-value for comparing groups is **0.0033**, which is less than the reference probability value of 0.05. You conclude that the average velocity is significantly different between the three types of gunpowder. If the ANOVA assumptions had not been reasonable, the Kruskal-Wallis test would lead to the same conclusion as the ANOVA, with *p*=0.0131.

Figure 9.20 Tukey-Kramer HSD Results for Bullets Data

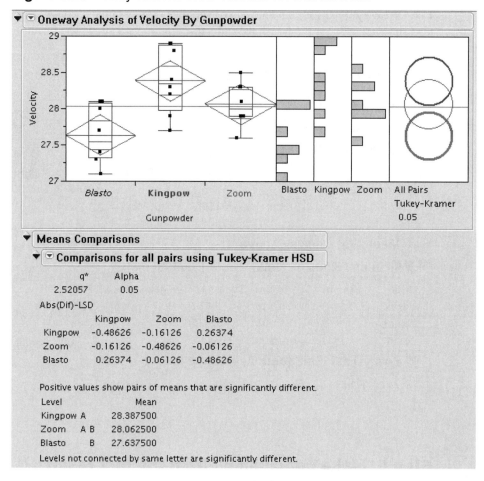

Next, perform the Tukey-Kramer HSD test. Figure 9.20 shows the results, with **Kingpow** selected in the comparison circles. Figure 9.20 removes the reports for the ANOVA and the Kruskal-Wallis test. In the Means Comparisons report, Figure 9.20 hides the Ordered Differences Report for the Tukey-Kramer HSD test.

Kingpow is selected in the comparison circles and is not significantly different from **Zoom**, but is significantly different from **Blasto**.

From the Connecting Letters Report, you conclude that the mean muzzle velocity for **Kingpow** is significantly different from **Blasto**. The mean muzzle velocities for other pairs of types of gunpowder are not significantly different.

Exploring the results further, the LSD Threshold Matrix has a positive value for only the **Kingpow–Blasto** value, indicating that this is the only significant difference. Because sample sizes for the three groups are the same, the values along the diagonal are the same. This value is the least significant difference (LSD).

In the hidden Ordered Differences Report, the confidence interval for **Kingpow–Blasto** does not include 0, again indicating a significant difference.

Because sample sizes are the same, you can use the overlap marks in the means diamonds. Click the crosshair tool (+) on the toolbar and place it on one of the overlap marks. If you do this for each means diamond, you will find that **Blasto** and **Zoom** are significantly different. These results are similar to the results for the Student's *t* multiple comparison test.

Summary

Key Ideas

To summarize data from more than two groups, separate the data into groups and get summary information for each group using the summaries in the **Oneway** platform.

- Regardless of the statistical test, the steps for analysis are:
    1. Create a JMP data table.

    2. Check the data table for errors.

    3. Choose the significance level for the test.

    4. Check the assumptions for the test.

    5. Perform the test.

    6. Make conclusions from the test results.

- An analysis of variance (ANOVA) is a test for comparing the means of several groups at once. This test assumes that the observations are independent samples from normally distributed populations, and that the groups have equal variances.

- If the assumptions for an ANOVA are not reasonable, the Kruskal-Wallis test provides a nonparametric analogue.

- Compare the *p*-value for the test with the significance level.

  □ If the *p*-value is less than the significance level, then reject the null hypothesis and conclude that the groups are significantly different. JMP helps you by displaying an asterisk next to *p*-values that are less than 0.05.

  □ If the *p*-value is greater than the significance level, then you fail to reject the null hypothesis. You conclude that the groups are not significantly different. Do not conclude that the groups are the same.

- Multiple comparisons are tests that show which group means are different from one another. Use these tests only after an ANOVA shows significant differences between groups. The Student's *t* test controls the comparisonwise error rate, but increases the overall risk of incorrectly concluding that the means are different. The Tukey-Kramer HSD test and Bonferroni approach control the experimentwise error rate. Dunnett's test and Hsu's MCB test are useful in specific situations.

JMP Steps

For summarizing data

To summarize data from multiple groups, you use **Distribution** with a **By** variable as described in Chapter 8. JMP provides a more compact report as follows:

1. In the JMP Starter window, click **Basic→Oneway**.

2. Click your response variable and then **Y, Response**. Click your grouping variable and then **X, Grouping**. Click **OK**.

3. Hold down the ALT key and click the hot spot for the Oneway Analysis of Annual Salary By Subject Area report.

4. Select the check boxes for: **Box Plots**, **Points Jittered**, **Histograms**, and **Means and Std Dev**. For easier viewing, deselect the check boxes for **Mean Error Bars** and **Std Dev Lines**. Click **OK**.

For analysis step 4, checking assumptions

- To check the assumption of independent observations, think about your data and whether this assumption is reasonable. This is not a step where using JMP will answer this question.

- To check the assumption of normality, use **Distribution** as described in Chapter 6. Check each group separately using a **By** variable.

- To test for equal variances for the ANOVA, follow steps 1 and 2 for summarizing groups. Then, click the hot spot for the Oneway Analysis of Annual Salary By Subject Area report. Select **UnEqual Variances**.

For analysis step 5, perform the test

- To compare groups, follow steps 1 through 3 for summarizing groups. Then, click the hot spot for the Oneway Analysis of Annual Salary By Subject Area report.

  If the ANOVA assumptions are reasonable, select **Means/Anova**.

  For non-normal data, select **Nonparametric→Wilcoxon**.

  If the equal variances assumption is not reasonable, use the Welch Anova test in the Tests that the Variances are Equal report. If the Welch Anova test is used, then multiple comparison tests are not appropriate.

- To enhance the continuous-by-nominal/ordinal plot for reporting, create the Oneway Analysis of Annual Salary By Subject Area report. Then:

  1. Hold down the ALT key and click the hot spot for the Oneway Analysis of Annual Salary By Subject Area report. Select the check boxes for: **Box Plots**, **Mean Diamonds**, **Connect Means**, **All Graphs**, **Grand Mean**, and **X Axis proportional**.

  2. Confirm that all other **Display Options** check boxes are deselected.

  3. Click **OK**.

For multiple comparison tests

- First, compare groups and perform multiple comparison tests only when you conclude that the groups are significantly different. In JMP, click the hot spot for the Oneway Analysis of Annual Salary By Subject Area report, select **Compare Means**, and select the test you want. Use the hot spots for each report to show or hide report tables.

Exercises

1. Click **Help→Tutorials** in the JMP menu bar. Work through the **Many Means** tutorial.

2. Use the statistics index and find **Kruskal-Wallis**. Review the example and discuss conclusions from the data. This is the Membrane data in the Sample Data Directory. Use **Distribution** to summarize the data. Are the assumptions for an ANOVA reasonable? If so, perform an analysis of variance. If not, perform a Kruskal-Wallis test. As appropriate, perform multiple comparison tests.

3. Perform a test for normality on the Salary data and comment on results. Is an ANOVA reasonable? If not, perform the steps for an appropriate analysis, define the null and alternative hypotheses, and test the assumptions. Use a 5% alpha level. Discuss your conclusions and answer the research question.

4. Use the Football data in the Sample Data Directory (under the Bivariate Analysis heading). The research question is whether there is a significant difference between mean player speeds (**Speed**) depending on position (**Position**). Perform the steps for analysis, define the null and alternative hypotheses, and test the assumptions. Use a 5% alpha level. Discuss your conclusions and answer the research question.

5. Using the Football data, suppose you decide to proceed based on the assumption of normality. Is the assumption for equal variances reasonable? Perform the appropriate analysis, discuss your conclusions, and answer the research question.

6. Use the Students data in the Sample Data Directory (under the Analysis of Variance heading). The research question is whether there is a significant difference between mean weights for the different ages of students. Perform the

steps for analysis, define the null and alternative hypotheses, and test the assumptions. Use a 5% alpha level. Discuss your conclusions and answer the research question.

7. Using the Students data, suppose you decide to proceed based on the assumption of normality. Is the assumption for equal variances reasonable? Perform the appropriate analysis. If the ANOVA shows a significant difference between groups, perform the Tukey-Kramer HSD test. Discuss your conclusions and answer the research question.

8. Use the Movies data in the Sample Data Directory (under the Business and Demographic heading). The research question is whether there is a significant difference between mean domestic revenue (**Domestic $**) for the different ratings of movies (**Rating**). Perform the steps for analysis, define the null and alternative hypotheses, and test the assumptions. Use a 5% alpha level. Discuss your conclusions and answer the research question.

9. Use the Cars Physical Data data in the Sample Data Directory (under the Exploratory Modeling heading). The research question is whether there is a significant difference in the mean weight (**Weight**) for the different country of origin (**Country**). Perform the steps for analysis, define the null and alternative hypotheses, and test the assumptions. Use a 5% alpha level. Discuss your conclusions and answer the research question.

10. Use the Lipid data in the Sample Data Directory (under the Medical Studies heading). Create a subset of this data that omits the two records with the value **>6** for the variable **Alcohol use**. Using this subset, the research question is whether there is a significant difference in the mean cholesterol for the three categories of alcohol use. Perform the steps for analysis, define the null and alternative hypotheses, and test the assumptions. Use a 10% alpha level. Discuss your conclusions and answer the research question.

11. Use the Scores data in the Sample Data Directory (under the Psychology and Social Science heading). The research question is whether there is a significant difference in the mean physics scores across the regions. Perform the steps for analysis, define the null and alternative hypotheses, and test the assumptions. Use a 5% alpha level. Discuss your conclusions and answer the research question.

12. Using the Scores data, suppose you decide to proceed based on the assumption of normality. Is the assumption for equal variances reasonable? Perform the appropriate analysis, discuss your results, and answer the research question.

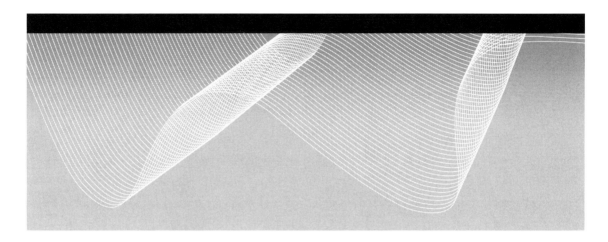

Part 4

Fitting Lines to Data

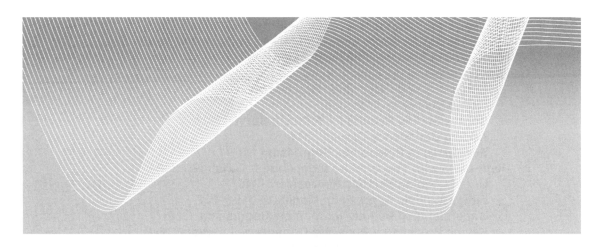

Chapter 10

Correlation and Regression

Can SAT scores be used to predict college grade-point averages? How does the age of a house affect its selling price? Is heart rate affected by the amount of blood cholesterol? How much of an increase in sales results from a specific increase in advertising expenditures?

These questions involve looking at two continuous variables and investigating if the variables are related. As one variable increases, does the other variable increase, decrease, or stay the same? Because both variables contain quantitative measurements, comparing groups is not appropriate. This chapter discusses:

- summarizing continuous variables using scatterplots and statistics.

- using correlation coefficients to describe the strength of the linear relationship between two continuous variables.

- performing least squares regression analysis to develop equations that describe how one variable is related to another variable. Sections discuss fitting straight lines, fitting curves, and fitting an equation with more than two continuous variables.

- enhancing the regression analysis by adding confidence curves.

The methods in this chapter are appropriate for continuous variables. Regression analyses that handle other types of variables exist, but they are outside the scope of this book. See "Further Reading" for suggested references.

Chapters 10 and 11 discuss the activities of regression analysis and regression diagnostics. Fitting a regression model and performing diagnostics are intertwined. In regression, you first fit a model. You then perform diagnostics to assess how well the model fits. You repeat this process until you find a suitable model. This chapter focuses on fitting models, and Chapter 11 focuses on performing diagnostics.

Summarizing Multiple Continuous Variables

This section discusses methods for summarizing continuous variables. Chapter 4 described how to use **Distribution** to view histograms, box plots, and reports to summarize each continuous variable. Interacting with the plots can give insight into how the variables relate to each other. Use the graphs and reports to check the data for errors before performing any statistical analyses.

For continuous variables, a *scatterplot* with one variable on the *y*-axis and another variable on the *x*-axis shows the possible relationship. Scatterplots provide another way to check the data for errors.

Suppose a homeowner was interested in the effect that using the air conditioner had on the electric bill. The homeowner recorded the number of hours the air conditioner was used for 21 days, and the number of times the dryer was used each day. The homeowner also monitored the electric meter for these 21 days, and computed the amount of electricity used each day in Kilowatt-hours.[1] Table 10.1 displays the data.

---

[1] Data is from Dr. Ramon Littell, University of Florida. Used with permission.

Table 10.1 Kilowatt Data

AC	Dryer	Kilowatt-hours
1.5	1	35
4.5	2	63
5	2	66
2	0	17
8.5	3	94
6	3	79
13.5	1	93
8	1	66
12.5	1	94
7.5	2	82
6.5	3	78
8	1	65
7.5	2	77
8	2	75
7.5	1	62
12	1	85
6	0	43
2.5	3	57
5	0	33
7.5	1	65
6	0	33

This data is available in the **Energy** data table in the sample data for the book.

Creating Scatterplots

JMP provides several ways to create scatterplots. The **Multivariate** platform provides both scatterplots and statistical reports. In JMP:

1. Open the Energy data table.

2. In the JMP Starter window, click **Multivariate→Multivariate**.

3. Click **AC**, **Dryer**, and **Kilowatt-hours** and then **Y, Columns**.

4. Click **OK**.

JMP generates and displays the Multivariate report, which contains the Scatterplot Matrix and the Correlations report. Figure 10.1 shows the scatterplot matrix. "Calculating Correlation Coefficients" discusses the Correlations report.

Figure 10.1 Scatterplot Matrix for Energy Data

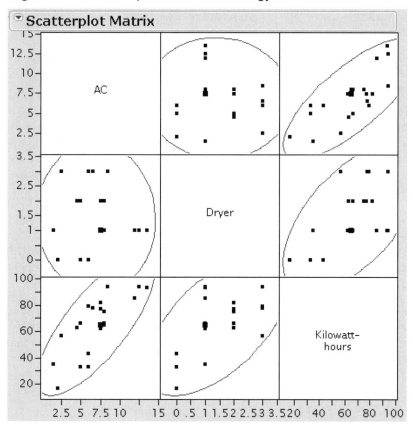

The scatterplot matrix shows all possible two-way scatterplots for the three variables. (For your data, the matrix will show all possible two-way plots for the variables you choose.) The center diagonal identifies the variables. Figure 10.2 helps decode the structure of the scatterplot matrix.

Figure 10.2 Understanding the Structure of the Scatterplot Matrix

AC	AC by Dryer	AC by Kilowatt-hours
Dryer by AC	Dryer	Dryer by Kilowatt-hours
Kilowatt-hours by AC	Kilowatt-hours by Dryer	Kilowatt-hours

The **AC by Kilowatt-hours** scatterplot in the upper-right corner shows **AC** on the *y*-axis and **Kilowatt-hours** on the *x*-axis. The lower-left corner shows the mirror image of this scatterplot, with **Kilowatt-hours** on the *y*-axis and **AC** on the *x*-axis. Kilowatt-hours is the *response variable*, or the variable whose values are impacted by the other variables. Typically, scatterplots show the response variable on the vertical *y*-axis and the other variables on the *x*-axis. For the **Multivariate** platform, JMP shows the full scatterplot matrix and you choose which scatterplot to use.

Look at the lower-left corner of Figure 10.1. The scatterplot shows that higher values of **Kilowatt-hours** tend to occur with higher values of **AC**. However, the relationship is not perfect because some days have higher **AC** values, but lower **Kilowatt-hours**. This is because of other factors—such as how hot it was or how many other appliances were used—that affect the amount of electricity that was used on a given day.

Similarly, the **Kilowatt-hours by Dryer** scatterplot shows that higher values of **Kilowatt-hours** tend to occur with higher values of **Dryer**. By just looking, this increasing relationship does not appear to be as strong as the increasing relationship between **Kilowatt-hours** and **AC**.

Enhancing the Scatterplot Matrix with Hot Spot Menu Choices

Figure 10.1 shows a *density ellipsis* for each scatterplot. If the two variables are normally distributed, the red outlines enclose about 95% of the data. You can remove the density ellipses, change the confidence interval, or change the color. In JMP:

1. Click the hot spot for Scatterplot Matrix.

2. Select **Ellipse α→90**. JMP updates the scatterplot matrix to show 90% density ellipses.

3. Click the hot spot again, select **Ellipse Color**, and select a color from the palette. JMP updates the scatterplot matrix with the new color.

4. Click the hot spot again and select **Density Ellipses** to remove them.

5. Repeat step 4 to re-display the density ellipses.

JMP provides two other choices from the Scatterplot Matrix hot spot. **Show Correlations** adds the correlation coefficients to the scatterplots, and **Show Histograms** adds histograms in the diagonal cells of the matrix.

Enhancing the Scatterplot Matrix with Right-Click Choices

Like many other JMP plots, the scatterplot matrix is interactive. You can double-click to change the axis settings and change the report title. You can right-click to display a menu of choices, some of which are available only after selecting data points in the plot. In JMP:

1. Click the **Lasso** tool on the toolbar. Click and drag a circle around the single point outside the density ellipse in the **Kilowatt-hours by AC** scatterplot (this assumes you have reset the density ellipses to 90% by following the earlier steps). JMP highlights the point in every scatterplot in the matrix and in the data table.

2. Right-click in one of the scatterplots, select **Row Colors**, and select a color from the palette. JMP colors the point in every scatterplot in the matrix.

3. Right-click in one of the scatterplots again, select **Row Markers**, and select a different marker from the palette. JMP updates the point in every scatterplot in the matrix. Using different markers helps distinguish the selected points when using a gray scale printer. The single selected point is on the edge of the density ellipses in the other scatterplots.

Figure 10.3 shows the results of enhancing the scatterplot matrix with hot spot menu choices and right-click choices. It shows other choices that are available when you right-click in a scatterplot in the matrix. See the JMP documentation for details on these additional choices.

Figure 10.3 Enhancing the Scatterplot Matrix

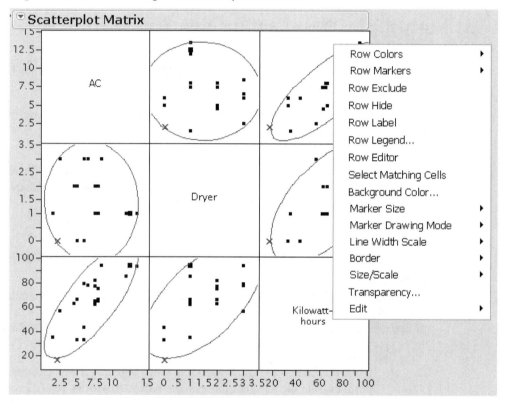

The highlighted point represents the lowest energy use in the data table, which was a day with no dryer use and only two hours of air conditioner use. This is a valid data point.

Figure 10.3 illustrates a benefit of a scatterplot matrix. It can highlight potential errors in the data by showing potential outlier points in two directions. For the **Energy** data, all of the data points are valid. Another example of where a scatterplot matrix could be useful is with blood pressure readings. A value of 95 for systolic blood pressure (the higher number of the two numbers) for a person is reasonable. Similarly, a value of 95 for diastolic blood pressure (the lower number of the two numbers) for a person is reasonable. However, a value of 95/95 for systolic/diastolic is not reasonable. Checking the two variables one at a time (with **Distribution**, for example) would not highlight the value of 95/95 for systolic/diastolic as an issue. The scatterplot matrix would highlight this value as a potential outlier point that should be investigated.

Using Summary Statistics to Check Data for Errors

As a final task of summarizing continuous variables, think about checking the data for errors. The scatterplot matrix is an effective way to find potential outlier points. Chapter 4 discussed using box plots for this purpose, and recommended checking the minimum and maximum values to confirm that they are reasonable. You could use **Distribution** and check the Moments report, but **Multivariate** gives similar statistics. In JMP:

1. Click the hot spot for Multivariate.

2. Select **Simple Statistics→Univariate Simple Statistics**.

JMP adds the Univariate Simple Statistics report to the Multivariate report. Figure 10.4 shows the Univariate Simple Statistics report.

Figure 10.4 Adding Simple Summary Statistics in Multivariate

▼ Univariate Simple Statistics

Column	N	Mean	Std Dev	Sum	Minimum	Maximum
AC	21	6.9286	3.1356	145.500	1.5000	13.5000
Dryer	21	1.4286	1.0282	30.0000	0.0000	3.0000
Kilowatt-hours	21	64.8571	21.8844	1362.00	17.0000	94.0000

Note: Statistics were calculated for each column independently without regard for missing values in other columns.

JMP lists the variables under the **Column** heading. See Chapter 4 for definitions of the statistics in the other columns. As with other JMP reports, you can double-click on a number in the column and change the decimal places that are displayed. Or, you can right-click and choose the columns to display in the report. You can change column headings or the report heading.

JMP adds a note to the bottom of the report. When your data has missing values, this note is very important. JMP uses all available values to calculate these statistics. Suppose the homeowner forgot to collect dryer information on one day, resulting in only 20 values for the variable. The Univariate Simple Statistics report would show **N** as **20** for **Dryer**, and **N** as **21** for the other two variables.

JMP Hint:

Suppose your data has missing values for some variables, and you want to calculate statistics for only those rows where all variables are non-missing. JMP does this automatically when you select **Simple Statistics→Multivariate Simple Statistics** from the **Multivariate** hot spot.

Calculating Correlation Coefficients

Figure 10.1 shows the scatterplot matrix that JMP automatically creates in the **Multivariate** platform. JMP also automatically creates the Correlations report, shown in Figure 10.5.

Figure 10.1 indicates that **AC** and **Kilowatt-hours** have an increasing relationship. Similarly, **Dryer** and **Kilowatt-hours** appear to have a weaker, but still increasing relationship. The *correlation coefficients* quantify the strength of the linear relationship between two variables.

Figure 10.5 Correlation Coefficients for Energy Data

▾ Correlations

	AC	Dryer	Kilowatt-hours
AC	1.0000	-0.0288	0.7653
Dryer	-0.0288	1.0000	0.5984
Kilowatt-hours	0.7653	0.5984	1.0000

The Correlations report contains the correlation coefficients for each pair of variables and displays the coefficients in a matrix. This matrix has the same structure as the scatterplot matrix. See Figure 10.2 to help understand the structure.

The Correlations report lists Pearson correlation coefficients. Statistics texts represent the Pearson correlation coefficient with the letter "r." Values of r range from -1.0 to +1.0. Figure 10.5 shows that the relationship between **AC** and **Kilowatt-hours** has a positive correlation with r=0.7653. Figure 10.5 shows that there is a weaker positive correlation between **Dryer** and **Kilowatt-hours** with r=0.5984. The Correlations report confirms the visual understanding from the scatterplot matrix.

When calculating correlations for the Correlations report, JMP uses observations with non-missing values for all variables. Because the Energy data has no non-missing values, JMP uses all the data. Suppose the data table had a missing value for **Dryer** for one day. Then, JMP would use only 20 observations to calculate the correlation coefficients in the Correlations report.

Understanding Correlation Coefficients

With positive correlation coefficients, the values of the two variables increase together. With negative correlation coefficients, the values of one variable increase, while the values of the other variable decrease. Values near 0 imply that the two variables do not have a linear relationship.

A correlation coefficient of 1 (r=+1) corresponds to a plot of points that fall exactly on an upward-sloping straight line. A correlation coefficient of r=-1 corresponds to a plot of points that fall exactly on a downward-sloping straight line. (Neither of these straight lines necessarily have a slope of 1.) The correlation of a variable with itself is always +1. Otherwise, values of +1 or -1 usually don't occur in real situations because plots of real data don't fall exactly on straight lines.

In reality, values of r are between -1 and +1. Relatively large positive values of r, such as 0.7, correspond to plots that have an upward trend. Relatively large negative values of r correspond to plots that have a downward trend.

What defines "near 0" or "relatively large?" How do you know whether the correlation coefficient measures a strong or weak relationship between two continuous variables? JMP provides these answers with the Pairwise Correlations report.

Graphs and Tests for Correlation Coefficients

JMP displays all possible correlations in the Correlations report. The Pairwise Correlations report provides more details and answers the above questions. In JMP:

1. Click the hot spot for Multivariate.

2. Select **Pairwise Correlations**.

Figure 10.6 shows the results.

Figure 10.6 Pairwise Correlations Report for Energy Data

Variable	by Variable	Correlation	Count	Signif Prob	-.8-.6-.4-.2 0 .2 .4 .6 .8
Dryer	AC	-0.0288	21	0.9014	
Kilowatt-hours	AC	0.7653	21	<.0001*	
Kilowatt-hours	Dryer	0.5984	21	0.0042*	

Understanding the Report

JMP lists each pair of variables and the correlation coefficient (**Correlation**). Compare the results in Figures 10.5 and 10.6, and you will notice that the correlation coefficients are the same.

The **Count** column in the Pairwise Correlations report is especially important for data with missing values. JMP uses all possible data when calculating pairwise correlation coefficients. Because the Energy data has no non-missing values, JMP uses all of the data. Suppose that the data table had a missing value for **Dryer** for one day. For the Pairwise Correlations report, JMP would use only 20 observations to calculate the **Dryer** by **AC** and **Kilowatt-hours** by **Dryer** coefficients. JMP would use all 21 observations for the **Kilowatt-hours** by **AC** coefficient. In contrast, JMP would use only 20 observations for all of the correlation coefficients in the Correlations report.

The **Signif Prob** column (short for "significance probability") displays a p-value. For this test, the null hypothesis is that the correlation coefficient is 0. The alternative hypothesis is that the correlation coefficient is different from 0. As usual, JMP highlights p-values less than 0.05 with an asterisk. This test provides answers to the questions of whether a coefficient is relatively large or near 0.

For the Energy data, focus on the two correlation coefficients including **Kilowatt-hours**. Both of these correlation coefficients are significantly different from 0. The results from the test confirm the visual understanding from the scatterplot matrix.

The results from the test for **AC** and **Dryer** show how JMP reports *p*-values greater than 0.05. The test confirms the visual understanding from the scatterplot matrix. You conclude that there is not a linear relationship between these two variables.

In general, if the *p*-value is less than the significance level, then reject the null hypothesis and conclude that the correlation coefficient is significantly different from 0. If the *p*-value is greater than the significance level, then you fail to reject the null hypothesis. You conclude that there is not enough evidence to say that the correlation coefficient is significantly different from 0.

Understanding the Plot

JMP creates a bar chart that is scaled from -1 to 1 and displays each pairwise correlation coefficient. JMP colors the bar from 0 to the value of the correlation coefficient. For each pairwise correlation coefficient, the bar chart helps you visualize how near 0 or relatively large the correlation coefficient is.

Unlike most plots in JMP, the bar chart that shows pairwise correlations is not interactive. You cannot click on the bar chart to change anything. You can, however, remove the bar chart and display only the pairwise correlations. Right-click in the Pairwise Correlations report and select **Columns→Plot Corr** to remove the bar chart. Repeat these steps again to display the bar chart.

Cautions about Correlations

There are two important cautions to remember when interpreting correlations.

First, correlation is not the same as causation. When two variables are highly correlated, it does not necessarily imply that one causes the other. In some cases, there might be an underlying causal relationship, but you don't know this from the correlation coefficient. In other cases, the relationship might be caused by a completely different variable. For example, consider a store owner who notices a high positive correlation between sales of ice scrapers and hot coffee. Coffee sales don't cause ice scraper sales, and the reverse is not true either. Perhaps the sales of both these items are caused by weather—drivers purchasing more hot coffee and more ice scrapers on cold, snowy days. Proving cause-and-effect relations is much more difficult than just showing a high correlation.

Second, "shopping for significance" in a large group of correlations is not a good idea. Researchers sometimes make the mistake of measuring many variables, finding the correlations between all possible pairs of variables, and choosing the significant correlations to make conclusions. Recall the interpretation of a significance level and you see the mistake: If a researcher performs 100 correlations and tests their significance at the 0.05 significance level, then about 5 significant correlations will be found by chance alone.

Questions Not Answered by Correlation

From the value of *r* in Figure 10.5 or 10.6, you conclude that as the use of the air conditioner increases, so do the Kilowatt-hours that are consumed. This is not a surprise. Some other important questions are:

- How many Kilowatt-hours are consumed for each hour of using the air conditioner?

- What is a prediction of the Kilowatt-hour consumption for a specific day when the air conditioner is used for a specified number of hours?

- What is an estimate of the average Kilowatt-hour consumption on days when the air conditioner is used for a specified number of hours?

- What are the confidence limits for the predicted Kilowatt-hour consumption?

A regression analysis of the data answers these questions. The next sections discuss fitting a straight line with regression analysis, fitting a curve, and regression analysis with multiple *x* variables.

Performing Straight-Line Regression

A correlation coefficient indicates that a linear relationship exists, and the *p*-value evaluates the strength of this linear relationship. However, a correlation coefficient does not fully describe the relationship between the two variables. Figure 10.7 shows a plot for two different *y* variables against the same *x* variable. The correlation coefficient between *y* and *x* is 1.0 in both cases. All of the points for each *y* variable fall exactly on a straight line. However, the relationships between *y* and *x* are quite different for the two *y* variables.

Figure 10.7 Correlation Coefficients of 1.0

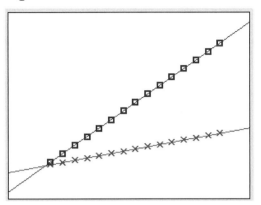

Look again at the **Kilowatt-hours by AC** scatterplot in Figure 10.1. You could draw a straight line through the data points. In a room of people, each person would draw a slightly different straight line. Which straight line is "best?" The next three topics discuss statistical methods and assumptions for fitting the "best" straight line to data.

Understanding Least Squares Regression

Least squares regression fits a straight line through the data points that minimizes the vertical differences between all of the points and the straight line. Figure 10.8 shows this process. For each point, calculate the vertical difference between the point and the line. Then, square the difference. This gives points above and below the line the same importance (squared differences are all positive). Finally, sum the squared differences. The "best" straight line is the line that minimizes the sum of squared differences, which is the basis of the name "least squares regression."

Figure 10.8 Process of Least Squares Regression

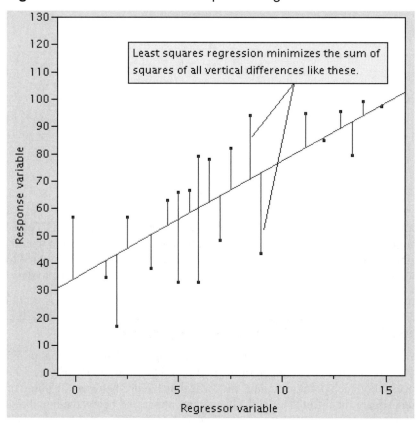

Regression Equations

The *regression equation* summarizes a straight-line relationship between two variables:

$$y = \beta_0 + \beta_1 x + \varepsilon$$

The *y* variable is the *dependent variable* or the *response variable*. The *x* variable is the *independent variable* or the *regressor*. The equation says that the dependent variable *y* is a straight-line function of *x*, with an *intercept* β_0 and a *slope* β_1. The intercept is the value of the *y*-axis when *x*=0. The slope is the amount of vertical increase for a one-unit horizontal increase; in algebra, this is called "the rise over the run." For the Energy data, the slope estimates the average number of Kilowatt-hours for running the air conditioner for one hour.

Because a given *x* value does not always lead to the same *y* value, the data has random variation. The equation uses ε to denote the random variation. For the Energy data, the homeowner knows how long the air conditioner was used each day. But, other appliances and lights consume electricity in varying amounts from day to day. This variation is the "error" in the model equation. For straight-line regression, the "error" includes both the random variation in the data, and other potential variables (such as **Dryer**) that are not included in the model.

Statisticians use the equation above when they have the entire population of values for *x* and *y*. In that case, the regression equation describes the entire population. In reality, you usually collect just a sample and use the sample data to estimate the straight line for the entire population. In this case, you use the equation:

$$\hat{y} = b_0 + b_1 x$$

b_0 and b_1 are the estimates of β_0 and β_1, respectively. The value b_0 gives the predicted value of *y* when *x* is 0. The value b_1 gives the increase in the *y* value that results from a one-unit increase in *x*. The value $\hat{y}$ indicates the predicted value of the response variable from the equation.

Assumptions for Least Squares Regression

Like all analyses, least squares regression requires some assumptions. These are:

- The data are measurements. Both the *x* and *y* variable are continuous.

- Observations are independent. The values from one pair of *x*-*y* observations are not related to the values from another pair. To check the assumption, think about your data and whether this assumption is reasonable. This is not a step where using JMP will answer this question.

- Observations are a random sample from the population. You want to make conclusions about a larger population, not about just the sample. For the Energy data, you want to make conclusions about **Kilowatt-hours** and **AC** use in general, not for just the 21 days in the data table. To check the assumption, think about your data and whether this assumption is reasonable. This is not a step where using JMP will answer this question.

- The values of *x* variables are known without error. To check the assumption, think about your data and whether this assumption is reasonable. This is not a step where using JMP will answer this question.

- The errors in the data are normally distributed, with a mean of 0 and a variance of σ^2. However, the regression equation has meaning even if the assumption is not reasonable. This assumption is needed for hypothesis tests and confidence intervals. (Chapter 11 discusses this assumption. For now, assume that it is reasonable.)

Steps in Fitting a Straight Line

The steps for regression analysis are basically the same as the steps for comparing groups:

1. Create a JMP data table.

2. Check the data table for errors.

3. Choose the significance level.

4. Check the assumptions.

5. Perform the test.

6. Make conclusions from the results.

Fitting a Straight Line Using JMP

As with scatterplots, JMP provides more than one way to fit a straight line to the data. In JMP:

1. Open the Energy data table.

2. In the JMP Starter window, click **Basic→Bivariate**.

3. Click **Kilowatt-hours→Y, Response**.

4. Click **AC→X, Regressor**.

5. Click **OK.** JMP creates a scatterplot. With only two variables, using **Bivariate** to create a scatterplot is often more useful than using the scatterplot matrix. Compare your results with Figure 10.9.

Figure 10.9 Scatterplot from Bivariate

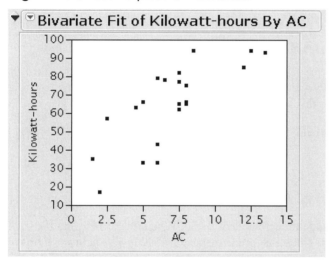

JMP Hints:

If you created this scatterplot after creating and highlighting points in the scatterplot matrix, JMP displays the colors and markers you selected in the scatterplot matrix. To remove these colors and markers, click **Rows→Clear Row States**.

For two variables, JMP provides a density ellipse, the correlation coefficient, and the *p*-value for testing if the correlation coefficient is different from 0. Click the hot spot for Bivariate Fit and select **Density Ellipse→.95**. JMP adds the density ellipse to the scatterplot and adds the Correlations report. The Correlations report contains the mean and standard deviation for each variable, the correlation coefficient, the *p*-value, and the number of rows used in calculating the statistics.

Continuing in JMP:

6. Click the hot spot for Bivariate Fit of Kilowatt-hours By AC.

7. Select **Fit Line**.

JMP fits the straight line and adds it to the scatterplot. JMP creates the Linear Fit report, which contains several report tables. Figure 10.10 shows the results. The next topics discuss these results, except for the results in the hidden Lack Of Fit report. (Chapter 11 discusses this report as one aspect of regression diagnostics.)

Finding the Equation for the Fitted Straight Line

Figure 10.10 shows the red fitted straight line in the scatterplot. Just below the scatterplot, JMP adds a legend for the line, and a hot spot next to the legend. "Enhancing the Scatterplot" uses this hot spot to enhance the scatterplot.

Just below the report title for the Linear Fit report in Figure 10.10, the fitted line equation is:

Kilowatt-hours = 27.85 + 5.34*AC

This equation rounds the JMP equation to two decimal places.

The fitted line has an intercept value of 27.85. When the homeowner does not use the air conditioner at all, the fitted line predicts that 27.85 Kilowatt-hours will be used that day.

Figure 10.10 Straight-Line Regression for Energy Data

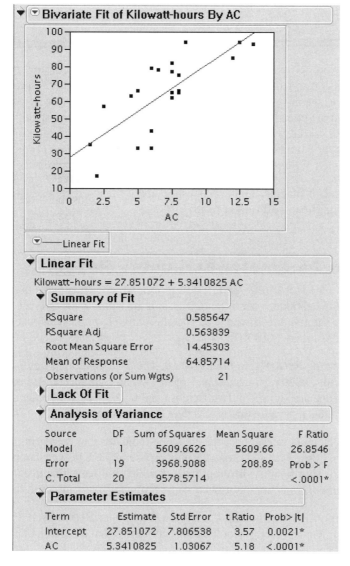

The fitted line has a slope of 5.34. The homeowner uses 5.34 Kilowatt-hours of electricity when the air conditioner runs for 1 hour. If the homeowner uses the air conditioner for 8 hours, the fitted line predicts that 42.72 (5.34 * 8) Kilowatt-hours of electricity are used.

For the entire day, the fitted line predicts:

Kilowatt-hours = 27.85 + (5.34*8)
= 27.85 + 42.72
= 70.57

Correlation coefficients could not provide an answer to the question of how many Kilowatt-hours are consumed for each hour's use of the air conditioner. The slope of the regression line gives the answer of 5.34 Kilowatt-hours. Another goal was to predict the Kilowatt-hours that are consumed when using the air conditioner for a specified number of hours. Again, the regression line gives the answer, as shown in the equation for using the air conditioner for 8 hours. (See "Displaying Confidence Limits on Predicted Values" and "Saving Predicted Values and Confidence Intervals" for more options.)

As with correlation coefficients, a natural question about the intercept and slope is whether they are significantly different from 0.

Understanding the Parameter Estimates Report

Figure 10.10 shows the **Parameter Estimates** report, which answers the question about the significance of the estimates for the intercept and the slope. JMP tests the null hypothesis that the parameter estimate is 0. The alternative hypothesis is that the parameter estimate is different from 0.

Look under the heading **Prob>|t|** in Figure 10.10. The p-values for the intercept and the slope are 0.0021 and <0.0001, respectively. Reject the null hypothesis, and conclude that the intercept and slope are significantly different from 0. Also, as with other statistical reports, JMP highlights a p-value that is less than 0.05 with an asterisk.

The statistical results make sense, because the slope indicates that increasing the number of hours the air conditioner is used produces an increase in the Kilowatt-hours for that day. The intercept is significantly different from 0, which indicates that even if the homeowner does not use the air conditioner, some Kilowatt-hours are used that day.

In general, to interpret JMP results, look at the p-values under **Prob>|t|**. If a p-value is less than your significance level, reject the null hypotheses that the parameter estimate is 0. If the p-value is greater, you fail to reject the null hypothesis.

The Parameter Estimates report provides other details on the parameters:

Term	Identifies the parameter. JMP identifies the intercept as **Intercept** and the slope of the line by the regressor variable (**AC** in this example).
Estimate	Lists the parameter estimate. It repeats the estimates that are in the regression equation at the top of the Linear Fit report.
Std Error	Standard error of the estimate. It measures how much the parameter estimates would vary from one collection of data to the next collection of data.
t Ratio	Gives the *t*-value for testing the hypothesis. JMP calculates the *t*-value as the parameter estimate divided by its standard error. For example, the *t*-value for the slope is 5.341/1.031, which is 5.18.

Understanding the Summary of Fit Report

Think about testing the parameter estimates. If neither the intercept nor slope is significantly different from 0, then the straight line does not fit the data very well. The Summary of Fit report provides statistical tools to assess the fit.

Find the value for **RSquare** in Figure 10.10. This statistic is the proportion of total variation in the *y* variable due to the *x* variables in the model. **RSquare** ranges from 0 to 1, with higher values indicating better-fitting models. For the Energy data, **RSquare** is **0.5856**. Statisticians often express this statistic as a percentage, saying that the model explains about "59% of the variation in the data" (for this example).

The Summary of Fit report provides other statistics. The **Mean of Response** is the average for the *y* variable. Compare the value in Figure 10.10 with the mean for **Kilowatt-hours** in Figure 10.4, and confirm that they are the same. See the JMP documentation for explanations of the other statistics in this report.

Understanding the Analysis of Variance Report

The Analysis of Variance report looks similar to reports in Chapter 9. For regression analysis, statisticians use this report to help assess whether the overall model explains a significant amount of the variation in the data. The report augments conclusions from the **RSquare** statistic. Statisticians typically inspect this report to evaluate the overall model before examining details for individual terms in the model.

When performing regression, the null hypothesis for the Analysis of Variance report is that the variation in the *y* variable is not explained by the variation in the *x* variable (for straight-line regression). The alternative hypothesis is that the variation in the *y* variable is explained by the variation in the *x* variable. Statisticians often refer to these hypotheses as testing whether "the model is significant or not."

Find the value for **Prob > F** in Figure 10.10. This gives the *p*-value for testing the hypothesis. For the Energy data, the *p*-value of **<.0001** leads you to conclude that the variation in **AC** explains a significant amount of the variation in **Kilowatt-hours**.

In general, to interpret JMP results, look at the *p*-value under **Prob > F** in the Analysis of Variance report. If the *p*-value is less than your significance level, reject the null hypotheses that the variation in the *y* variable does not explain the variation in the *x* variable. If the *p*-value is greater, you fail to reject the null hypothesis.

Chapter 9 describes the other information in the Analysis of Variance report. In Chapter 9, see the topic "Understanding Other Items in the Report" in "Performing a One-way Analysis of Variance."

Figure 10.10 shows the **DF** for **Model** equal to **1**. When fitting a straight line with a single independent variable, the **DF** for **Model** will always be **1**.

Figure 10.10 shows that the **Sum of Squares** for **Model** and **Error** add to be the **C. Total Sum of Squares**. Statisticians usually abbreviate "sum of squares" as "SS," and describe the sum of squares with this equation:

Total SS = Model SS + Error SS

This is a basic and important equation in regression analysis. Regression partitions total variation into variation due to the variables in the model, and variation due to error.

The model cannot typically explain all of the variation in the data. For example, Table 10.1 shows three observations with **AC** equal to **8** and with **Kilowatt-hours** values of **66**, **65**, and **75**. Because the three different **Kilowatt-hours** values occurred on days with the same value (8) for **AC**, the straight-line regression model cannot explain the variation in these points. This variation must be due to error (or due to factors other than the use of the air conditioner).

Enhancing the Reports

Double-click on a column in any report and change the format of the numbers that are displayed. As with other reports in JMP, you can change the report titles.

Click on the equation at the top of the Linear Fit report and edit it. Because JMP displays the equation with many decimal places, you might want to round the parameter estimates for easier display in a presentation or report.

As with other statistical reports in JMP, position the mouse pointer near a *p*-value and move it around in a very small circle. JMP displays a pop-up window, which includes text explaining the *p*-value. To close the window, move your mouse pointer again. As with other statistical reports, JMP highlights *p*-values less than 0.05 with an asterisk.

To hide a report, click the disclosure diamond next to the report title.

To remove the entire report, click the hot spot next to the equation for the line. Figure 10.10 shows this hot spot immediately below the scatterplot. This hot spot is next to the Linear Fit label. Select **Report** so that it is unchecked, and JMP removes the report and its title.

Enhancing the Scatterplot

Like most plots in JMP, the scatterplot is interactive. As with the scatterplot matrix earlier in this chapter, you can use the **Lasso** tool to select points and then highlight them with colors or markers.

Double-click on an axis to display the Axis Specification window and change the scale of the axis.

Click on an axis label and JMP displays a text box in which you can enter new text for the axis label. When you are finished, click outside the text box and JMP shows your new text as the axis label.

Chapter 4 discussed using the **Annotate** tool to add sticky notes to reports and graphs. This can be helpful for explaining outlier points in the scatterplot, or for adding the regression equation in the white space in the scatterplot.

Saving Predicted Values

"Finding the Equation for the Fitted Straight Line" showed how to predict how many Kilowatt-hours are consumed when the air conditioner is used for eight hours. You can manually use the equation to predict other values, or you can let JMP save the predictions. In JMP:

1. Click the hot spot next to the line labeled **Linear Fit**. (Figure 10.10 shows this hot spot.)

2. Select **Save Predicteds**.

> **JMP Hint:**
>
> The steps assume that you still have the straight-line regression results available. If you do not, and if you are in the same JMP session, click **Basic→Bivariate** in the JMP Starter window. Click **Recall** and JMP fills in your choices from the previous regression analysis. Click **OK** and click the hot spot for the scatterplot to fit the regression line.

JMP adds the predicted values to the data table. The graphs and reports from regression are the same. Figure 10.11 shows a portion of the Energy data table with the new column that contains the predicted values (**Predicted Kilowatt-hours**). Figure 10.11 shows rows 7 through 15 of the data table, with the rows where **AC** equals **8** selected. (These rows were selected manually to show the same predicted value. The next two topics on confidence intervals refer to these rows.)

Figure 10.11 Predicted Values Added to a Data Table

	AC	Dryer	Kilowatt-hours	Predicted Kilowatt-hours
7	13.5	1	93	99.9556847
8	8	1	66	70.5797312
9	12.5	1	94	94.6146023
10	7.5	2	82	67.90919
11	6.5	3	78	62.5681075
12	8	1	65	70.5797312
13	7.5	2	77	67.90919
14	8	2	75	70.5797312
15	7.5	1	62	67.90919

Displaying Confidence Limits on Predicted Values

Correlations could not provide confidence limits for an individual predicted Kilowatt-hour consumption. Figure 10.11 highlights the three days in the data where the homeowner used the air conditioner for eight hours (**AC** equals **8**). The regression equation predicts the same **Kilowatt-hours** for these three days. But, the actual values for the days range from 65 to 75. Suppose you want to put confidence limits on the predicted value of 70.57. These *confidence limits on individual values* need to account for possible error in the fitted regression line. They need to account for variation in the *y* variable for observations that have the same value of the *x* variable. Statisticians often refer to confidence limits on individual values as "prediction limits." JMP calls these limits **Confid Curves Indiv** in menu choices. In JMP:

1. Click the hot spot next to the line labeled **Linear Fit**. (Figure 10.12 shows this hot spot.)

2. Click the hot spot again, and select **Confid Curves Indiv**. JMP adds the confidence limits to the scatterplot.

3. Select **Confid Shaded Indiv**. JMP shades the area inside the confidence limits.

Figure 10.12 shows the results.

Figure 10.12 Adding Confidence Limits on Predicted Values

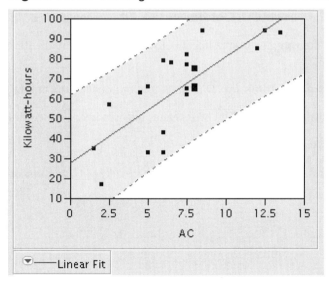

Estimating the Mean and Confidence Limits for the Mean

Suppose you want to estimate the average Kilowatt-hours that are consumed on all days when the air conditioner is used for a given number of hours. This task is essentially the same task as estimating the average Kilowatt-hours that are consumed on a given day.

For example, suppose you want to estimate the mean Kilowatt-hour consumption for all days when the air conditioner is used for eight hours. To get an estimate for each day, insert the value **AC=8** into the fitted regression equation. Because **AC** is the same for all of these days, the equation produces the same predicted value for **Kilowatt-hours**, as Figure 10.11 shows. It makes sense to use this predicted value as an estimate of the mean Kilowatt-hours consumed for all of these days. In other words, to predict either a single future value, or to estimate the mean response for a given value of the independent variable, use the same value from the regression equation.

Next, add confidence limits on the average Kilowatt-hours that are consumed when the air conditioner is used for eight hours. These confidence limits will differ from the prediction limits.

Because the mean is a population parameter, the mean value for all the days with a given value for **AC** does not change. Because the mean does not vary and the actual values do vary, it makes sense that a *confidence interval for the mean* would be smaller than the confidence interval for a single predicted value. With a single predicted value, you need to account for the variation between actual values, as well as for any error in the fitted regression line. With the mean, you need to account for only the error in the fitted regression line. JMP refers to the confidence interval for the mean as "confidence curves for the fitted equation," and calls it **Confid Curves Fit** in menu choices. In JMP:

1. Click the hot spot next to the line labeled **Linear Fit**. (Figure 10.13 shows this hot spot.)

2. Select **Confid Curves Fit**. JMP adds the confidence limits to the scatterplot.

3. Select **Confid Shaded Fit**. JMP shades the area inside the confidence limits.

Figure 10.13 shows the results.

Figure 10.13 Adding Confidence Limits for the Mean

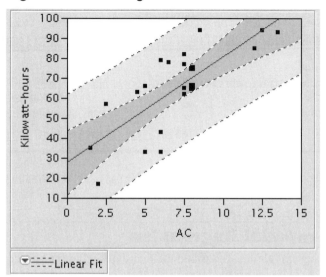

Figure 10.13 shows the confidence limits for the mean as the inner, dashed, red lines and dark-pink shaded area. The confidence limits for individual predicted values are the outer, dashed, red lines and light-pink shaded areas.

Summarizing Straight-Line Regression

Straight-line regression uses least squares to fit a line through a set of data points. Predicted values for the *y* variable for a given *x* value are computed by inserting the value of *x* into the equation for the fitted line. Prediction limits account for the error in fitting the regression line, and the variation between values for a given *x* value. Confidence limits on the mean account for the error in fitting the regression line because the mean does not vary. Plots of the observed values, fitted regression line, and confidence limits on the mean or prediction limits are useful in summarizing the regression.

After fitting a regression line, your next step is to perform regression diagnostics. The diagnostic tools help you decide whether the regression equation is adequate, or if you need to add more terms to the equation. Perhaps another variable needs to be added, or a curve fits the data better than a straight line. Chapter 11 discusses a set of basic tools for regression diagnostics.

The next section discusses fitting curves to data.

Fitting Curves

Understanding Polynomial Regression

For the Energy data, a straight line described the relationship between air conditioner use and Kilowatt-hours. In other cases, the relationship between two variables is not represented well by a straight line. Sometimes, a curve does a better job of describing the relationship. A *quadratic polynomial* has the equation:

$$\hat{y} = b_0 + b_1 x + b_2 x^2$$

With least squares regression, b_0, b_1, and b_2 are estimates of unknown population parameters. If you could measure all of the values in the entire population, you would know the exact relationship between x and y. Because you can measure only values in a sample, you estimate the relationship using regression. Least squares regression for curves minimizes the sum of squared differences between the points and the curve, as shown in Figure 10.14.

Figure 10.14 Least Squares Regression for a Curve

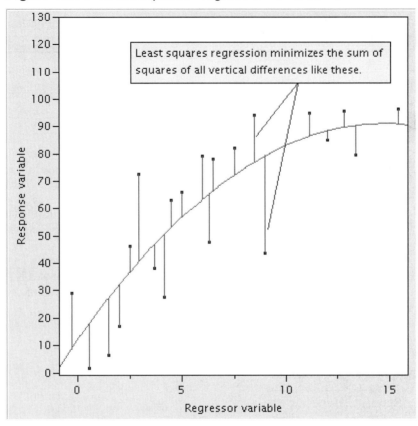

The assumptions for fitting a curve with least squares regression are the same as the assumptions for fitting a straight line. Similarly, the steps for fitting a curve are the same as the steps for fitting a straight line. As with fitting a straight line, the **Bivariate** platform provides one way to fit a curve to data.

Fitting Curves in JMP

An engineer conducted an experiment to test the performance of an industrial engine. The experiment used a mixture of diesel fuel and gas derived from distilling organic materials. The engineer measured horsepower produced from the engine at several speeds, where speed is measured in hundreds of revolutions per minute (rpm × 100).[2] Table 10.2 shows the data.

The steps for fitting a curve are:

1. Create a JMP data table.

2. Check the data table for errors. Assume you have performed this step and found no errors.

3. Choose the significance level. Choose a 95% significance level. This level implies a 5% chance of concluding that the regression coefficients are different from 0 when, in fact, they are not.

4. Check the assumptions.

5. Perform the analysis.

6. Make conclusions from the results.

Table 10.2 Engine Data

Speed	Horsepower
22.0	64.03
20.0	62.47
18.0	54.94
16.0	48.84
14.0	43.73
12.0	37.48
15.0	46.85
17.0	51.17
19.0	58.00
21.0	63.21

[2] Data is from Dr. Ramon Littell, University of Florida. Used with permission.

Table 10.2 Engine Data (*continued*)

Speed	Horsepower
22.0	64.03
20.0	59.63
18.0	52.90
16.0	48.84
14.0	42.74
12.0	36.63
10.5	32.05
13.0	39.68
15.0	45.79
17.0	51.17
19.0	56.65
21.0	62.61
23.0	65.31
24.0	63.89

This data is available in the Engine data table in the sample data for the book.

Checking the Assumptions

In thinking about the assumptions:

- Both the variables are continuous and the data contains measurements.

- The observations are independent because the measurement for one observation of speed and power is unrelated to the measurement for another observation.

- The observations are a random sample from the population. Because this is an experiment, the engineer selected the levels of **Speed** in advance, selecting levels that made sense in the industrial environment where the engine would be used.

- The engineer can set the value for **Speed** precisely, so assume that the x variable is known without error.

- The assumption about testing the errors in the data is discussed in Chapter 11. For now, assume that this assumption is reasonable.

Steps in JMP

To perform the analysis, in JMP:

1. Open the Engine data table.

2. In the JMP Starter window, click **Basic→Bivariate**.

3. Select **Power→Y, Response**.

4. Select **Speed→X, Regressor**.

5. Click **OK**.

JMP creates a scatterplot. Compare your results with Figure 10.15.

Figure 10.15 Scatterplot Showing Curve for Engine Data

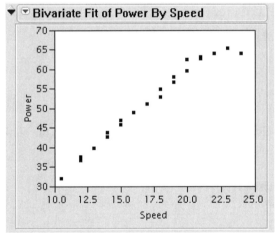

Looking at the data in Figure 10.15, it seems like a straight line would not fit the data well. **Power** increases with **Speed** up to about 21, and then it levels off or curves downward. Instead of fitting a straight line, fit a curve to the data. Continuing in JMP:

6. Click the hot spot for Bivariate Fit of Power By Speed.

7. Select **Fit Special…**. JMP displays the Specify Transformation or Constraint window (see Figure 10.16).

8. Click the menu for **Degree** and select **2 Quadratic**. This option tells JMP to fit a curve. Compare your window with Figure 10.16.

9. Clear the check box for **Centered Polynomial** so that it is deselected. (See "Technical Details: Centering" for more discussion.)

10. Compare your window with Figure 10.16. Click **OK**.

Figure 10.16 Fitting a Curve in JMP

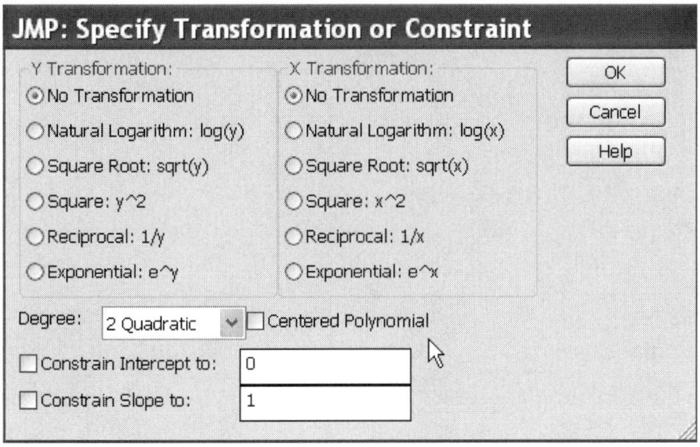

Figure 10.17 shows the results.

Figure 10.17 Fitting a Curve to the Engine Data

Bivariate Fit of Power By Speed

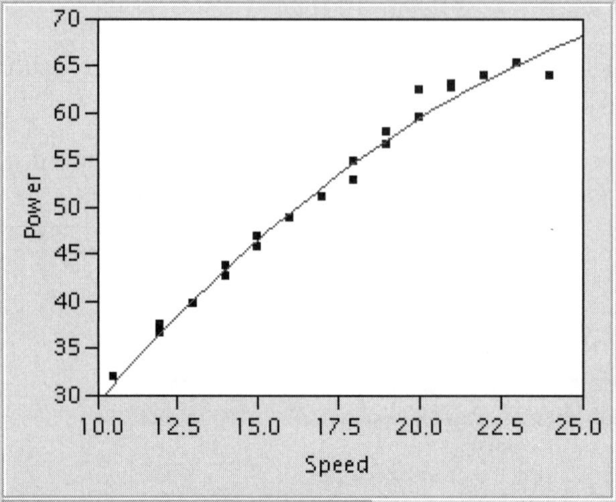

—— Polynomial Fit Degree=2

Polynomial Fit Degree=2

Power = -17.66377 + 5.5377602 Speed - 0.0840715 Speed^2

Summary of Fit

RSquare	0.98619
RSquare Adj	0.984875
Root Mean Square Error	1.234542
Mean of Response	52.19333
Observations (or Sum Wgts)	24

Lack Of Fit

Analysis of Variance

Source	DF	Sum of Squares	Mean Square	F Ratio
Model	2	2285.6454	1142.82	749.8372
Error	21	32.0060	1.52	Prob > F
C. Total	23	2317.6513		<.0001*

Parameter Estimates

Term	Estimate	Std Error	t Ratio	Prob>|t|
Intercept	-17.66377	5.435977	-3.25	0.0038*
Speed	5.5377602	0.644853	8.59	<.0001*
Speed^2	-0.084072	0.01852	-4.54	0.0002*

Figure 10.17 for fitting a curve shows the same JMP graphs and reports as Figure 10.10 for fitting a straight line. The key difference is in the report title, where JMP uses **Linear Fit** for the straight line and **Polynomial Fit Degree=2** for the quadratic curve. See the explanations earlier in the chapter for understanding the details of these JMP reports. The next two topics focus on explaining the conclusions for the Engine data.

JMP Hint:

As you become familiar with JMP, you might want to select **Analyze→Fit Y by X** from the menu instead of selecting **Bivariate** from the JMP Starter window. Both selections launch the same JMP platform.

One advantage of **Bivariate** is that JMP reminds you that the *y* variable is the response variable and the *x* variable is the regressor variable.

Understanding Results for Fitting a Curve

At the top of the Polynomial Fit Degree=2 report in Figure 10.17, the fitted JMP equation is:

$$\text{Power} = -17.66 + 5.54*\text{Speed} - 0.08*\text{Speed}^2$$

Speed^2 is **Speed** multiplied by itself. The equation rounds the JMP equation to two decimal places. JMP shows superscripts with a caret or $^\wedge$. Figure 10.17 shows **Speed^2** at the end of the formula for the fitted curve and in the reports that follow. In presentations and written reports, researchers typically use superscripts instead.

From the Parameter Estimates report, you conclude that all three coefficients are significantly different from 0. All three *p*-values are less than 0.05. At first, this might not make sense, because 0.08 seems close to 0. Remember that the **t Ratio** divides **Estimate** by **Std Error**. Figure 10.17 shows a very small standard error for the coefficient of **Speed^2** and a correspondingly large **t Ratio**. This coefficient is multiplied by the square of the **Speed** value. Even though the coefficient is small, the impact of this term on the curve is important.

The Summary of Fit report shows **RSquare** is about 0.99, meaning that the fitted curve explains about 99% of the variation in the data. This is an excellent fit.

The Analysis of Variance report leads you to conclude that the fitted curve for **Speed** explains a significant amount of the variation in **Power**. The *p*-value for the *F* test is **<.0001**. Statisticians typically examine the overall test of the fitted model before reviewing the details of parameter estimates.

Technical Details: Centering

When fitting polynomials or models with interactions between two variables, JMP automatically centers the model. From a statistical view, this improves the model when the regressor variables are related to each other. From a practical view, when fitting a curve with a single regressor variable, the resulting equation changes. For example, the equation for a centered polynomial fit for the Engine data is:

Power = 7.90 + 2.61*Speed – 0.08*(Speed–17.44)2

Compare the equation with the equation in Figure 10.17. For the quadratic term, the equation subtracts the overall average for **Speed**, which impacts both the intercept and linear coefficients. Some basic statistics texts use polynomial centering, and some do not. This chapter shows the classical approach that does not use polynomial centering, but JMP performs either approach.

Adding Confidence Curves

Just as when you fit a straight line, when you fit a curve, you can add confidence limits for the mean and confidence limits on an individual predicted value. Continuing in JMP:

1. Hold down the ALT key and click the hot spot next to the line labeled **Polynomial Fit Degree=2**. (Figure 10.18 shows this hot spot.)

2. Select **Confid Curves Fit**. JMP adds the confidence limits on the mean to the scatterplot.

3. Select **Confid Shaded Fit**. JMP shades the area inside the confidence limits for the mean.

4. Select **Confid Curves Indiv**. JMP adds the confidence limits on an individual predicted value (prediction limits) to the scatterplot.

5. Select **Confid Shaded Indiv**. JMP shades the area inside the prediction limits.

6. Click **OK.**

Figure 10.18 shows the results.

Figure 10.18 Adding Confidence Curves for the Engine Data

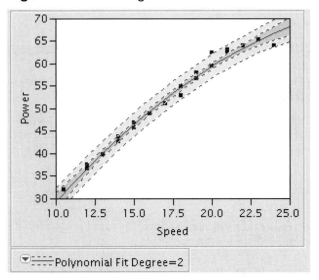

Figure 10.18 illustrates the narrow confidence curves for a model that fits very well. The dark-pink shaded area for the confidence limits for the mean is very close to the fitted curve. The light-pink shaded area for prediction limits is fairly narrow. Compare these confidence limits for a model with **RSquare** of about 0.99, with a model that doesn't fit as well in Figure 10.13 (where **RSquare** is about 0.59). This illustrates a general principle: poorly fitting models generate wider confidence limits.

Summarizing Polynomial Regression

Fitting a curve to data involves a single dependent *y* variable, and a single *x* variable with a linear and quadratic term. The same assumptions for fitting a straight line and the same analysis steps apply. Use the same JMP platform to create reports and graphs, and interpret the results in the same way. You can add confidence limits on the mean and on individual predicted values to the scatterplot. Although this is not shown, you can save predicted values using the same steps as you did when fitting a straight line. JMP fits equations with higher-order polynomials (cubes, for example). See the JMP documentation for more details.

After you fit a curve, the next step is to perform diagnostics to check the fit of your model. Chapter 11 discusses a set of basic tools for regression diagnostics.

The next section discusses regression with more than one *x* variable.

Regression with Two or More Independent Variables

Understanding Multiple Regression

This chapter discussed how to fit a straight line and a curve using regression. Both cases involved a single *y* variable and a single *x* variable. The curve included linear and quadratic (squared) terms for **Speed** in the Energy data, but the model included a single *x* variable.

Remember the homeowner recorded dryer use for the Energy data? Suppose you want to add the **Dryer** variable to the model. In this case, you are no longer fitting a straight line to the data, because both **AC** and **Dryer** are independent variables. *Multiple regression* is a regression model with multiple independent variables.

Multiple regression is difficult to picture in a simple scatterplot. For two independent variables, think of a three-dimensional picture. Figure 10.19 shows multiple regression, where the two independent variables are on the axes labeled **X1** and **X2**, and the dependent variable is on the axis labeled **Y**. Multiple regression is the process of finding the best-fitting plane through the data points. Here, "best-fitting" is defined as the plane that minimizes the squared distances between all of the data points and the plane.

Figure 10.19 Multiple Regression with Two Independent Variables

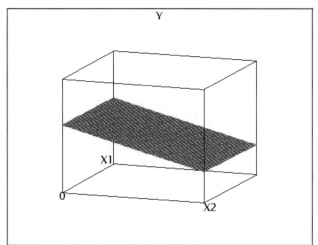

With two independent variables, the estimated regression equation is:

$$\hat{y} = b_0 + b_1 x_1 + b_2 x_2$$

b_0, b_1, and b_2 estimate the population parameters β_0, β_1, and β_2. The two independent variables are x_1 and x_2.

The assumptions for multiple regression are the same as the assumptions for fitting a straight line. Similarly, the steps for multiple regression are the same as the steps for fitting a straight line.

Fitting Multiple Regression Models in JMP

For the Energy data, fit a multiple regression model with both **AC** and **Dryer** as independent variables. You have already considered the assumptions for multiple regression, because you considered these assumptions earlier when fitting a straight line to the data. The only new assumption to consider for multiple regression is whether the homeowner measured **Dryer** without error. Assume the homeowner correctly recorded the number of times the dryer was used each day.

In JMP, the options under **Fit Y by X** in the JMP Starter window allow for a single **Y** variable and a single **X** variable. (This is also true when choosing **Fit Y by X** from the **Analyze** menu choice.) Multiple regression involves multiple *x* variables, so these choices are not appropriate. In JMP, the **Fit Model** platform is appropriate for multiple regression. This is a powerful platform that provides both simple and complex tools for regression analyses. This chapter discusses the basic aspects of multiple regression. Chapter 11 discusses using the **Fit Model** platform to perform regression diagnostics. The references in "Further Reading" provide recommendations for guidance on using the more complex tools in **Fit Model**.

To perform multiple regression for the Energy data in JMP:

1. Open the Energy data table.

2. Click **Analyze→Fit Model** from the menu. (In the JMP Starter window, click **Model→Fit Model**.) Either way, JMP displays exactly the same window.

3. Click **Kilowatt-hours→Y**.

4. Click and drag to select **AC** and **Dryer** and click **Add** in the Construct Model Effects area.

5. Click the menu for **Emphasis** and select **Minimal Report**. Compare your window with Figure 10.20.

6. Click **Run Model**.

For most other analyses in JMP, you click **OK** and JMP closes the window where you specify the options for analysis. With the Fit Model window, you click **Run Model** instead, and JMP leaves the Fit Model window open. This is useful for more advanced analyses, where you might want to change the aspects of how the model is fit, change the variables in the model, and so on. This example no longer requires the Fit Model window. Click the **X** in the upper-right corner to close the window.

Figure 10.20 Specifying the Multiple Regression Model for the Energy Data

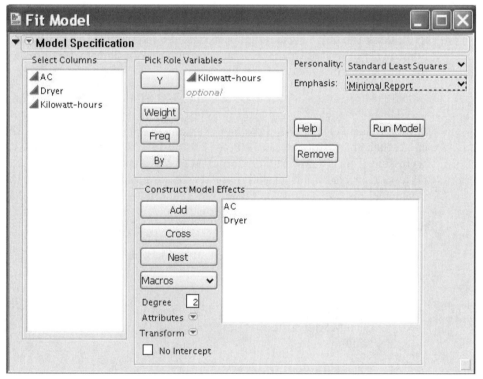

Figure 10.21 displays the results.

Figure 10.21 Multiple Regression Results for Energy Data

Response Kilowatt-hours

Summary of Fit

RSquare	0.970897
RSquare Adj	0.967663
Root Mean Square Error	3.93538
Mean of Response	64.85714
Observations (or Sum Wgts)	21

Analysis of Variance

Source	DF	Sum of Squares	Mean Square	F Ratio
Model	2	9299.8015	4649.90	300.2412
Error	18	278.7699	15.49	Prob > F
C. Total	20	9578.5714		<.0001*

Lack Of Fit

Source	DF	Sum of Squares	Mean Square	F Ratio
Lack Of Fit	14	211.26989	15.0907	0.8943
Pure Error	4	67.50000	16.8750	Prob > F
Total Error	18	278.76989		0.6130
				Max RSq
				0.9930

Parameter Estimates

Term	Estimate	Std Error	t Ratio	Prob>|t|
Intercept	8.1053853	2.480851	3.27	0.0043*
AC	5.4659032	0.280755	19.47	<.0001*
Dryer	13.2166	0.856219	15.44	<.0001*

Effect Tests

Effect Details

Understanding Results for Multiple Regression

Finding the Regression Equation

From the Parameter Estimates report in Figure 10.21, the fitted equation is:

Kilowatt-hours = 8.11 + 5.47*AC + 13.22*Dryer

The equation rounds the JMP equation to two decimal places. Interpret the coefficients as follows:

- The intercept is 8.11. It estimates the number of Kilowatt-hours that were consumed on days when neither the air conditioner nor the dryer was used.

- The second term in the equation, **5.47*AC**, indicates that the air conditioner uses 5.47 Kilowatt-hours of energy an hour.

- The third term in the equation, **13.22*Dryer**, indicates that each dryer load uses 13.22 Kilowatt-hours of energy.

You can specify values for **AC** and **Dryer** and use the regression equation to predict the **Kilowatt-hours** that are consumed.

JMP Hints:

The order of regressors does not matter in the Fit Model window for the models discussed in this chapter. JMP gives the same results whether you specify **AC** and then **Dryer**, or whether you specify **Dryer and** then **AC**. When you click to select and then drag and drop to add terms to the model, JMP uses the order of the variables in the data table.

To display the equation, click the hot spot for Response Kilowatt-hours, and select **Estimate→Show Prediction Expression**. JMP adds the Prediction Expression report, which displays the fitted equation.

Testing for Significance of Parameters

From the Parameter Estimates report in Figure 10.21, you conclude that all three coefficients are significantly different from 0. All three p-values are less than 0.05. The values for **AC** and **Dryer** are both **<.0001**. These values provide overwhelming evidence of the significant effect of these variables on the Kilowatt-hours that are consumed. The p-value for the intercept is **0.0043**. This value provides evidence that a significant (non-0) number of Kilowatt-hours are consumed even when neither the air conditioner nor the dryer is used.

A significant regressor in multiple regression indicates that the variation explained by the regressor is significantly larger than the random variation in the data. For the Energy data, the electricity consumed by the **AC** and **Dryer** is significantly larger than the random variation. Suppose the homeowner measured the number of times a small appliance, such as a coffee maker, was used. The amount of electricity the coffee maker uses is so small that it would probably not be detected. If you added **Coffeemaker** to the model, you would probably find a large *p*-value, indicating that the coffee maker is not a significant source of variation.

Checking the Fit of the Model

In Figure 10.21, the Summary of Fit report shows **RSquare** is about 0.97, indicating that the fitted curve explains about 97% of the variation in the data. This is an excellent fit. Compare this fit with the **RSquare** of 0.59 in Figure 10.10, for the model that contained only **AC**. Adding **Dryer** to the model significantly improved the fit.

The Analysis of Variance report leads you to conclude that the fitted model with **AC** and **Dryer** as regressors explains a significant amount of the variation in **Kilowatt-hours**. The *p*-value for the *F* test is <0.0001. Statisticians typically examine the overall test of the fitted model before reviewing the details of parameter estimates.

JMP automatically displays the Lack Of Fit report. Chapter 11 discusses this report in the context of regression diagnostics.

Saving Predicted Values and Confidence Intervals

You can manually use the equation to predict other values, or you can let JMP save the predictions. You can save the confidence limits on the mean and the confidence limits on individual predicted values. In JMP:

1. Hold down the ALT key and click the hot spot for Response Kilowatt-hours.

2. Select **Predicted Values, Mean Confidence Interval,** and **Indiv Confidence Interval**. These options are in the third column. Compare your window with Figure 10.22. (This figure highlights the many options that are available in **Fit Model**. See "Further Reading" for references that explain these options in detail.)

3. Click **OK**.

Figure 10.22 Options in Multiple Regression

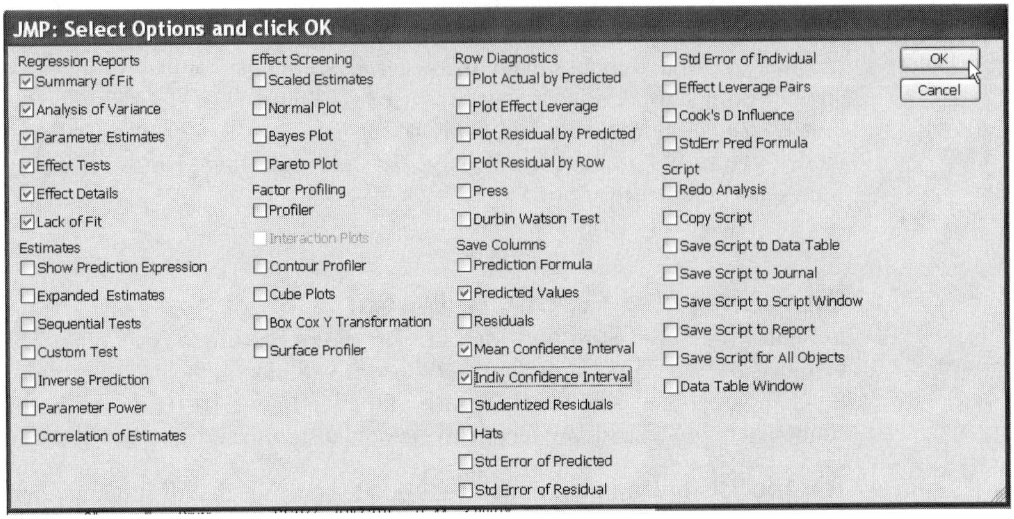

JMP Hint:

Holding down the ALT key and clicking the hot spot is a faster way to save multiple columns at once. For saving only a single column, such as predicted values, click the hot spot, and select the column to save.

Figure 10.23 shows the first 10 rows of the **Energy** data table, with the new columns at the right.

Figure 10.23 Energy Data with Saved Results from Multiple Regression

	AC	Dryer	Kilowatt-hours	Predicted Kilowatt-hours	Lower 95% Mean Kilowatt-hours	Upper 95% Mean Kilowatt-hours	Lower 95% Indiv Kilowatt-hours	Upper 95% Indiv Kilowatt-hours
1	1.5	1	35	29.5208398	25.7466366	33.2950429	20.4322084	38.6094711
2	4.5	2	63	59.1351491	56.629364	61.6409342	50.4958453	67.7744528
3	5	2	66	61.8681007	59.5147073	64.221494	53.2717602	70.4644412
4	2	0	17	19.0371918	14.7081625	23.3662211	9.70450166	28.3698819
5	8.5	3	94	94.2153616	90.7145272	97.716196	85.2368065	103.193917
6	6	3	79	80.5506035	77.1658475	83.9353595	71.6166691	89.4845379

Summarizing Multiple Regression

Multiple regression involves two or more independent variables to estimate the dependent variable. The same assumptions for fitting a straight line or fitting a curve and the same analysis steps apply. JMP provides a different platform for multiple regression, which has many advanced features. You can save predicted values, confidence limits on the mean, and prediction limits to the data table.

After you fit the multiple regression, the next step is to perform diagnostics to check the fit of your model. Chapter 11 discusses a set of basic tools for regression diagnostics. Usually, the process of fitting a model is an iterative one. First, you fit a model, and then you look at the fit, revise the fit according to what you have learned from the tools, look at the revised fit, and so on.

Summaries

Key Ideas

- Scatterplots show the relationship between two variables. A scatterplot matrix shows multiple relationships between pairs of variables.

- The Pearson correlation coefficient, r, measures the strength of the relationship between two variables. However, it does not describe the form of the relationship, and it does not show that one of the variables causes the other.

- Regression analysis describes relationships between variables. The simplest model fits a straight line that relates one dependent variable (y) to one independent variable (x). Fitting a curve relates one y variable to an x variable and the square of x. Multiple regression relates one y variable to two or more x variables.

- Least squares regression provides the best-fitting models. Here "best-fitting" means that the fitted model minimizes the sum of squared differences between the data points and the fitted line, fitted curve, or multidimensional plane.

- Once regression analysis has been performed, use the fitted equation to predict future values at a given value of the independent variable.

- Prediction limits, or confidence limits for individual values, put bounds around a future value.

- Confidence limits for the mean put limits around the mean value of the dependent variable at a given value of the independent variable.

- Plots of the actual data points, regression equation, and prediction or confidence limits are useful in seeing how the regression equation fits the data.

- Regression analysis and regression diagnostics are intertwined. First, fit a model. Next, perform diagnostics to assess how well the model fits. Then, fit another model, and repeat the process as needed.

- Using the **Bivariate** platform is the simplest way to fit a straight line or a curve to data. For multiple regression, use the **Fit Model** platform. The results from both platforms perform a test for overall significance of the model, provide parameter estimates and significance tests for the estimates, and provide the R-Square statistic. Both platforms provide features for saving predicted values and confidence limits on the mean and on predicted values.

JMP Steps

To create a scatterplot matrix and Correlations report for two or more continuous variables:

1. In the JMP Starter window, click **Multivariate→Multivariate**.

2. Click variables and then **Y, Columns**.

3. Click **OK**.

To enhance the scatterplot matrix:

1. Click the hot spot for Scatterplot Matrix.

2. Select **Ellipse α→90**. JMP updates the scatterplot matrix to show 90% density ellipses. Click other values to change the density ellipses.

3. Click the hot spot again, select **Ellipse Color**, and select a color from the palette. JMP updates the scatterplot matrix with the new color.

4. Click the hot spot again and select **Density Ellipses** to remove them.

5. Click the **Lasso** tool on the toolbar. Click and drag a circle around interesting points in a scatterplot. JMP highlights the points in every scatterplot in the matrix and in the data table.

6. Right-click in one of the scatterplots, select **Row Colors**, and select a color from the palette. JMP colors the point in every scatterplot in the matrix.

7. Right-click in one of the scatterplots again, select **Row Markers**, and select a different marker from the palette. JMP updates the point in every scatterplot in the matrix.

To enhance the multivariate reports:

1. Click the hot spot for Multivariate.

2. Click **Simple Statistics→Univariate Simple Statistics**. JMP adds statistics for each variable.

3. Click the hot spot and select **Simple Statistics→Multivariate Simple Statistics**. JMP adds statistics for each variable for only those rows where all variables are non-missing.

4. Click the hot spot and select **Pairwise Correlations**. JMP uses all possible non-missing values to calculate pairwise correlation coefficients.

5. Right-click in the Pairwise Correlations report and select **Columns→Plot Corr** to remove the plot of pairwise correlation coefficients.

To fit a straight line to data:

1. In the JMP Starter window, click **Basic→Bivariate**.

2. Click the response variable and then **Y, Response**.

3. Click the independent (regressor) variable and then **X, Regressor**.

4. Click **OK**. JMP creates a scatterplot.

5. Click the hot spot for Bivariate Fit.

6. Select **Fit Line**.

To fit a quadratic curve to data:

1. In the JMP Starter window, click **Basic→Bivariate**.

2. Click the response variable and then **Y, Response**.

3. Click the independent (regressor) variable and then **X, Regressor**.

4. Click **OK**. JMP creates a scatterplot.

5. Click the hot spot for Bivariate Fit.

6. Click **Fit Special**.

7. Click the menu for **Degree** and select **2 Quadratic**.

8. Clear the check box for **Centered Polynomial** so that it is deselected.

9. Click **OK**.

Saving predicted values for regression to fit a straight line or a curve:

1. Click the hot spot next to the line (labeled **Linear Fit** for a line or **Polynomial Fit Degree=2** for a curve).

2. Select **Save Predicteds**. JMP saves the predicted values to a new column in the data table.

Enhancing plots and reports for regression to fit a straight line or a curve:

1. Hold down the ALT key and click the hot spot next to the line (labeled **Linear Fit** for a line and **Polynomial Fit Degree=2** for a curve).

2. Select **Confid Curves Indiv**. JMP adds the confidence limits on individual predicted values (prediction limits) to the scatterplot.

3. Select **Confid Shaded Indiv**. JMP shades the area inside the prediction limits.

4. Select **Confid Curves Mean**. JMP adds confidence limits for the mean to the scatterplot.

5. Select **Confid Shaded Mean**. JMP shades the area inside the confidence limits for the mean.

6. Click **OK**.

To fit a multiple regression model:

1. Click **Analyze→Fit Model** from the menu.

2. Click the response variable and then **Y**.

3. Click and drag to select the regressor variables and click **Add** in the Construct Model Effects area.

4. Click the menu for **Emphasis** and select **Minimal Report**.

5. Click **Run Model**.

6. Click the **X** in the upper-right corner to close the window.

Saving predicted values and confidence intervals for multiple regression:

1. Hold down the ALT key and click the hot spot for the response variable. JMP titles this hot spot with the word **Response** and then the name of the variable.

2. Select **Predicted Values**. JMP adds a new column with the predicted values to the data table.

3. Select **Mean Confidence Interval**. JMP adds two new columns with the upper and lower prediction limits to the data table.

4. Select **Indiv Confidence Interval**. JMP adds two new columns with the upper and lower confidence limits on the predicted values to the data table.

5. Click **OK**.

Exercises

1. Fit a straight-line model to the Engine data. Add confidence limits for the mean and prediction limits. Discuss the results and compare them with the results for the fitted curve.

2. From the Sample Data Directory, click the disclosure diamond for Multivariate Analysis and open the Body Measurements data table. Create a scatterplot matrix of **Mass**, **Waist**, **Height**, and **Thigh**. Discuss the correlation coefficients, focusing on the correlations between **Mass** and the other variables.

3. With the Body Measurements data, fit a straight line with **Mass** as the response variable and **Waist** as the regressor variable. Discuss the results, including whether the assumptions for regression are reasonable.

4. From the Sample Data Directory, click the disclosure diamond for Exploratory Modeling and open the Cars 1993 data table. Create a scatterplot matrix of **Maximum Price ($1000)**, **Maximum Horsepower**, **Highway Mileage (MPG)**, and **Luggage Capacity (cu. ft.)**. Discuss the correlation coefficients, focusing on the correlations between **Maximum Price ($1000)** and the other variables.

5. With the Cars 1993 data, fit a straight line with **Maximum Price ($1000)** as the response variable and **Maximum Horsepower** as the regressor. Add

prediction limits and confidence limits for the mean. Discuss the results, including whether the assumptions for regression are reasonable.

6. From the Sample Data Directory, click the disclosure diamond for Business and Demographics and open the Grandfather Clocks data table. Fit a straight line with **Price** as the response variable and **Age** as the regressor variable. Add prediction limits and confidence limits for the mean. Discuss the results, including whether the assumptions for regression are reasonable.

7. From the Sample Data Directory, click the disclosure diamond for Sciences and open the Sleeping Animals data table. Create a scatterplot matrix of **Total Sleep**, **Gestation**, **Lifespan**, and **Danger**. Discuss the correlation coefficients, focusing on the correlations between **Total Sleep** and the other variables.

8. With the Sleeping Animals data, fit a straight line with **Total Sleep** as the response variable and **Gestation** as the regressor. Add prediction limits and confidence limits for the mean. Discuss the results, including whether the assumptions for regression are reasonable.

9. From the Sample Data Directory, click the disclosure diamond for Regression and open the Anscomb data table. Create a scatterplot for **Y2** and **X2**. Use **Bivariate** to fit an appropriate model. Add prediction limits and confidence limits for the mean. Discuss the results, including whether the assumptions for regression are reasonable.

10. From the Sample Data Directory, click the disclosure diamond for Sciences and open the Pendulum data table. Create a scatterplot for **Length** and **Period**. Use **Bivariate** to fit an appropriate model, with **Length** as the response variable. Add prediction limits and confidence limits for the mean. Discuss the results, including whether the assumptions for regression are reasonable.

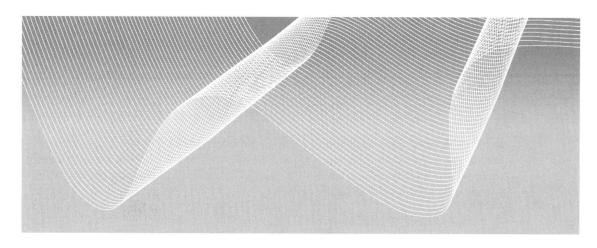

Chapter 11

Basic Regression Diagnostics

How do you determine whether your regression model adequately represents your data? How do you know when more terms should be added to the model? How do you identify outlier points, where the model doesn't fit well? These questions can be answered using regression diagnostics. This chapter discusses:

- understanding residuals plots

- using residuals plots and lack of fit tests to decide whether to add terms to the model

- using residuals plots to identify outlier points

- using residuals plots to detect a time sequence in the data

Chapters 10 and 11 discuss the activities of regression analysis and regression diagnostics. Fitting a regression model and performing diagnostics are intertwined. In regression, you first fit a model. You then perform diagnostics to assess how well the model fits. You repeat this process until you find a suitable model. Chapter 10 focused on fitting models, and this chapter focuses on performing diagnostics.

Concepts in Plotting Residuals

A regression model fits an equation to an observed set of data points. Chapter 10 showed how to use the equation to get predicted values. The differences between the observed and predicted values are *residuals* (residual=observed–predicted). Residuals can help show you if your model fits the data well. The next four topics discuss plots using residuals. All plots use residuals on the *y*-axis. Statisticians often refer to this group of plots as *residuals plots*.

Plotting Residuals against Predicted Values

A plot of residuals against predicted values should look like a random scattering of points, or a horizontal band. If your model needs another term, then a plot of residuals can suggest what type of term should be added to the model. Figure 11.1 shows some possible patterns in the plots.

Figure 11.1 Possible Patterns in Plots of Residuals

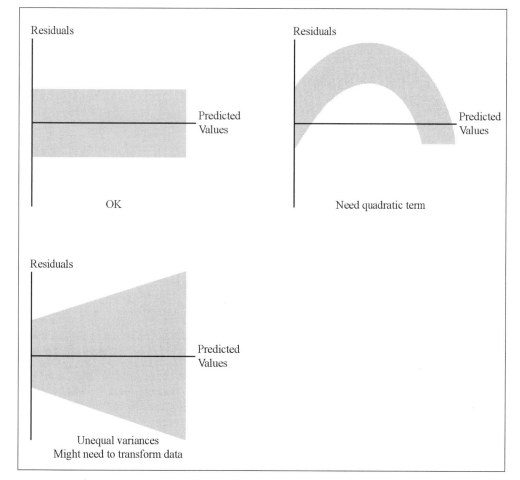

Residuals, Predicted Values, and Outlier Points

A plot of residuals against predicted values sometimes looks like a horizontal band, with the exception of one or two points. Figure 11.2 shows an example of a possible outlier point. All points except for one point fall in the random pattern indicated by the gray horizontal band.

A large residual occurs when the predicted value is substantially different from the observed value. The meaning of "large" refers to the absolute value of the residual, because residuals can be either positive or negative. Observations with large residuals are possible outlier points. As with possible outlier points in the data, you need to investigate the residuals further. The possible outlier point might simply be due to chance, or it might be due to a special cause.

Figure 11.2 Residuals Plot Showing Pattern for a Possible Outlier Point

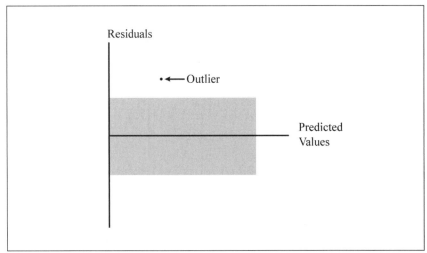

Plotting Residuals against Independent Variables

Plotting residuals against independent variables (*x* variables or regressors) helps show whether the model fits the data well. For a good-fitting model, plots of residuals against regressors show a random scattering of points.

Plots that show an obvious pattern indicate that another term needs to be added to the model. A curved pattern indicates that a quadratic term needs to be added to the model. A plot with a definite increasing or decreasing trend indicates that a regressor variable needs to be added to the model. For multiple regression, plot the residuals against regressor variables in the model, and against independent variables not in the model.

Plotting Residuals in Time Sequence

When data is collected all at once, a time sequence is unlikely. For example, the homebuyer collected the **Mortgage** data (in Chapter 7) in a single day. Typically, data is collected over time. This is especially true for data used in regression. For the **Energy** data, the homeowner collected data over 21 days. For the **Engine** data, the engineer measured **Power** and **Speed** for 24 data points. When data is collected over time, the conditions that change over time might impact the model.

For data without a measurable time trend, the plot of residuals against the time sequence in which the data was collected shows a random pattern of points. For data with a measurable time trend, the plot often shows an up-and-down, or wavy, pattern. Figure 11.3 shows an example.

Here, the main focus is the relationship between dependent and regressor variables. You are not focused on time as a regressor, but you are checking for a possible time sequence effect. In contrast, suppose you are interested in modeling changes in the stock market over the past five years. In that case, time is a regressor variable, and more advanced statistical techniques are required.

Figure 11.3 Residuals Plot Showing Pattern for a Time Trend

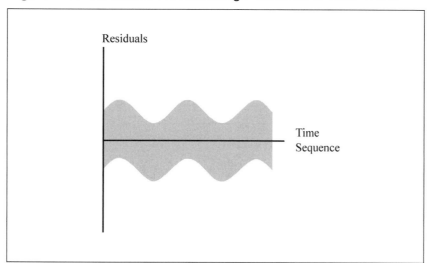

Creating Residuals Plots for the Energy Data

Chapter 10 discussed the straight line and multiple regression fits for the Energy data. This section shows the residuals plots for the straight-line model, and then shows the plots for the multiple regression model.

Residuals Plots for Straight-Line Regression

Chapter 10 used **Bivariate** to fit a straight line to the **Energy** data, and created the results in Figure 10.10. In this topic, the JMP steps start after this figure is created. (Refer to "Fitting a Straight Line Using JMP" in Chapter 10 for the steps to create Figure 10.10.)

Plotting Residuals against Independent Variables

To check the fit of the straight-line model, plot the residuals against both the variable in the model (**AC**) and the variable not in the model (**Dryer**). In JMP:

1. Click the hot spot next to the line labeled **Linear Fit**.

2. Select **Plot Residuals**. JMP adds a plot of **Residual by AC** to the **Parameter Estimates** report.

Figure 11.4 shows the plot.

Figure 11.4 Residual by AC for the Straight-Line Model

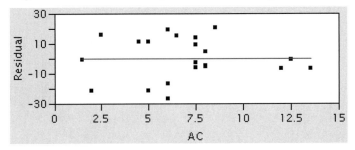

Figure 11.4 shows a random scatter of points, indicating that no additional term for **AC** is needed.

To plot the residuals against variables not in the model, first, save the residuals to the data table. Then, use the **Graph** platform to create the plot. Continuing in JMP:

3. Click the hot spot next to the line labeled **Linear Fit**.

4. Select **Save Residuals**. JMP adds the **Residuals Kilowatt-hours** column to the data table. The next display shows the first few rows of the data table.

	AC	Dryer	Kilowatt-hours	Residuals Kilowatt-hours
1	1.5	1	35	-0.8626952
2	4.5	2	63	11.1140574
3	5	2	66	11.4435162
4	2	0	17	-21.533236
5	8.5	3	94	20.7497276

5. Click **Graph→Overlay Plot** in the JMP menu bar.

6. Click **Residuals Kilowatt-hours** and then **Y**.

7. Click **Dryer** and then **X**. Compare your window with the following window.

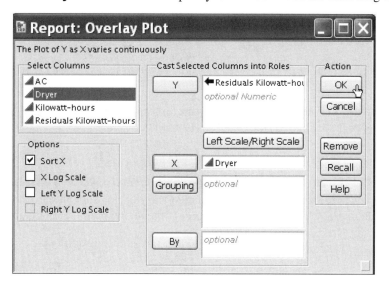

8. Click **OK**.

Figure 11.5 shows the plot.

Figure 11.5 Residuals by Dryer for the Straight-Line Model

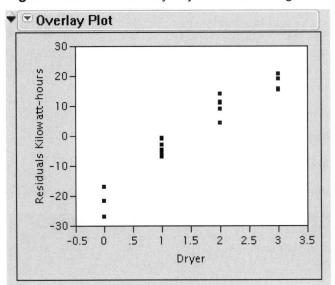

Figure 11.5 shows a definite increase in residuals with an increase in Dryer. This pattern sends a message to add Dryer to the model.

Plotting Residuals against Predicted Values

To plot the residuals against predicted values, first, save the predicted values to the data table. Then, use the Graph platform to create the plot. Continuing in JMP:

9. Click the hot spot next to the line labeled Linear Fit.

10. Select **Save Predicteds**. JMP adds the Predicted Kilowatt-hours column to the data table. The next display shows the first few rows of the data table.

	AC	Dryer	Kilowatt-hours	Residuals Kilowatt-hours	Predicted Kilowatt-hours
1	1.5	1	35	-0.8626952	35.8626952
2	4.5	2	63	11.1140574	51.8859426
3	5	2	66	11.4435162	54.5564838
4	2	0	17	-21.533236	38.5332365

11. Click **Graph→Overlay Plot** in the JMP menu bar.

12. Click **Residuals Kilowatt-hours** and then **Y**.

13. Click **Predicted Kilowatt-hours** and then **X**. Compare your window with the following window.

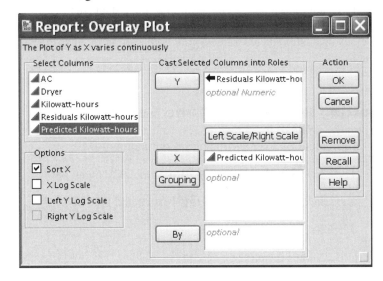

14. Click **OK**.

Figure 11.6 shows the plot.

Figure 11.6 Residuals by Predicted Values for the Straight-Line Model

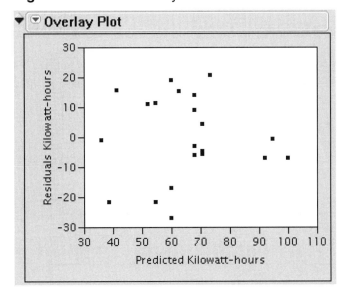

The points in Figure 11.6 appear in a horizontal band, with no obvious outlier points. This plot indicates that the model fits the data reasonably well. From Chapter 10, the model explains about 59% of the variation in the data (see Figure 10.10). This shows why looking at more than one residuals plot is important. If you looked at only the plot of residuals against predicted values, you would probably miss the need to add Dryer to the model.

Plotting Residuals in Time Sequence

To plot the residuals in time sequence, first, save the residuals to the data table. Then, use the Graph platform to create the plot. Continuing in JMP:

15. Click **Graph→Overlay Plot** in the JMP menu bar.

16. Click **Residuals Kilowatt-hours** and then **Y**.

17. Click **OK**.

Figure 11.7 shows the plot.

> **JMP Hint:**
>
> When Graph→Overlay has only a Y variable, JMP plots the data points in the order they appear in the data table. When the data is sorted in time sequence, creating the residuals plot against time requires only a Y variable. When the data is not sorted in time sequence, use the appropriate time sequence variable for X.

Figure 11.7 Residuals in Time Sequence for the Straight-Line Model

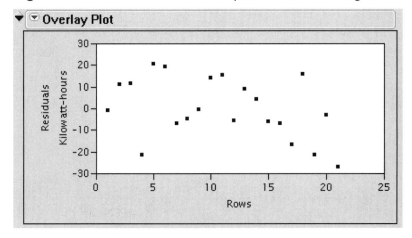

The points in Figure 11.7 appear in a horizontal band. Some people see a slightly curved pattern, indicating a possible time sequence effect. Looking carefully at the data in Table 10.1, notice that the days with the lowest air conditioner use are at the beginning and end of the 21-day period. Perhaps this is due to cooler days, or to the homeowner's knowledge that data was being collected, or to something else. This example shows the subjective nature of residuals plots. When the message is weak, the plots are more subjective than when the message is strong. Look at Figure 11.5 again. The message to add Dryer to the model is obvious from the plot because it's a strong message.

Summarizing Residuals Plots for the Straight-Line Model

For the straight-line model, residuals plotted against AC show that no additional term for AC is needed. Plotting residuals against Dryer shows a definite increasing pattern, which sends a message to add Dryer to the model. Plotting residuals against predicted values shows a random pattern, indicating an adequate model. Plotting residuals in time sequence indicates no obvious pattern.

Residuals Plots for Multiple Regression

Chapter 10 used Fit Model for multiple regression with the Energy data, and created the results in Figure 10.21. In this topic, the JMP steps start after this figure is created. (Refer to "Fitting Multiple Regression Models in JMP" in Chapter 10 for the steps to create Figure 10.21.)

Plotting Residuals against the Independent Variables

To check the fit of the model, plot the residuals against the variables in the model (AC and Dryer). First, save the residuals to the data table. Then, use the Graph platform to create the plot. Use the same approach for independent variables in the model and for other independent variables that are not included in the model. In JMP:

1. Click the hot spot for Response Kilowatt-hours.

2. Select **Save Columns→Residuals**.

   JMP adds the Residual Kilowatt-hours column to the data table. The window shows the first few rows of the data table.

	AC	Dryer	Kilowatt-hours	Residuals Kilowatt-hours	Predicted Kilowatt-hours	Residual Kilowatt-hours
1	1.5	1	35	-0.8626952	35.8626952	5.47916022
2	4.5	2	63	11.1140574	51.8859426	3.86485092
3	5	2	66	11.4435162	54.5564838	4.13189931

JMP uses a different name for residuals that are saved from **Bivariate** and for residuals that are saved from **Fit Model**. For Fit Model, JMP starts the name of the new column with **Residual**, instead of **Residuals**. Because this subtle difference might cause confusion, rename the column.

3. Right-click on the **Residual Kilowatt-hours** column in the columns panel.

4. Select **Column Info**. JMP displays information about the column.

5. Enter **Residual KWH Multiple** in the Column Name field, as shown in the window.

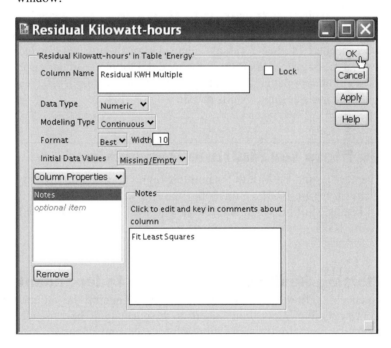

6. Click **OK** to close the window. The following window shows the first few rows of the data table with the renamed column.

	AC	Dryer	Kilowatt-hours	Residuals Kilowatt-hours	Predicted Kilowatt-hours	Residual KWH Multiple
1	1.5	1	35	-0.8626952	35.8626952	5.47916022
2	4.5	2	63	11.1140574	51.8859426	3.86485092
3	5	2	66	11.4435162	54.5564838	4.13189931

7. Click **Graph→Overlay Plot** in the JMP menu bar.

8. Click **Residual KWH Multiple** and then **Y**.

9. Click **AC** and then **X**.

10. Click **OK**.

Figure 11.8 shows the plot.

Figure 11.8 Residuals by AC for Multiple Regression

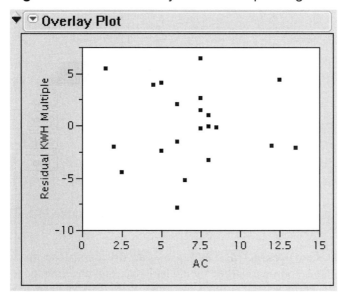

Figure 11.8 shows a random pattern. No additional term for AC (such as a quadratic term) is needed.

Continuing in JMP:

11. Click **Graph→Overlay Plot** in the JMP menu bar.

12. Click **Residual KWH Multiple** and then **Y**.

13. Click **Dryer** and then **X**.

14. Click **OK**.

Figure 11.9 shows the plot.

Figure 11.9 Residuals by Dryer for Multiple Regression

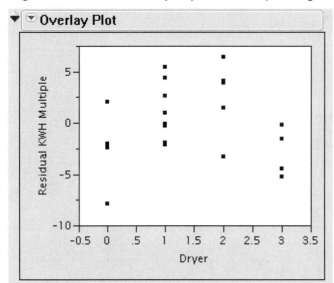

Figure 11.9 shows a curved pattern. Compare this pattern with Figure 11.1. The curvature in the plot indicates a need for a quadratic term for Dryer.

These results might seem unexpected. If each use of the dryer consumes the same amount of electricity, then the response to Dryer should be linear, and no quadratic term should be needed for Dryer. Perhaps smaller loads of clothes were dried on days when several loads were washed, requiring less electricity per load on these days. See the exercises at the end of the chapter to explore the impact of adding a quadratic term for Dryer to the model.

Plotting Residuals against Predicted Values

To plot residuals against predicted values, you could use the same approach that you used for the straight-line model: first, save the predicted values to the data table, and then use the Graph platform to create the plot. However, Fit Model provides a quicker way. Continuing in JMP:

15. Click the hot spot for Response Kilowatt-hours.

16. Select **Row Diagnostics→Plot Residual by Predicted**.

Figure 11.10 shows the plot.

Figure 11.10 Residuals by Predicted Values for Multiple Regression

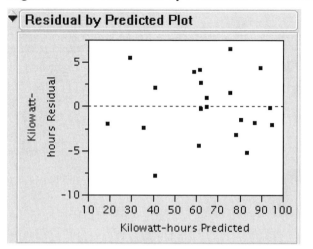

The points in Figure 11.10 appear in a horizontal band, with no obvious outlier points. This plot indicates that the model fits the data well.

JMP Hint:

Position your mouse pointer over the options in Row Diagnostics. JMP gives a summary of the benefits of the plot, and what to look for in a model that fits the data well.

Plotting Residuals in Time Sequence

To plot residuals against a time sequence, you could use the same approach that you used for the straight-line model: first, save the residuals to the data table, and then use the Graph platform to create the plot. However, Fit Model provides a quicker way. Continuing in JMP:

17. Click the hot spot for Response Kilowatt-hours.

18. Select **Row Diagnostics→Plot Residual by Row**.

Figure 11.11 shows the plot.

Figure 11.11 Residuals in Time Sequence for Multiple Regression

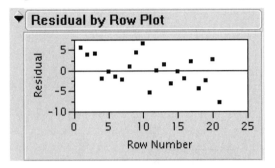

The points in Figure 11.11 appear in a horizontal band. Some people see a slightly decreasing trend. This trend indicates that the use of electricity might have decreased slightly with time. Perhaps the homeowner's overall use of electricity was affected by the knowledge that data was being collected. Or, perhaps the days near the end of the experiment were cooler, and the air conditioner was used less. Just as with your own data, the true answers to these questions might be unknown, or careful sleuthing might reveal a cause for the time sequence effect.

Summarizing Residuals Plots for Multiple Regression

For the multiple regression model, plotting residuals against AC shows a horizontal band, indicating that there is no need for a quadratic term. Plotting residuals against Dryer indicates the possible need for a quadratic term. Plotting residuals by predicted values shows a horizontal band, indicating that the model fits the data well and that no obvious outlier points exist. Plotting the residuals in time sequence might show a slight time sequence effect in the data. This might be due to either a cooling trend during the time the data was collected, or to some other cause, such as the homeowner's knowledge that the use of electricity was being monitored.

> **JMP Hint:**
>
> Saving the data table with the new variables is a good idea because you can recreate plots in a later JMP session without doing the analyses again. The sample data for the book includes the Energy data with saved residuals and predicted values from both the straight-line and multiple regression fits. This data table is named Energy_Ch11.

Creating Residuals Plots for the Engine Data

Chapter 10 discussed fitting a curve to the Engine data. Suppose the engineer didn't see the slight curvature in the scatterplot, and fit a straight line to the data. The residuals plots would help show that the model needed more terms. The next two topics show the plots for fitting a straight line and for fitting a curve.

Residuals Plots for Straight-Line Regression

Chapter 10 did not fit a straight line to the Engine data. However, one of the exercises involved fitting a straight line and discussing the results. Figure 11.12 shows the results of a straight-line regression for the Engine data. To generate these results, follow the JMP steps for fitting a straight line (provided in Chapter 10 for the Energy data). Substitute Power as the *y* variable and Speed as the *x* variable.

Figure 11.12 Straight-Line Regression Results for Engine Data

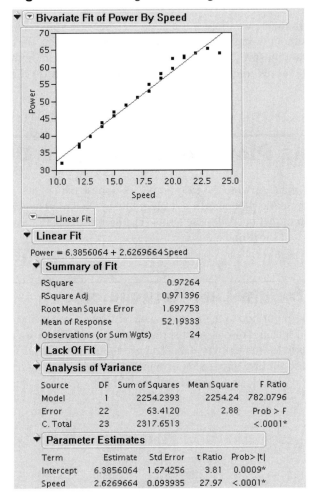

Briefly, the model is significant, and both the intercept and slope parameters are significantly different from 0. The model fits the data quite well, explaining over 97% of the variation in the data.

In the scatterplot, points near both ends of the line appear below the fitted line. Points in the middle appear above the fitted line. This subtle curvature is an indication that a quadratic term needs to be added to the model. Because the amount of curvature in the data is small, the indication is subtle. However, with a more dramatic curvature, this type of plot would clearly show that a quadratic term needs to be added the model. The residuals plots can provide a clearer picture of what needs to happen in the next steps.

Plotting Residuals against the Independent Variable

The model has only one independent variable. Following similar JMP steps as the steps for the Energy data, plotting residuals against Speed creates Figure 11.13.

Figure 11.13 Residuals by Speed for Straight-Line Fit to Engine Data

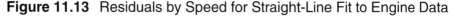
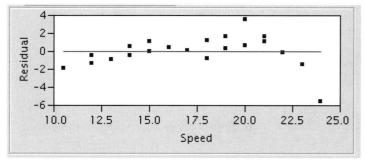

Figure 11.13 shows curvature. It starts on the left with negative values, changes to positive values, and reverts to negative values. This pattern indicates that a quadratic term needs to be added to the model.

Plotting Residuals against Predicted Values

To plot residuals against predicted values, first, save both the residuals and predicted values to the data table. Then, use the Graph platform to create the plot. Follow similar JMP steps as the steps for the Energy data, and create Figure 11.14.

Figure 11.14 Residuals by Predicted Values for Straight-Line Fit to Engine Data

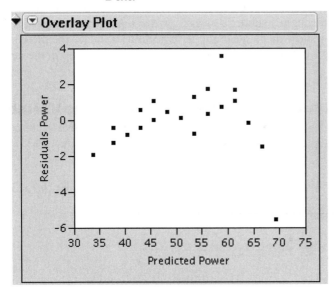

Figure 11.14 shows a much more obvious curvature than Figure 11.13. This pattern reinforces that a quadratic term for **Speed** needs to be added to the model.

Plotting Residuals in Time Sequence

To plot residuals against a time sequence, use the **Graph** platform and the saved residuals. Follow similar JMP steps as the steps for the **Energy** data, and create Figure 11.15.

Figure 11.15 Residuals in Time Sequence for Straight-Line Model for Engine Data

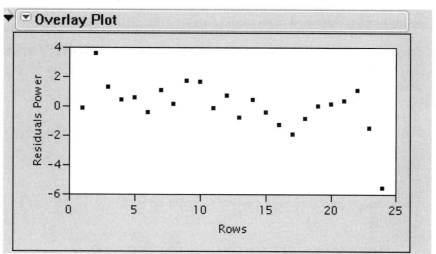

Figure 11.15 shows a wavy pattern similar to what was depicted in Figure 11.3. The wavy pattern is more obvious toward the end of the time period. This plot sends a message to add a term to the model.

Summarizing Residuals Plots for Straight-Line Fit

For the straight-line model, the scatterplot of the data with the regression line gives a subtle signal that a quadratic term for Speed needs to be added to the model. Plotting the residuals against Speed strengthens the signal. Plotting the residuals against predicted values strengthens the signal even more. Plotting the residuals in time sequence also indicates that the model needs another term.

The residuals plots all lead to the same conclusion—add a quadratic term to the model.

Residuals Plots for Fitting a Curve

Chapter 10 fit a curve to the Engine data and created the results in Figure 10.17. The residuals plots discussed in this topic start after this figure is created.

Plotting Residuals against the Independent Variable

To plot the residuals against **Speed**, follow similar steps as the steps for the Energy data to create Figure 11.16.

Figure 11.16 Residuals by Speed for Fitting a Curve to the Engine Data

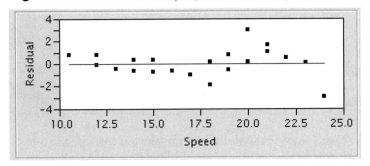

Figure 11.16 shows a horizontal band with two possible outlier points. The plot shows a point higher than the other points above **Speed** equal to 20, and a point much lower than the other points at **Speed** equal to 24. Because JMP is interactive, clicking on these points in the plot highlights the points. In JMP:

1. Right-click on the outlier point above **Speed** equal to 20. Select **Row Colors** and select a color from the palette. JMP colors the point.

2. Right-click on the outlier point again. Select **Row Markers** and select a different marker from the palette. Using different markers helps distinguish the selected points when using a gray scale printer. JMP changes the marker for the point.

3. Repeat these steps for the outlier point at **Speed** equal to 24.

Figure 11.17 shows the plot.

Figure 11.17 Highlighting Possible Outlier Points in Residuals by Speed Plot

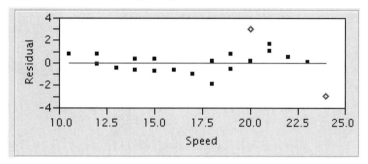

JMP shows the colors and markers for these two points in the data table. The next steps are to create other residuals plots to see whether they indicate possible outlier points.

Plotting Residuals against Predicted Values

To plot residuals against predicted values, first, save the residuals and predicted values to the data table. Then, use the **Graph** platform to create the plot shown in Figure 11.18.

Suppose you create residuals plots for the straight-line and quadratic fits in the same JMP session. JMP adds a "2" to the ends of the names of the second set of residuals and predicted values. To avoid confusion, change the name to clarify the fitted model. Figures 11.18 and 11.19 reflect renaming the residuals to **Residuals Power Curve** for the quadratic model. (Refer to the JMP steps in "Plotting Residuals against the Independent Variables" in "Residuals Plots for Multiple Regression" for saving and renaming residuals and predicted values.)

JMP Hint:

Saving the data table with the new variables is a good idea because you can recreate plots in a later JMP session without doing the analyses again. The sample data for the book includes the **Engine** data with saved residuals and predicted values from both the straight-line and quadratic regression fits. This data table is named **Engine_Ch11**.

Figure 11.18   Residuals by Predicted Values for Fitting a Curve to the Engine Data

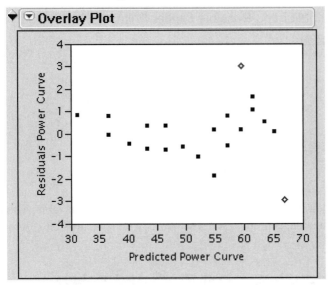

Figure 11.18 shows the benefits of highlighting points in one plot. JMP uses the highlighting in other plots. The points in Figure 11.18 form a rough horizontal band, except for the two possible outlier points shown as red diamonds. This plot sends the same message as the Residuals by Speed plot. Investigate the two possible outlier points.

Plotting Residuals in Time Sequence

To plot residuals in time sequence, first, save the residuals to the data table. (You might have already saved the residuals to create the plot of residuals against predicted values.) Then, use the Graph platform to create the plot shown in Figure 11.19.

Figure 11.19 Residuals in Time Sequence for Fitting a Curve to the Engine Data

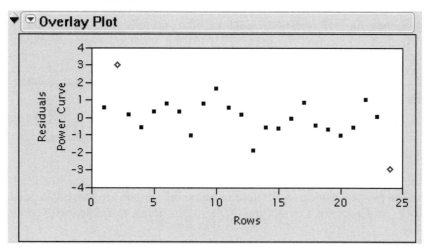

The points in Figure 11.19 form a rough horizontal band, except for the two possible outlier points shown as red diamonds. The large positive residual is the second point, and the large negative residual is the last point. This plot sends the same message as other residuals plots. Investigate the two possible outlier points.

Summarizing Residuals Plots for Fitting a Curve to the Engine Data

For the curved model, plotting residuals against Speed forms a mostly horizontal band, with two possible outlier points. Plotting residuals against predicted values has the same results. Plotting residuals against a time sequence reinforces these results. The plot doesn't show an overall time sequence effect, but it does show that one of the outlier points occurred near the beginning of the experiment, and the other outlier point occurred at the end of the experiment.

These results highlight the subjective nature of residuals plots. If you highlight the same potential outlier points for the straight-line fit, you might have different interpretations for those residuals plots. (See the exercise at the end of the chapter.)

Using the Lack Of Fit Report

In Chapter 10, JMP created the Lack Of Fit report for both the Bivariate and Fit Model platforms. This section discusses how to use the report as a tool in diagnosing models.

Concepts for Lack of Fit

Chapter 10 discussed the concepts for least squares regression, and explained how the variation in the data was separated into variation due to the model and variation due to error.

The error variation can be separated even further. When the data contains observations with the same x value and different y values, the variation in these data points is *pure error*. No matter what model you fit, these data points associated with pure error will still vary.

For example, Chapter 10 introduced this issue for the Energy data, which has three points with AC equal to 8. These three points have the same x value and different observed y values. The straight-line regression equation predicts the same y value for these three points.

Lack of fit tests are a statistical way of separating the error variation into pure error and *lack of fit* error. The null hypothesis for the lack of fit test is that the lack of fit error is 0. The alternative hypothesis is that the lack of fit error is different from 0. With a significant p-value, you conclude that the model has significant lack of fit, and other models should be investigated. Statisticians usually perform lack of fit tests with a reference probability of 0.05. This gives a 5% chance of incorrectly concluding that the model has significant lack of fit when, in fact, it does not.

Understanding Reports for the Energy Data

Straight-Line Regression

Figure 10.10 showed results of the straight-line regression for the Energy data, but hid the Lack Of Fit report. Figure 11.20 shows this report.

Figure 11.20 Lack Of Fit Report from Straight-Line Regression for Energy Data

Lack Of Fit				
Source	DF	Sum of Squares	Mean Square	F Ratio
Lack Of Fit	11	1920.0755	174.552	0.6816
Pure Error	8	2048.8333	256.104	Prob > F
Total Error	19	3968.9088		0.7281
				Max RSq
				0.7861

Find the value for **Prob > F**. This gives the *p*-value for the lack of fit test. Figure 11.20 shows a *p*-value of 0.7281. Because this value is greater than the reference probability of 0.05, you conclude that the model does not have significant lack of fit.

In general, to perform the lack of fit test at the 5% significance level, you conclude that the lack of fit is significant if the *p*-value is less than 0.05.

Look at the **Pure Error** row for **Source**. This shows 8 for the degrees of freedom (**DF**). Looking at the data table shows how these 8 degrees of freedom are derived:

AC Value	Number of Rows	Degrees of Freedom
5	2	1
6	3	2
7.5	4	3
3	8	2
		Total=8

For each case with duplicate values of the *x* variable, the degrees of freedom are one less than the number of duplicate rows. (Table 10.1 in Chapter 10 shows the **Energy** data.)

When looking at lack of fit results, check the degrees of freedom for pure error. The lack of fit test is less useful when the data has only a few duplicate *x* values. With only a few duplicate *x* values, the estimate for pure error is not as good as for data that has many duplicate *x* values. The straight-line fit to the **Energy** data has enough duplicate points.

For more details on the other items in the report, see the JMP Help or documentation.

From the **Lack Of Fit** report, you conclude that the model is adequate. This example shows why multiple diagnostics are important. If you review only this report, instead of the report and the residuals plots, you miss the need to add **Dryer** to the model.

Multiple Regression

Figure 10.21 showed results from multiple regression for the **Energy** data, and showed the **Lack Of Fit** report. Figure 11.21 shows this report.

Figure 11.21 Lack Of Fit Report from Multiple Regression for Energy Data

▼ **Lack Of Fit**				
Source	DF	Sum of Squares	Mean Square	F Ratio
Lack Of Fit	14	211.26989	15.0907	0.8943
Pure Error	4	67.50000	16.8750	Prob > F
Total Error	18	278.76989		0.6130
				Max RSq
				0.9930

Figure 11.21 shows a *p*-value of 0.6130. This value leads you to conclude that the model is adequate.

Look at the **Pure Error** row for **Source**. This shows 4 for the degrees of freedom (**DF**). Looking at the data table shows how these 4 degrees of freedom are derived:

AC Value	Dryer Value	Number of Rows	Degrees of Freedom
6	0	2	1
7.5	1	2	1
7.5	2	2	2
8	1	2	1
			Total=4

This might be a case where the data does not have enough duplicate *x* values. If this were a designed experiment instead of an observational study, the design could be improved by adding more duplicate *x* values.

JMP Hint:

JMP creates the **Lack Of Fit** report only when the data has duplicate *x* values. If your data has unique *x* values for every data point, JMP cannot create the report.

Understanding Reports for the Engine Data

Straight-Line Regression

Figure 11.12 showed results of the straight-line regression for the Engine data, but hid the Lack Of Fit report. Figure 11.22 shows this report.

Figure 11.22 Lack Of Fit Report from Straight-Line Regression for Engine Data

▼ **Lack Of Fit**

Source	DF	Sum of Squares	Mean Square	F Ratio
Lack Of Fit	12	54.794093	4.56617	5.2984
Pure Error	10	8.617950	0.86180	Prob > F
Total Error	22	63.412043		0.0064*
				Max RSq
				0.9963

Figure 11.22 shows a *p*-value of 0.0064. This leads you to conclude that the model is inadequate. JMP highlights *p*-values that are less than 0.05 with an asterisk.

Looking at the data table shows where the 10 degrees of freedom come from. Most of the *x* values appear in the data table twice. The 10 degrees of freedom come from duplicate *x* values for Speed values of 12, 14, 15, 16, 17, 18, 19, 20, 21, and 22. This planned experiment was designed with enough duplicate *x* values to test for lack of fit.

Fitting a Curve

Figure 10.17 showed results from fitting a curve to the Engine data, but hid the Lack Of Fit report. Figure 11.23 shows this report.

Figure 11.23 Lack Of Fit Report from Fitting a Curve to the Engine Data

▼ **Lack Of Fit**

Source	DF	Sum of Squares	Mean Square	F Ratio
Lack Of Fit	11	23.388032	2.12618	2.4672
Pure Error	10	8.617950	0.86180	Prob > F
Total Error	21	32.005982		0.0830
				Max RSq
				0.9963

Figure 11.23 shows a *p*-value of 0.0830, which leads you to conclude that the model is adequate.

Testing the Regression Assumption for Errors

Chapter 10 defined the last assumption for regression to be that the errors in the data are normally distributed with a mean of 0 and a variance of σ^2. Chapter 10 did not test this assumption, because testing involves the residuals from the regression model. Specifically, testing this assumption involves testing that the residuals are normally distributed with a given mean and variance. In practice, many statisticians rely on the theory behind regression, and often don't test this assumption. The theory behind least squares ensures that the mean of the residuals is 0. The least squares theory also ensures that the Root Mean Square Error from the regression fit is the best estimate of the standard deviation of the residuals. As a result, many statisticians test this last assumption for regression by testing the normality of the residuals. However, it's a good idea to know how to test the entire assumption.

Chapter 6 discussed testing for normality, and Chapter 8 discussed testing that the mean difference was 0. Testing the errors assumption uses these same JMP steps. The only new steps are for testing the assumption about the variance, which uses the Distribution platform. The next two topics show how to test the errors assumption for the final models for the Energy and Engine data.

Testing Errors Assumption for the Energy Data

The regression assumption is that the errors have a variance of σ^2. In JMP, this translates to testing that the residuals have a standard deviation of σ. The regression analysis provides the estimate of σ in the Summary Of Fit report. The Root Mean Square Error estimates σ, regardless of whether you are fitting a line, a curve, or a multiple regression model. For fitting the multiple regression model for the Energy data, Figure 10.21 shows Root Mean Square Error as 3.94 (rounded to two decimal places).

In JMP, use the Energy_Ch11 data table and Distribution for the Residual KWH Multiple variable. Following steps similar to the steps in Chapter 6, fit a normal distribution and test for goodness of fit. Figure 11.24 shows the histogram with a fitted normal curve, Fitted Normal report, and results from the goodness of fit test.

Figure 11.24 Testing for Normality of Residuals for Multiple Regression for Energy Data

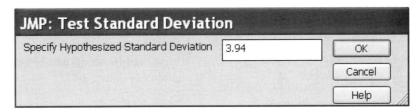

For the Goodness-of-Fit Test, the *p*-value is 0.9589, which is not significant. You can proceed with the assumption that the residuals are normally distributed. (Refer to Chapter 6 for more details on this report.)

To test the mean, follow similar steps as the steps in Chapter 8. Testing that the mean of the residuals is 0 uses the same JMP steps as testing that the mean of a difference variable is 0. Select **Test Mean** from the hot spot for Residual KWH Multiple and accept the automatic choice of 0 for the hypothesized mean. Figure 11.25 shows the results.

To test the standard deviation in JMP:

1. Click the hot spot for Residual KWH Multiple.

2. Select **Test Std Dev**.

3. In the Test Standard Deviation window, enter **3.94** for the hypothesized standard deviation. Compare your window with the following window.

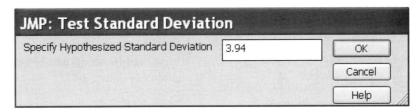

4. Click **OK**.

Figure 11.25 shows the tests for the mean and the standard deviation of the residuals.

Figure 11.25 Testing Errors Assumption for Multiple Regression for Energy Data

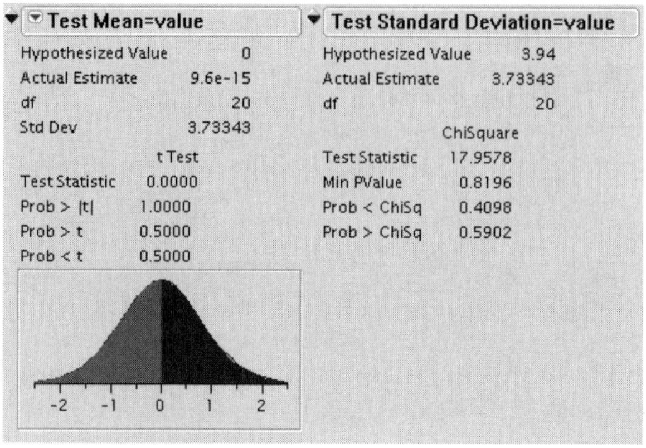

For testing the mean, the two-sided *p*-value is 1.0000. You can proceed with the assumption that the residuals have a mean of 0. This result is expected, because the least squares theory ensures that the mean of the residuals is 0. (Refer to Chapter 8 and using Distribution to test a difference variable for more details on this report.)

For testing the standard deviation, find the Min PValue in the Test Standard Deviation=value report. This is the *p*-value for the two-sided test that the standard deviation is significantly different from the hypothesized value (3.94 in this example). Figure 11.25 shows the *p*-value as 0.8196. You can proceed with the assumption that the residuals have a standard deviation of 3.94. This result is as expected, because it is supported by the least squares theory.

The report provides other details:

Hypothesized Value	Shows the value entered in the Test Standard Deviation window.
Actual Estimate	Actual standard deviation from the data. This also appears in the Moments report.
df	Degrees of freedom, which are one less than the number of data points.
Test Statistic	Gives the Chi Square value for testing the hypothesis.
Prob < ChiSq **Prob > ChiSq**	Give the one-tailed tests for the standard deviation.

Testing Errors Assumption for Engine Data

Follow the same steps shown previously. However, use the Engine_Ch11 data and use the Residuals Power Curve variable. For fitting a curve to the Engine data, Figure 10.17 shows Root Mean Square Error as 1.23 (rounded to two decimal places). JMP creates the results shown in Figures 11.26 and 11.27.

Figure 11.26 Testing for Normality of Residuals from Fitting a Curve to the Engine Data

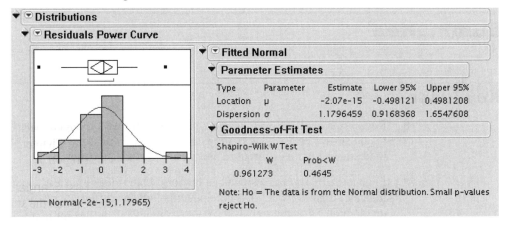

For the Goodness-of-Fit Test, the *p*-value is 0.4645, which is not significant. You can proceed with the assumption that the residuals are normally distributed.

Figure 11.27 Testing Errors Assumption from Fitting a Curve to the Engine Data

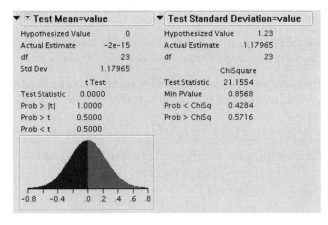

For testing the mean, the two-sided *p*-value is 1.0000. You can proceed with the assumption that the residuals have a mean of 0. This result is expected, because it is supported by the least squares theory.

For testing the standard deviation, the *p*-value is 0.8568. You can proceed with the assumption that the residuals have a standard deviation of 1.23. This result is expected, because it is supported by the least squares theory.

Summaries

Key Ideas

- Regression analysis is an iterative process of fitting a model and performing diagnostics. Residuals plots show inadequacies in models. Lack of fit tests indicate whether a different model would fit the data better.

- In general, in plots of residuals, a random scatter of points (a horizontal band) indicates a good model. Definite patterns indicate different situations, depending on the plot. Stronger signals have more obvious patterns than weak signals.

- Plot residuals against independent variables in the model and independent variables not in the model. Curved patterns indicate that a quadratic term needs to be added to the model. Linear patterns indicate that a variable needs to be added to the model.

- Plot residuals against predicted values. A horizontal band of points indicates a good model. Investigate obvious outlier points to determine whether they are due to a special cause.

- Plot residuals against the time sequence in which the data was collected. An obvious pattern shows a possible time sequence effect in the data.

- Lack of fit tests separate error variation into pure error and lack of fit error. A significant *p*-value for a lack of fit test indicates the need to fit a different regression model.

- Use residuals from the regression model to test the regression assumption that errors in the data are normally distributed with a mean of 0 and a variance of σ^2.

JMP Steps

To plot residuals against regressors in the model with Bivariate:

1. Fit the model using the Bivariate platform.

2. Click the hot spot next to the line for the fit. For fitting a straight line, the line is labeled Linear Fit. For fitting a curve, the line is labeled Polynomial Fit Degree=2.

3. Select **Plot Residuals**.

To plot residuals against variables not in the model with Bivariate:

1. Fit the model using the Bivariate platform.

2. Click the hot spot next to the line for the fit.

3. Select **Save Residuals**.

4. Click **Graph→Overlay Plot** in the JMP menu bar.

5. Click the new **Residuals** variable and then **Y**.

6. Click the independent variable not in the model and then **X**.

7. Click **OK**.

8. Repeat, as needed, for the other independent variables in the data table, but not in the model.

To plot residuals against predicted values with Bivariate:

1. Fit the model using the Bivariate platform.

2. Click the hot spot next to the line for the fit.

3. Select **Save Residuals**.

4. Click the hot spot again and select **Save Predicteds**.

5. Click **Graph→Overlay Plot** in the JMP menu bar.

6. Click the new **Residuals** variable and then **Y**.

7. Click the new **Predicteds** variable and then **X**.

8. Click **OK**.

To plot residuals in time sequence with Bivariate:

1. Fit the model using the Bivariate platform.

2. Click the hot spot next to the line for the fit.

3. Select **Save Residuals**.

4. Click **Graph→Overlay Plot** in the JMP menu bar.

5. Click the new **Residuals** variable and then **Y**.

6. Assuming that the data is sorted in time sequence, click **OK**. (If not, supply an X variable that identifies the time sequence and click **OK**.)

To plot residuals against independent variables with Fit Model:

1. Fit the model using the Fit Model platform.

2. Click the hot spot next to the response variable.

3. Select **Save Columns→Residuals**. JMP adds the new column to the data table. Rename the column as needed. The following steps assume a name of "Residuals" for the new column.

4. Click **Graph→Overlay Plot** in the JMP menu bar.

5. Click **Residuals** and then **Y**.

6. Click an independent variable and then **X**. Use this approach for independent variables in the model and for independent variables not in the model.

7. Click **OK**.

8. Repeat, as needed, for other independent variables.

To plot residuals against predicted values with Fit Model:

1. Fit the model using the Fit Model platform.

2. Click the hot spot next to the response variable.

3. Select **Row Diagnostics→Plot Residual by Predicted**.

To plot residuals in time sequence with Fit Model:

1. Fit the model using the Fit Model platform.

2. Click the hot spot next to the response variable.

3. Click **Row Diagnostics→Plot Residual by Row**.

To enhance plots:

1. Select the points in the plot. For a single point, click on the point. For several points, use the **Lasso** tool on the toolbar.

2. Right-click on the point and select **Row Colors**. Select a color from the palette.

3. Right-click on the point and select **Row Markers**. Select a different marker from the palette.

To test the errors assumption for regression:

1. Fit the regression model, either with Bivariate or Fit Model. Save the residuals to the data table. The following steps assume a name of Residuals for the new column.

2. Use Distribution on the Residuals variable, and test for normality following steps similar to the steps in Chapter 6. Briefly, click the hot spot in the Distributions window and select **Fit Distribution→Normal**. Next, click the hot spot in the Fitted Normal report title and select **Goodness of Fit**.

3. Use Distribution on the Residuals variable, and test that the mean of the residuals is 0 following steps similar to the steps in Chapter 8. Briefly, select **Test Mean** from the hot spot and accept the automatic choice of 0 for the hypothesized mean.

4. Use Distribution on the Residuals variable to test the standard deviation of the residuals. In the report, click the hot spot for Residuals.

5. Select **Test Std Dev**.

6. In the Test Standard Deviation window, enter the appropriate value for the hypothesized standard deviation. "Appropriate" is the Root Mean Square Error from the Summary Of Fit report for the regression.

7. Click **OK**.

Exercises

1. From the Sample Data Directory, click the disclosure diamond for Multivariate Analysis, and open the Body Measurements data table. Chapter 10 exercises fit a straight line with **Mass** as the response variable and **Waist** as the regressor. Use residuals plots to perform regression diagnostics. Explain whether plotting the data in time sequence makes sense. Discuss the lack of fit test. Plot the residuals against **Thigh** and discuss whether this regressor should be added to the model.

2. From the Sample Data Directory, click the disclosure diamond for Exploratory Modeling, and open the Cars 1993 data table. Chapter 10 exercises fit a straight line with **Maximum Price** as the response variable and **Maximum Horsepower** as the regressor. Use residuals plots to perform regression diagnostics. Explain whether plotting the data in time sequence makes sense. Discuss the lack of fit test.

3. With the Cars 1993 data, plot the residuals against **Highway MPG** and discuss whether this regressor should be added to the model.

4. With the Cars 1993 data, investigate the potential outlier point in the residuals plots. Suppose this luxury car should be deleted from the model. Create a subset of the data that deletes this point, and fit the regression model again. Perform regression diagnostics and discuss the results.

5. From the Sample Data Directory, click the disclosure diamond for Business and Demographics, and open the Grandfather Clocks data table. Chapter 10 exercises fit a straight line with **Price** as the response variable and **Age** as the regressor. Use residuals plots to perform regression diagnostics. Explain whether plotting the data in time sequence makes sense. Discuss the lack of fit test.

6. From the Sample Data Directory, click the disclosure diamond for Sciences, and open the Sleeping Animals data table. Chapter 10 exercises fit a straight line with **Total Sleep** as the response variable and **Gestation** as the regressor. Use residuals plots to perform regression diagnostics. Explain whether plotting the data in time sequence makes sense. Discuss the lack of fit test.

7. With the Sleeping Animals data, plot the residuals against **Danger**. Use **Fit Model** and add this term to the regression. Perform regression diagnostics, including residuals plots and the lack of fit test. Discuss the results.

8. From the Sample Data Directory, click the disclosure diamond for Sciences, and open the Pendulum data table. Chapter 10 fit an appropriate model with **Length** as the response variable. Use residuals plots to perform regression diagnostics. Explain whether plotting the data in time sequence makes sense. Discuss why JMP does not create the lack of fit test.

9. For the Energy data, fit a multiple regression model with **AC**, **Dryer**, and **Dryer*Dryer**. Use the residuals plots to perform regression diagnostics. Discuss the results and explain whether or not adding the quadratic term for **Dryer** is worthwhile. Hint: In **Fit Model**, the easiest way to add the quadratic term is to first select **Dryer** in the **Select Columns** area. Second, click the **Macros** button and select **Polynomial to Degree**. JMP's automatic choice of **2** adds both the **Dryer** and **Dryer*Dryer** terms to the model.

10. For the Engine data, regression diagnostics for fitting a curve showed two possible outlier points. Recreate the JMP results and regression diagnostics for fitting a line, and highlight the points for rows 2 and 24 as possible outliers. Does thinking about these points as possible outliers change your interpretation of the residuals plots?

11. For the Engine data, suppose the researcher discovers an error in data entry. The point for **Speed** equal to **24** should be 68.39, not 63.89. Change the value in the data table, and fit a curved model to the data. Create residuals plots and discuss the results. Is the model a better fit? Does this change solve all potential problems with outlier points?

Special Topic: Leverage Plots

You can use many diagnostic tools to decide whether your regression model fits the data well. This chapter concentrates on residuals plots and lack of fit tests. However, JMP provides more advanced tools, especially in Fit Model. This section introduces leverage plots.

Leverage plots for an effect graph the significance test for the effect. The plot shows the residuals with and without the effect in the model. Figure 10S.1 shows a leverage plot. The blue horizontal dotted line is the mean for the response variable. The distance between a point and the blue line is the residual that would occur without the effect in the model. The red solid line is the fitted regression equation with the effect in the model.

The red dotted lines are confidence curves. When interpreting leverage plots, look at two issues:

- The relationship between the red confidence curves and the blue horizontal line. If the confidence curve crosses the horizontal line, then the effect is significant. If the confidence curve encloses the horizontal line, then the effect is not significant. In Figure 10S.1, the effect is significant.

- Influential points. Points that appear to be outliers on the leverage plot have more impact on the model. Just like outliers, investigate these points to see whether they are due to a special cause. In Figure 10S.1, the point outside the confidence curve is an influential point.

Figure 10S.1 Sample Leverage Plot

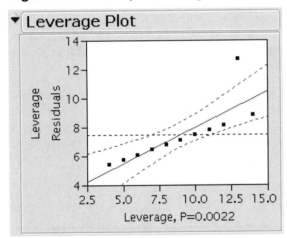

JMP provides leverage plots in the Fit Model platform. For the Energy data, start with the multiple regression results (see Figure 10.21 in Chapter 10). In JMP:

1. Click the hot spot for Response Kilowatt-hours.

2. Select **Row Diagnostics→Plot Effect Leverage**.

3. Click the disclosure diamond to reveal the Effect Details report.

Figure 10S.2 shows the leverage plots.

Figure 10S.2 Leverage Plots from Multiple Regression for Energy Data

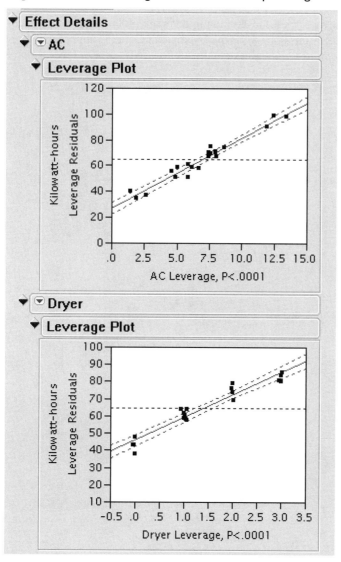

For both leverage plots, the confidence curve crosses the horizontal line. The effects for AC and Dryer are both significant. Neither leverage plot has an influential point. The *p*-values at the bottom of each leverage plot are the same *p*-values that appear in the Parameter Estimates report from Fit Model.

This topic gives a very brief introduction to leverage plots. See the references in "Further Reading" for more discussion. Also, the "Statistical Details" appendix in the *JMP Statistics and Graphics Guide* gives details on how JMP creates leverage plots.

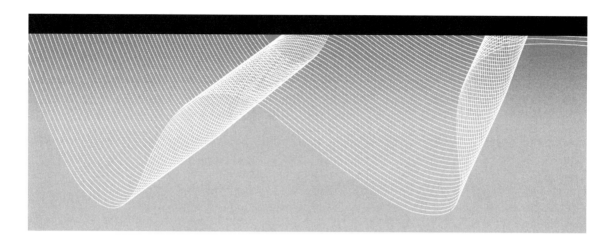

Part 5

Data in Summary Tables

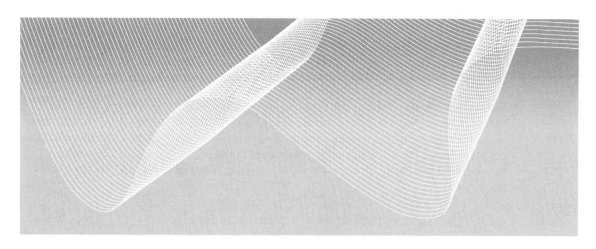

Chapter 12

Creating and Analyzing Contingency Tables

Do Democrats and Republicans have the same responses to a survey question asking about campaign reforms? Do rural and urban residents own different types of vehicles (sports cars, sedans, SUVs, and trucks)? Do graduate and undergraduate students differ in whether they share an apartment, have their own apartment, or live in a dorm?

These questions involve looking at two classification variables, and testing if the variables are related. Neither variable contains quantitative measurements; instead, both variables identify the respondent as belonging to a group. For example, one respondent might be "rural, truck", and another respondent might be "urban, sedan". The two variables can be character or numeric, and are either nominal or ordinal. This chapter discusses:

- summarizing classification data using tables and plots

- testing for independence between the classification variables

- using measures of association between classification variables

The methods in this chapter are appropriate for nominal and ordinal variables.

Defining Contingency Tables

Suppose you have nominal or ordinal variables that classify the data into groups. You want to summarize the data in a table. To make discussing summary tables easier, this section introduces some notation.

Tables that summarize two or more classification variables are called *contingency tables.* These tables are also called *crosstabulations*, *summary tables*, or *pivot tables* (in Microsoft Excel). Tables that summarize two variables are called *two-way tables*, tables that summarize three variables are called *three-way tables*, and so on. A special case of the two-way table occurs when both variables have only two levels. This special case is called a *2×2 table*. Although this chapter shows how to create contingency tables involving several variables, the analyses are appropriate only for two-way tables. Figure 12.1 shows the parts of a contingency table.

Figure 12.1 Parts of a Contingency Table

	Columns			
	column 1	**column 2**	**...**	**column c**
row 1	cell$_{11}$	cell$_{12}$	...	cell$_{1c}$
row 2	cell$_{21}$	cell$_{22}$	...	cell$_{2c}$
...	...	...	...	...
row r	cell$_{r1}$	cell$_{r2}$	...	cell$_{rc}$

(Label: **Rows** on the left spanning the row entries)

The table consists of rows and columns. Figure 12.1 contains r rows and c columns, and is an $r{\times}c$ table. The rows and columns form *cells*. Each cell of a table is uniquely indexed by its row and column. For example, the cell in the second row and first column is cell$_{21}$. A contingency table usually shows the number of observations in each cell, or the *cell frequency*. The total number of observations in the table is n. The number of observations in each cell follows the same notation pattern as the cells. For example, the number of observations in cell$_{21}$ is n_{21}.

The contingency table in Figure 12.1 is a two-way table because it summarizes two variables. **The phrase "two-way" does not refer to the number of rows or columns; it refers to the number of variables that are included in the table.**

Sometimes, you have the raw data and you want to summarize the data in a table and analyze it. Other times, you already have a summary table and you want to analyze it. The next three sections discuss summarizing data in tables. The rest of the chapter discusses analyses for two-way tables.

Summarizing Raw Data in Tables

Suppose you have raw data that you want to summarize in a table. Table 12.1 shows data from an introductory statistics class. The instructor collected data on the gender of each student, and whether the student was majoring in Statistics[1].

---

[1] Data is from Dr. Ramon Littell, University of Florida. Used with permission.

Table 12.1 Class Data

Student	Gender	Major
1	Male	Statistics
2	Male	Other
3	Female	Statistics
4	Male	Other
5	Female	Statistics
6	Female	Statistics
7	Male	Other
8	Male	Other
9	Male	Statistics
10	Female	Statistics
11	Male	Other
12	Female	Statistics
13	Male	Statistics
14	Male	Statistics
15	Male	Other
16	Female	Statistics
17	Male	Statistics
18	Male	Other
19	Female	Other
20	Male	Statistics

This data is available in the **Stat Majors** data table in the sample data for the book.

To summarize the data table in JMP:

1. Open the **Stat Majors** data table.

2. In the **JMP Starter** window, click **Basic→Contingency**.

3. Click **Major→Y, Response Category**. This variable forms the columns of the summary table.

4. Click **Gender→X, Grouping Category**. This variable forms the rows of the summary table.

5. Click **OK**.

Figure 12.2 shows the results, with the Tests report hidden. ("Performing Tests for Independence" in this chapter discusses this hidden report.) JMP displays both a graph and a text report. The title of the report identifies the column variable (**Major**) and the row variable (**Gender**). The next two topics discuss the graphs and reports in Figure 12.2.

Understanding the Mosaic Plot

Figure 12.2 shows a *two-way mosaic plot*. JMP documentation calls this a *contingency analysis mosaic plot* or a *mosaic plot*.

The left axis of the plot identifies proportions. The right axis shows color coding for the column variable (**Major**). The right axis also shows the relative proportions for the column variable, combined across the levels of the row variable. In Figure 12.2, the bar at the right axis shows the relative proportions of **Statistics** and **Other** majors, combined across the **Male** and **Female** students.

For variables with two levels, JMP uses red and blue color coding. For variables with more levels, JMP selects a color scheme.

JMP uses the data to scale the width of the columns in the mosaic plot. For the Stat Majors data, 8 of the 20 students are female, and JMP scales the **Female** column accordingly.

Look at the left side of the plot. The left side shows that over 75% of the **Female** students are majoring in **Statistics** (the blue rectangle). The right side of the two-way mosaic plot shows that half of the **Male** students are majoring in **Statistics**. This difference gives a visual hint that the pattern of majoring in **Statistics** or **Other** differs for **Male** and **Female** students. Later, "Performing Tests for Independence" shows how to check this visual hint to see whether it leads to a statistical conclusion.

The two-way mosaic plot provides a visual summary of the two variables. If the pattern for the row variable is the same across the values of the column variable, then the color patterns—and the relative proportion for each color—is the same from left to right across the mosaic plot. If the pattern differs, then the relative proportion for each color differs also.

Figure 12.2 Contingency Results for Stat Majors Data

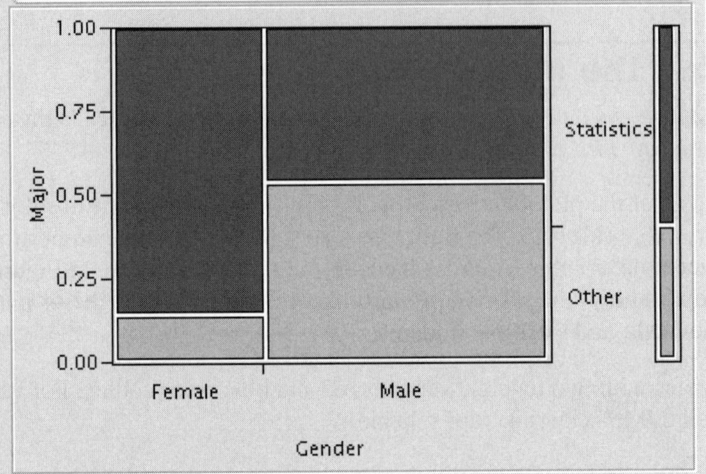

Understanding the Contingency Table Report

The Contingency Table report summarizes the data table. The top row shows the values for the column variable, and the leftmost column shows the values for the row variable.

The outside edges of the table give *row totals* and *column totals*. Looking at the row totals, 7 students are **Female**, and 13 are **Male**. Looking at the column totals, 12 students are majoring in **Statistics**, and 8 are majoring in something else (**Other**). The outside edges also give the *row percentages* and *column percentages*. Looking at the row percentages, 35% (calculated from 7/20) of the students are **Female**. Looking at the column percentages, 60% (calculated from 12/20) of the students are majoring in **Statistics**.

The lower-right corner cell gives the overall total for the table, which is **20**. Because there are no missing values, this number matches the number of observations in the data table. However, if the data table contained the **Gender** and not the **Major** for a student, the summary table would contain only 19 observations.

The top-left corner cell gives a key to understanding the main body of the table. The list gives details:

Count	Number of observations in each cell. This class has 1 female student who is majoring in **Other**.
Total %	Percentage of the total number of observations represented by the cell count. The single **Female** student majoring in **Other** represents 5% of the class. The class has 20 students, so 1/20=5%.
Col %	Percentage of observations in the column represented by the cell frequency. The single **Female Other** student represents 12.5% of the **Other** majors in the class. The class has 8 students majoring in **Other**, so 1/8=12.5%.
	The **Col %** values sum to 100% for each column.
Row %	Percentage of observations in the row represented by the cell frequency. The single **Female Other** student represents 14.29% of the females in the class. The class has 7 female students, so 1/7=14.29%.
	The **Row %** values sum to 100% for each row.

Enhancing the Report

The Contingency Table report has a hot spot that provides options for hiding the summary statistics that JMP automatically displays, and for adding more statistics. In JMP, click the hot spot for Contingency Table. Select a checked item to hide it. Select an unchecked item to display it. JMP uses the three unchecked items (**Expected**, **Deviation**, and **Cell Chi Square**) when performing statistical tests.

The Contingency Table report differs from most other reports in JMP. You cannot double-click on the cells in the summary table to change their appearance. JMP displays percentages to two decimal places.

The Contingency Analysis of Major By Gender report title (at the top of the window) has a hot spot. It provides options for closing the Mosaic Plot, the Contingency Table report, and the Tests report that JMP automatically displays. This hot spot also has options for adding more analyses. See the JMP documentation for more details.

The Contingency Analysis of Major By Gender hot spot provides a feature for changing the display. Suppose you want to rotate the mosaic plot so that the row variable displays as rows in the plot. Some people find this easier to view, because the rows of the mosaic plot are the same as the rows in the Contingency Table report. In JMP:

1. Click the hot spot for the Contingency Analysis of Major By Gender report.

2. Select **Display Options→Horizontal Mosaic**.

Figure 12.3 shows the results.

Figure 12.3 Horizontal Mosaic Plot

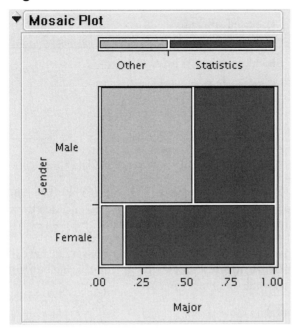

Creating a JMP Contingency Table from an Existing Summary Table

Sometimes, you already have a summary table of the data. You can create a JMP data table that matches the summary table, and then analyze it. It is not necessary to expand the summary table into a data table that has one row for every observation in the summary table. Table 12.2 shows frequency counts for several court cases. The columns show the defendant's race, and the rows identify whether the death penalty was imposed after the defendant was convicted of homicide.[2]

Table 12.2 Death Penalty Data

Defendant's Race

Decision	Black	White
No	149	141
Yes	17	19

This data is available in the Penalty data table in the sample data for the book.

To create the data table in JMP, follow the steps in Chapter 3. Your data table will have four rows, one for each cell in the table. It will have three columns, one for decision, one for race, and one for count.

The data table itself summarizes the data because it displays a spreadsheet-like view. However, the results from **Contingency** provide more features, including the two-way mosaic plot, percentages, and statistical tests. In JMP:

1. Open the Penalty data table.

2. In the JMP Starter window, click **Basic→Contingency**.

3. Click **Defendant Race→Y, Response Category**.

4. Click **Decision→X, Grouping Category**.

5. Click **Count→Freq**.

6. Click **OK**.

As with the raw data table, the *y* variable forms the columns of the summary table, and the *x* variable forms the rows of the summary table. The **Freq** variable tells JMP the frequency count for each cell. Without a **Freq** variable, JMP shows a single observation for each cell.

Figure 12.4 shows the results, with the Tests report hidden.

Figure 12.4 Contingency Results with a Freq Variable

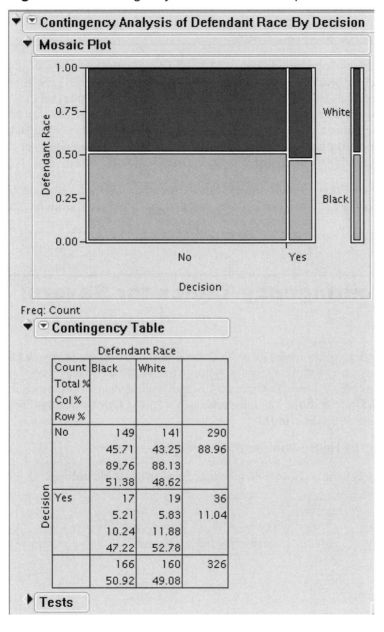

JMP produces the same plots and reports with a **Freq** variable as it does when creating a summary table from raw data. Look at Figure 12.4, between the Mosaic Plot and the Contingency Table report, and you see the only difference. JMP identifies the **Freq** variable with the text **Freq: Count**.

Compare the mosaic plots in Figures 12.2 and 12.4. For the Penalty data, the proportion of red and blue blocks (black and white defendants) is roughly the same for both the **Yes** and **No** decisions. Figure 12.4 might lead you to initially conclude that the two variables are not related. "Performing Tests for Independence" uses a statistical test to check this initial conclusion. Figure 12.4 scales the width of the columns according to the values of the **X, Grouping Category** variable. The **Yes** column is much narrower than the **No** column, reflecting the small percentage of **Yes** decisions.

When using a **Freq** variable, you can change the statistics displayed in the Contingency Table report just as you can for summary tables that are created from raw data.

Creating Contingency Tables for Several Variables

To create contingency tables for several variables, start with the approach for creating contingency tables for two variables. Select a row variable and a column variable, and add **By** variables to create multiple contingency tables. Chapter 8 shows how to use a **By** variable in **Distribution**. The same approach works in **Contingency**. For an example, use the Cars 1993 data. In JMP:

1. Click **Help→Sample Data Directory**.

2. Click the disclosure diamond for **Exploratory Modeling**.

3. Select **Cars 1993** and JMP opens the data table.

4. Click the **X** in the upper-right corner of the Sample Data Directory window to close the window.

5. In the JMP Starter window, click **Basic→Contingency**.

6. Click **Passenger Capacity→Y, Response Category**.

7. Click **Vehicle Category→X, Grouping Category**.

8. Click **Domestic Manufacturer→By**.

9. Click **OK**.

    JMP displays a warning message, informing you that **Passenger Capacity** is not a nominal or ordinal variable. The message asks you to consider canceling the action. In this case, **Passenger Capacity** is defined as a continuous variable in the data table, but it is actually an ordinal variable. As a result, the warning message can be ignored. In contrast, the multiple Cost and Mileage variables are correctly defined as continuous variables, and using these variables in a summary table is inappropriate.

10. Click **Continue**.

JMP creates a summary table for each level (**0** and **1**) of **Domestic Manufacturer**. This variable follows a coding convention where 0 means 'no' and 1 means 'yes'. When a row in the data table has Domestic Manufacturer=0, that row corresponds to a foreign car. Figure 12.5 displays results, with the Contingency Table and Tests reports hidden.

Figure 12.5 Contingency Results Using a By Variable

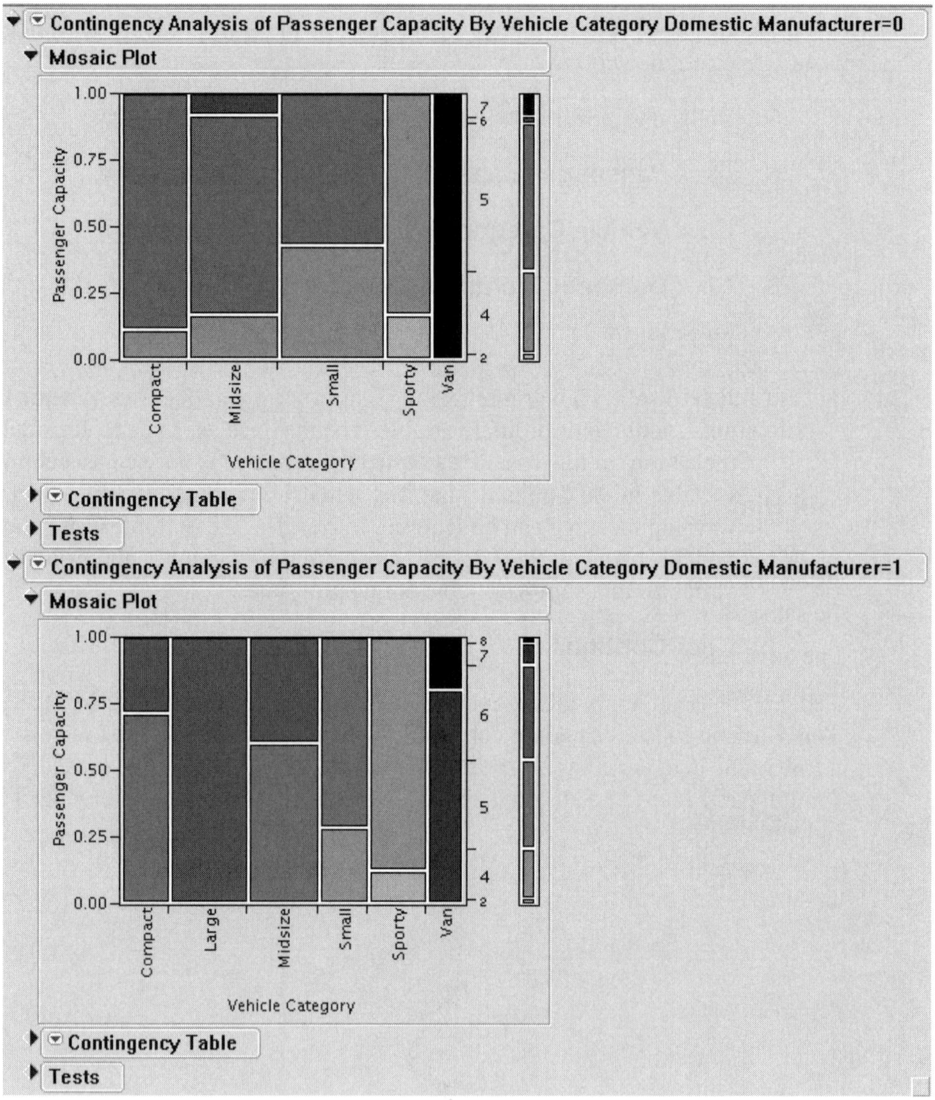

JMP displays the summaries for the two levels of **Domestic Manufacturer** in separate reports. Figure 12.5 displays the mosaic plots for each level of **Domestic Manufacturer**. The mosaic plots show that the domestic cars (**1**) differ from foreign cars (**0**). As one example of a difference, there are no **Large** foreign cars.

JMP uses multiple colors in the mosaic plot because the variables have more than two levels. Using a **By** variable has no effect on the colors in the mosaic plot. See "Revising Colors in Mosaic Plots" for a way to enhance the mosaic plot.

You can enhance reports with a **By** variable using the same JMP features discussed earlier.

At the end of this chapter, see "Special Topic: Statistical Summary Tables" for a way to summarize several variables in a single table. See "Further Reading" at the end of the book or refer to JMP documentation for references on analyses involving more than two classification variables.

JMP Hint:

As you become familiar with JMP, you might want to select **Analyze→Fit Y by X** instead of selecting **Contingency** from the JMP Starter window. Both choices launch the same JMP platform.

One advantage of **Contingency** is that JMP provides a warning window when you select a continuous variable. With **Fit Y by X**, JMP assumes that you want to perform a different analysis and does not create the contingency table.

Revising Colors in Mosaic Plots

JMP uses a red and blue color scheme for variables with two levels in mosaic plots. For variables with multiple levels, JMP uses multiple colors. When printing these mosaic plots on a gray scale printer, the colors can be difficult to distinguish. You can revise the colors to use shades of gray. In JMP:

1. Right-click on the mosaic plot and select **Set Colors**. If the **Set Colors** option does not display, carefully place your mouse pointer so that it is on the mosaic plot.

2. JMP shows the old and new colors in the **Select Colors for Values** window. When the window first appears, the two colors are the same because you have not changed the colors yet, as shown in the following window.

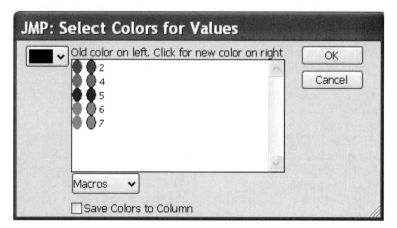

3. Click the right colored oval for **2** and select the lightest shade of gray from the color palette, as shown in the following window.

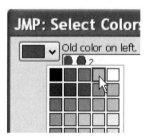

4. Click the right colored oval for **7** and select black from the color palette.

5. Click the **Macros** button and select **Gradient between ends**, as shown in the following window.

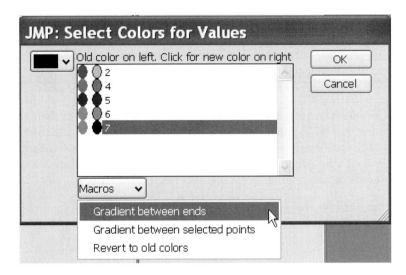

6. When you are finished changing colors, click **OK**.

JMP updates the mosaic plot to use the new colors. When changing colors and using a **By** variable, JMP changes the colors for one mosaic plot at a time. To change the colors for all of the mosaic plots, change them for each level of the **By** variable.

JMP Hints:

If you want to return to the automatic color choices, click the **Macros** button and select **Revert to old colors**.

If you find that selecting the colored oval is difficult, select the row and select the color button at the far-left side of the window. This displays a color palette and you can change colors from it.

Performing Tests for Independence

When you collect classification data, you want to know whether the variables are related in some way. For the Penalty data, is the defendant's race related to the verdict? Does knowing the defendant's race tell you anything about the likelihood that the defendant will receive the death penalty?

In statistical terms, the null hypothesis is that the row and column variables are independent. The alternative hypothesis is that the row and column variables are not independent. To test for independence, you compare the observed cell frequencies with the cell frequencies that would occur in the situation where the null hypothesis is true. (See "Technical Details: Expected Cell Frequencies" at the end of this section.)

One commonly used test is a Chi Square test, which tests the hypothesis of independence. A test statistic is calculated and compared with a critical value from a Chi-Square distribution. Suppose you want to test the hypothesis of independence at the 10% significance level for the **Penalty** data. (For more information, see the general discussion about building hypothesis tests in Chapter 6.)

The steps for analysis are the same as the steps for comparing groups:

1. Create a JMP data table.

2. Check the data table for errors.

3. Choose the significance level for the test.

4. Check the assumptions for the test.

5. Perform the test.

6. Make conclusions from the test results.

To check the data table for errors, use **Distribution** and the tools from Chapter 4.

To test for independence with two classification variables, the assumptions are:

- Data are counts. Practically, this requires that the variables are nominal or ordinal. JMP performs these tests in the **Contingency** platform for nominal and ordinal variables.

- Observations are independent. The values for one observation are not related to the values for another observation. To check the assumption of independent observations, think about your data and whether this assumption is reasonable. This is not a step where using JMP will answer this question.

- Observations are a random sample from the population. You want to make conclusions about a larger population, not about just the sample. For the statistics class, you want to make conclusions about statistics classes in general, not for just this single class. To check this assumption, think about your data and whether this assumption is reasonable. This is not a step where using JMP will answer this question.

- Sample size is large enough for the tests. As a general rule, the sample size should be large enough to expect five responses in each cell of the summary table. JMP prints warning messages when this assumption is not met.

JMP automatically performs appropriate tests when creating results from **Contingency**. Figure 12.6 shows the **Tests** report for the **Penalty** data. Figure 12.4 shows the other results, with the **Tests** report hidden.

Figure 12.6 Testing for Independence with the Penalty Data

▼ Tests

Source	DF	-LogLike	RSquare (U)
Model	1	0.11073	0.0005
Error	324	225.80004	
C. Total	325	225.91076	
N	326		

Test	ChiSquare	Prob>ChiSq
Likelihood Ratio	0.221	0.6379
Pearson	0.221	0.6379

Fisher's Exact Test	Prob	Alternative Hypothesis
Left	0.7412	Prob(Defendant Race=White) is greater for Decision=No than Yes
Right	0.3843	Prob(Defendant Race=White) is greater for Decision=Yes than No
2-Tail	0.7246	Prob(Defendant Race=White) is different across Decision

The first report in Figure 12.6 (with **Source** as the first column heading) is similar to an analysis of variance table for a continuous response variable. See the JMP documentation for more details. The test for independence does not use this report.

Before making decisions about the test, think about the assumptions. The data are counts, so the first assumption is reasonable. The observations are independent, because the race of and decision for a defendant is unrelated to the race of and decision for another defendant. The second assumption is reasonable. The observations are a random sample from the population of defendants convicted of homicide, so the third assumption is reasonable. In the Contingency Table report, use the hot spot to display the **Expected** values, and confirm that the fourth assumption is reasonable. Also, when this assumption is not met, JMP prints a warning message. Now, look at the results from the test for independence.

Understanding Chi Square Test Results

In the mosaic plot, the proportion of white and black defendants was roughly the same for the **Yes** and **No** decisions. The mosaic plot led to an initial conclusion that the variables were unrelated. The Chi Square test for independence quantifies the initial conclusion.

Look under the heading **Test** in Figure 12.6. JMP displays two Chi Square tests. The **Pearson** and **Likelihood Ratio** tests both have the same assumptions. The Pearson test uses the observed and expected cell frequencies, and the Likelihood Ratio test uses a more complex formula.

Look at the number under **Prob>ChiSq**. This value is **0.6379**, which is greater than the significance level of 0.10. You conclude that there is not enough evidence to reject the null hypothesis of independence between the defendant's race and the decision. (Refer to Agresti in "Further Reading" for an additional analysis of this data that considers the race of the victim.) Although the *p*-values for the two tests are identical in Figure 12.6, this is not always true. Typically, the *p*-values are similar, but are not identical.

In general, to interpret JMP results, look at the *p*-value under **Prob>ChiSq**, in the line for **Pearson**. If the *p*-value is less than the significance level, reject the null hypothesis that the two variables are independent. If the *p*-value is greater, you fail to reject the null hypothesis.

Understanding Fisher's Exact Test Results

Fisher's exact test was developed for the special case of a 2×2 table. This test is very useful when the assumptions for a Chi Square test are not reasonable, and is especially useful for tables with small cell frequencies. JMP automatically performs this test for 2×2 tables, but it isn't available for larger tables.

Look under the heading **Fisher's Exact Test** in Figure 12.6. JMP displays results for both one-sided tests and the two-sided test. Look at the line labeled **2-Tail**. The p-value is **0.7246**, so you fail to reject the null hypothesis that the two variables are independent.

In general, to interpret JMP results, look at the **2-Tail** p-value, which tests for independence between the two variables. The one-sided **Left** and **Right** p-values might be useful in specific situations. Interpret the p-value the same way you do for the Chi Square test.

Enhancing the Tests Report

You can double-click on a column in the Tests report and change the format of the numbers that are displayed. As with other reports in JMP, you can change the report titles.

Position the mouse pointer near a p-value and move it around in a very small circle. JMP displays a pop-up window, which includes text explaining the p-value. To close the window, move your mouse pointer again. JMP highlights p-values less than 0.05 with an asterisk.

To hide the Tests report, click the disclosure diamond next to the report title.

To remove the Tests report, click the hot spot at the top of the Contingency report. Click the **Tests** selection so that it is deselected, and JMP removes the report and its title.

Technical Details: Expected Cell Frequencies

The Chi Square test compares the observed cell frequencies with the expected cell frequencies, assuming the null hypothesis that the variables are independent. Click the hot spot for the Contingency Table report to display the **Expected** frequencies. To calculate the expected cell frequencies, multiply the row total and column total, and divide by the total number of observations. For the **Black-No** cell, the formula is:

[(row total for **No**)×(column total for **Black**)]/total **N**

$= (290 \times 166) / 326$

$= 147.67$

The Chi Square test is always valid if there are no empty cells (no cells with a cell frequency of 0), and if the expected cell frequency for all cells is 5 or greater.

Because these conditions are true for the Penalty data, the Chi Square test is a valid test. If these two conditions are not true, JMP prints a message warning that the Chi Square test might not be valid.

There is some disagreement among statisticians about exactly when the test should not be used, and what to do when the test is not valid. Two practical recommendations are to collect more data, or to combine low-frequency categories.

Combine low-frequency categories only when it makes sense. For example, consider a survey that asked people how often they called a Help Desk in the past month. Suppose the categories are: 0 (no calls), 1-2, 3-5, 6-8, 9-11, 12-15, 16-20, and "over 20". Now, suppose the expected cell counts for the last four categories are less than 5. It makes sense to combine these last four categories into a new category of "9 or more".

Measures of Association with Ordinal Variables

When you reject the null hypothesis for either the Chi Square test or Fisher's exact test, you conclude that the two variables are not independent. But, you do not know how the two variables are related. When both variables are ordinal, *measures of association* give more insight into your data. As defined in Chapter 3, ordinal variables have values that provide names and an implied order.

Two measures of association are Kendall's *tau* and Spearman's rank correlation coefficient. Both measures range from -1.0 to 1.0. Values close to 1.0 indicate a positive association, and values close to -1.0 indicate a negative association. (The Spearman's rank correlation coefficient is similar to correlation coefficients discussed in Chapter 10. This correlation coefficient is essentially the Pearson correlation, applied to ranks instead of to actual values.)

An animal epidemiologist tested dairy cows for the presence of a bacterial disease[3]. The disease is detected by analyzing blood samples, and the disease severity for each animal was classified as none (0), low (1), or high (2). The size of the herd that each cow belonged to was classified as small (10), medium (100), or large (1000). Table 12.3 shows the number of cows in each herd size, and in each disease severity category. Both the herd size and disease severity variables are ordinal. The disease is transmitted from cow to cow by bacteria, so the epidemiologist wanted to know whether disease severity is affected by herd size. As the herd size gets larger, is there either an increasing or a decreasing trend in disease severity?

The epidemiologist tested for independence using the Chi Square test. However, she still does not know whether there is a trend in disease severity that is related to an increase in herd size. Kendall's *tau* or Spearman's rank correlation coefficient can answer this question.

Table 12.3 Cow Disease Data

Disease Severity

Herd Size	None (0)	Low (1)	High (2)
Small (10)	9	5	9
Medium (100)	18	4	19
Large (1000)	11	88	136

This data is available in the **Cow Disease** data table in the sample data for the book. The icons for **Herd Size** and **Disease** indicate that these two variables are ordinal, as shown in the following window. The variables are also numeric, which JMP requires for the **Multivariate** platform.

---

[3] Data is from Dr. Ramon Littell, University of Florida. Used with permission.

Cow Disease			Herd Size	Disease	Number
		1	1000	0	11
		2	1000	1	88
Columns (3/0)		3	1000	2	136
Herd Size		4	100	0	18
Disease		5	100	1	4
Number		6	100	2	19
Rows		7	10	0	9
All rows	9	8	10	1	5
Selected	0	9	10	2	9

To create the data table in JMP, follow the steps in Chapter 3. Your data table will have 9 rows, one for each cell in the table. It will have 3 columns, one for herd size, one for disease severity, and one for number.

JMP requires numeric variables to create Kendall's *tau* and Spearman's rank correlation coefficient. JMP provides these statistics in the **Multivariate** platform. This platform automatically creates a scatterplot matrix that is useful for investigating multiple continuous variables. To create the measures of association in JMP:

1. Open the Cow Disease data table.

2. In the JMP Starter window, click **Multivariate→Multivariate**.

3. Click **Herd Size** and **Disease** and then **Y, Columns**.

4. Click **Number→Freq**.

5. Click **OK**.

   JMP displays a warning message, informing you that **Herd Size** and **Disease** are not continuous variables. The message asks you to consider canceling the action. In this case, both variables are ordinal. As a result, the warning message can be ignored. Using these two variables to create the measures of association is appropriate.

6. Click **Continue**. JMP creates the results.

7. Hold down the ALT key and click the hot spot for the Multivariate report.

8. Select **Correlations Multivariate** to close this report. It makes sense for continuous variables.

9. Select **Scatterplot Matrix** to close the plot. It makes sense for continuous variables.

10. Select **Nonparametric Correlations→Spearman'sρ**. (The ρ is the Greek letter rho, which is how statisticians often refer to Spearman's rank correlation coefficient.)

11. Select **Nonparametric Correlations→Kendall'sτ**. (The τ is the Greek letter tau.)

12. Click **OK**.

Figure 12.7 shows the results.

Figure 12.7 Measures of Association for the Cow Disease Data

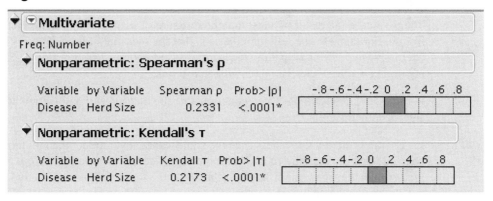

Figure 12.7 highlights the **Freq** variable by showing **Freq: Number** just below the Multivariate report title. JMP performs exactly the same analyses with raw data. The only difference in the results is that the report does not show a **Freq** variable. The plots and reports are similar to the Pairwise Correlations results, discussed in Chapter 10.

Understanding the Plot

For both measures of association, JMP creates a bar chart scaled from -1 to 1. JMP colors from the value 0 to the bar segment that matches the value of the measure of association. Both Spearman's rank correlation coefficient and Kendall's *tau* have a value of about 0.2, so the same area is colored for each plot.

Understanding the Report

For each measure of association, JMP lists the two variables involved, the measure, and a p-value.

A positive measure of association indicates an increasing trend between the two variables. As the ordinal levels of one variable increase, so do the ordinal levels of the other variable. For the Cow Disease data, the epidemiologist can conclude that disease severity increases with increasing herd size.

A negative measure of association indicates a decreasing trend between the two variables. As the ordinal levels of one variable increase, the ordinal levels of the other variable decrease.

The closer a measure of association is to 0, the weaker the strength of the relationship. A value of -0.8 or 0.8 indicates a stronger relationship than a value of -0.1 or 0.1.

The p-value is the result of a test that the measure of association is significantly different from 0. For this test, the null hypothesis is that the measure of association is 0. The alternative hypothesis is that the measure of association is different from 0. JMP highlights p-values less than 0.05 with an asterisk.

For the Cow Disease data, you conclude that the measures of association are significantly different from 0.

In general, if the p-value is less than the significance level, reject the null hypothesis and conclude that the measure of association is significantly different from 0. If the p-value is greater than the significance level, fail to reject the null hypothesis. Conclude that there is not enough evidence to say that the measure of association is significantly different from 0.

JMP Hint:

As you become familiar with JMP, you might want to select **Analyze→ Multivariate Methods→Multivariate** instead of selecting **Multivariate→Multivariate** from the JMP Starter window. Both choices launch the same JMP platform.

One advantage of selecting **Multivariate** in the JMP Starter window is that JMP provides a warning window for an ordinal variable. Click **Continue** and create reports with measures of association for ordinal variables. When you select **Analyze** from the menu, JMP requires continuous variables in the **Multivariate** platform.

Summaries

Key Ideas

- Contingency tables are tables that summarize two or more classification variables. The rows and columns of a contingency table form cells, and the number of observations in a cell is the cell frequency for that cell.

- The **Basic→Contingency** choice in the JMP Starter window creates contingency tables and a two-way mosaic plot, and performs statistical tests on the two variables. Use nominal or ordinal variables in the **Contingency** platform. As you become familiar with JMP, you might want to select **Analyze→Fit Y by X** from the menu instead of selecting **Contingency** in the JMP Starter window.

- Use **By** variables to summarize more than two variables. JMP creates separate reports for each level of the **By** variable. With multiple **By** variables, JMP creates a separate report for each combination of levels of the multiple **By** variables.

- Both the Chi Square test and Fisher's exact test are used to test for independence between two classification variables. Generally, the Chi Square test should not be used if there are empty cells or if cells have expected cell frequencies of less than 5. One option is to collect more data, which increases the expected cell frequency. Another option is to combine levels that have only a few observations.

- Regardless of the test, the steps for analysis are:

  1. Create a JMP data table.

  2. Check the data table for errors.

  3. Choose the significance level for the test.

  4. Check the assumptions for the test.

  5. Perform the test.

  6. Make conclusions from the test results.

- Regardless of the test, to make conclusions, compare the *p*-value for the test with your significance level.

    □ If the *p*-value is less than the significance level, reject the null hypothesis that the two variables are independent. JMP displays an asterisk next to *p*-values that are less than 0.05.

    □ If the *p*-value is greater than the significance level, fail to reject the null hypothesis.

- Kendall's *tau* and Spearman's rank correlation coefficient are both measures of association that provide information about how strongly related ordinal variables are. Use these statistics to decide whether there is an increasing or a decreasing trend in the two variables, or if there is no trend at all. JMP tests whether the measure of association is significantly different from 0, and reports the *p*-value.

- The **Multivariate→Multivariate** choice in the JMP Starter window creates measures of association for the two variables. Use numeric ordinal variables in the **Multivariate** platform. As you become familiar with JMP, you might want to select **Analyze→Multivariate Methods** from the menu instead of selecting **Multivariate** in the JMP Starter window, but remember that it requires numeric continuous variables.

JMP Steps

To summarize two nominal or ordinal variables in a contingency table:

1. In the JMP Starter window, click **Basic→Contingency**.

2. Click the column variable and then **Y, Response Category**.

3. Click the row variable and then **X, Grouping Category**.

4. If your data already form a summary table, click **Count→Freq**.

5. Click **OK**.

To summarize three or more variables in a contingency table:

1. Complete steps 1 through 4 above.

2. Before step 5, click the additional variables and then **By**. JMP creates a contingency table for each combination of levels of the additional variables.

3. Click **OK**.

To rotate the mosaic plot:

1. Click the hot spot for the Contingency Analysis report.

2. Click **Display Options→Horizontal Mosaic**.

To revise colors to gray scale in the mosaic plot:

1. Right-click on the mosaic plot and select **Set Colors**. If the **Set Colors** option does not display, carefully place your mouse pointer so that it is on the mosaic plot.

2. JMP shows the old and new colors in the Select Colors for Values window. When the window first appears, the two colors are the same because you have not changed colors yet.

3. Click the right colored oval for the top color in the list and select the lightest shade of gray.

4. Click the right colored oval for the bottom color in the list and select black from the color palette.

5. Click the **Macros** button and select **Gradient between ends**.

6. Click **OK**.

To perform tests for independence:

Follow the steps above for creating a contingency table. JMP automatically creates the Tests report, which contains results for the Chi Square test. For 2×2 tables, JMP includes results from Fisher's exact test. However, see the steps for analysis in "Key Ideas." Although JMP automatically performs the tests, you still need to check assumptions and think about your data.

To generate measures of association:

The measures of association discussed in this chapter require two ordinal variables. JMP requires numeric variables.

1. In the JMP Starter window, click **Multivariate→Multivariate**.

2. Click the row variable and column variable and then **Y, Columns**.

3. If the data already form a summary table, click the **Count→Freq**.

4. Click **OK**.

   If your variables are ordinal, JMP displays a warning message, informing you that the variables are not continuous variables. The message asks you to consider canceling the action. When the variables are numeric ordinal variables, creating measures of association is appropriate.

5. Click **Continue**. JMP creates the results.

6. Hold down the ALT key and click the hot spot for the Multivariate report.

7. Select **Correlations Multivariate** to close this report. It makes sense for continuous variables.

8. Select **Scatterplot Matrix** to close the plot. It makes sense for continuous variables.

9. Select **Nonparametric Correlations→Spearman's**ρ.

10. Select **Nonparametric Correlations→Kendall's**τ.

11. Click **OK**.

Exercises

1. Perform a test for independence for the Stat Majors data. Are the assumptions for the test reasonable? Define the null and alternative hypotheses. Use a 10% alpha level. Discuss your conclusions.

2. Test for independence with the Cow Disease data. Are the assumptions for the test reasonable? Define the null and alternative hypotheses. Use a 5% alpha level. Discuss your conclusions. Does it make a difference in the reports and graphs if you make the variables ordinal? Do the results of the statistical test change?

3. Create a new data table for the Cow Disease data. Use **10**, **20**, and **30** for the **Small**, **Medium**, and **Large** values of **Herd Size**. Use **0**, **4**, and **8** for the **None**, **Low**, and **High** values of **Disease Severity**. Repeat the analysis in the chapter, creating Kendall's *tau* and Spearman's rank correlation coefficient. Do the results differ? Do the values used for a variable have an effect on these statistics?

4. From the Sample Data Directory, click the disclosure diamond for Categorical Models and open the Alcohol data table. Create a summary table of **Relapsed** by **Alcohol Consumption**. Rotate the mosaic plot.

5. From the Sample Data Directory, click the disclosure diamond for Business and Demographic and open the Movies data table. Create a summary table of **Type** by **Rating**. Are the assumptions for the test for independence reasonable? If so, define the null and alternative hypotheses and use a 5% alpha level. Discuss your conclusions. Does it make sense to create measures of association for this data? If so, generate them and discuss your conclusions.

6. From the Sample Data Directory, click the disclosure diamond for Business and Demographic and open the Titanic data table. Create a summary table of **Survived** by **Class**. Are the assumptions for the test for independence reasonable? If so, define the null and alternative hypotheses and use a 5% alpha level. Discuss your conclusions. Does it make sense to create measures of association for this data? If so, generate them and discuss your conclusions.

7. From the Sample Data Directory, click the disclosure diamond for Exploratory Modeling and open the Cars 1993 data table. Create a summary table of **Vehicle Category** by **Passenger Capacity**. Are the assumptions for the test for independence reasonable? If so, define the null and alternative hypotheses and use a 5% alpha level. If not, explain whether it makes sense to combine categories and discuss which categories you would combine.

8. With the Cars 1993 data table from exercise 7, create a summary table of **Vehicle Category** by **Domestic Manufacturer**. Are the assumptions for the test for independence reasonable? If so, define the null and alternative hypotheses and use a 5% alpha level. Discuss your conclusions. Does it make sense to create measures of association for this data? If so, generate them and discuss your conclusions.

9. From the sample data for the book, open the Cereal Revised data table. Create a summary table of **Enriched** by **Fiber Gr**. Are the assumptions for the test for independence reasonable? If so, define the null and alternative hypotheses and use a 5% alpha level. Perform the test. Create measures of association for these variables. Discuss your conclusions.

10. From the Sample Data Directory, click the disclosure diamond for Exploratory Modeling and open the Mushroom data table. Create a summary table of **Odor** by **Habitat** for each level of **Edibility**. (Use **Edibility** as a **By** variable.) Are the assumptions for the test for independence reasonable? If so, define the null and alternative hypotheses and use a 5% alpha level. Discuss your conclusions, and whether results differ for edible and poisonous mushrooms.

Special Topic: Statistical Summary Tables

The **Contingency** platform with **By** variables summarizes three or more classification variables. JMP provides two other tools that summarize multiple variables in a single table. This section gives a brief introduction to the **Tables→Summary** platform. JMP also provides the **Tables→Tabulate** platform, which has a drag-and-drop interface for creating tables. The **Tabulate** platform has some similarities with creating pivot tables in Microsoft Excel.

This example uses the Cars 1993 data and creates a summary table. The table condenses the two tables from the **Contingency** platform (used with a **By** variable earlier in the chapter) into a single table. In JMP:

1. Click **Help→Sample Data Directory**.

2. Click the disclosure diamond for **Exploratory Modeling**.

3. Click **Cars 1993.jmp**. JMP opens the data table.

4. Click the **X** in the upper-right corner of the Sample Data Directory window to close it.

5. Click **Tables→Summary**.

6. Click **Domestic Manufacturer→Group**.

7. Click **Vehicle Category→Group**.

8. Click **Passenger Capacity→Group**. Compare your window with Figure 11S.1 to confirm your choices.

9. Click **OK**.

Figure 11S.1 Window for Summary Table

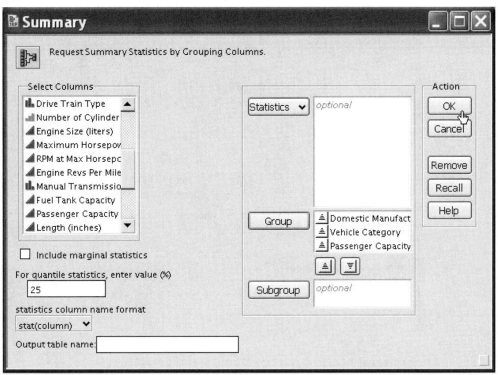

Figure 11S.2 shows the results.

The **N Rows** column gives the frequency count for the combination of levels for the three variables in that row. For example, the first row in the data table reports a single car that is from a foreign manufacturer (**Domestic Manufacturer** equal to **0**), is **Compact**, and can carry **4** passengers.

Figure 11S.2 Summary Table for Cars 1993 Data

	Domestic Manufacturer	Vehicle Category	Passenger Capacity	N Rows
1	0	Compact	4	1
2	0	Compact	5	8
3	0	Midsize	4	2
4	0	Midsize	5	9
5	0	Midsize	6	1
6	0	Small	4	6
7	0	Small	5	8
8	0	Sporty	2	1
9	0	Sporty	4	5
10	0	Van	7	4
11	1	Compact	5	5
12	1	Compact	6	2
13	1	Large	6	11
14	1	Midsize	5	6
15	1	Midsize	6	4
16	1	Small	4	2
17	1	Small	5	5
18	1	Sporty	2	1
19	1	Sporty	4	7
20	1	Van	7	4
21	1	Van	8	1

Window title: Cars 1993 By (Domestic Manufacturer, Vehicle Category, Passenger Capacity)

Side panel:
- Cars 1993 By (Domestic Ma
- Source
- Columns (4/0)
  - Domestic Manufacturer
  - Vehicle Category
  - Passenger Capacity
  - N Rows
- Rows
  - All rows 21
  - Selected 0
  - Excluded 0
  - Hidden 0
  - Labelled 0

JMP Hint:

The order of variables is important in the **Tables→Summary** platform. JMP uses the order to create the columns in the new data table. If you hold down the CTRL key and click to select variables in the **Select Columns** area, JMP uses the columns in the order they appear in the data table. This might not be what you want.

One advantage of using **Tables→Summary** is that the results are in a data table. You can create bar charts, or use the data in any appropriate JMP platform.

This special topic is an extremely brief introduction to summarizing multiple variables in tables. The **Summary** platform can create very complex tables, with means, standard deviations, and other statistics in columns. The **Tabulate** platform can create similarly complex tables, with the distinction that these tables are in a report window, rather than in a data table. Discussing all of the features of these two platforms would require another book!

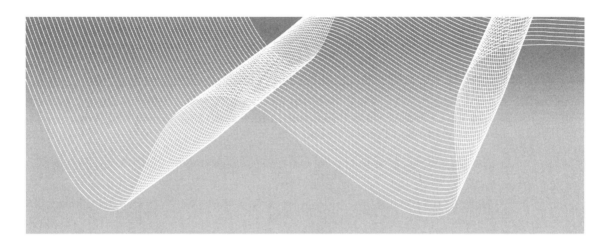

Appendix 1

Further Reading

This appendix includes a brief list of books that provide more detail on the statistical topics that are discussed in this book. It is not intended to provide a complete bibliography; instead, it is intended to provide a few reference books to get you started. Many of the books listed do contain exhaustive bibliographies of books and articles for the statistical topics that are discussed in this book.

Statistics References

For more information about using graphs and summary statistics to explore data, see the following:

Cleveland, W. S. 1994. *The Elements of Graphing Data, Second Edition*. Chapman & Hall/CRC.

Tufte, E. R. 1983. *The Visual Display of Quantitative Information*. Cheshire, CT: Graphics Press.

Tufte, E. R. 1990. *Envisioning Information*. Cheshire, CT: Graphics Press.

Tufte, E. R. 1997. *Visual Explanations: Images and Quantities, Evidence and Narrative*. Cheshire, CT: Graphics Press.

For a non-technical discussion of how statistics can be used incorrectly, see the following:

Gonick, L., and W. Smith. 1993. *The Cartoon Guide to Statistics*. New York: HarperCollins Publishers, Inc.

Hooke, R. 1983. *How to Tell the Liars from the Statisticians*. New York: Marcel Dekker, Inc.

Huff, D. 1954. *How to Lie with Statistics*. New York: W. W. Norton & Company, Inc.

Spirer, H. F., L. Spirer, and A. J. Jaffe. 1998. *Misused Statistics, Second Edition*. New York: Marcel Dekker, Inc.

For general introductions to statistics and statistical thinking, see the following. Many of these books also discuss testing for normality.

Brook, R., G. Arnold, T. Hassard, and R. Pringle, eds. 1986. *The Fascination of Statistics*. New York: Marcel Dekker, Inc.

Fraenkel, J. R., E. I. Sawin, and N. E. Wallen. 1999. *Visual Statistics*. Needham Heights, MA: Allyn & Bacon.

Freedman, D., R. Pisani, and R. Purves. 2007. *Statistics, Fourth Edition*. W. W. Norton & Company, Inc.

Gonick, L., and W. Smith. 1993. *The Cartoon Guide to Statistics*. New York: HarperCollins Publishers, Inc.

Moore, D., and G. McCabe. 2005. *Introduction to the Practice of Statistics, Fifth Edition*. W. H. Freeman & Company.

Utts, J. M. 1999. *Seeing Through Statistics*. Pacific Grove, CA: Brooks/Cole Publishing Company.

For more information about the statistical methods that are discussed in Chapters 6 through 12 of this book, see the following:

De Veaux, R., P. Velleman, and D. Bock. 2005. *Intro Stats, Second Edition*. Reading, MA: Addison-Wesley.

Lehman, A., N. O'Rourke, L. Hatcher, and E. J. Stepanski. 2005. *JMP for Basic Univariate and Multivariate Statistics*. Cary, NC: SAS Institute Inc.

Sall, J., L. Creighton, and A. Lehman. 2004. *JMP Start Statistics, Third Edition.* Boston, MA: Duxbury Press, PWS/Kent.

For more information about the Kruskal-Wallis test and other nonparametric analyses, see the following:

Conover, W. J. 2001. *Practical Nonparametric Statistics, Third Edition.* New York: John Wiley & Sons, Inc.

Hollander, M., and D. A. Wolfe. 1999. *Nonparametric Statistical Methods, Second Edition.* New York: John Wiley & Sons, Inc.

Siegel, S., and N. J. Castellan, Jr. 1988. *Nonparametric Statistics for the Behavioral Sciences, Second Edition.* New York: McGraw-Hill, Inc.

For more information about ANOVA and multiple comparison procedures, see the following:

Box, G. E. P., W. G. Hunter, and J. S. Hunter. 2005. *Statistics for Experimenters: Design, Innovation, and Discovery, Second Edition.* New York: John Wiley & Sons, Inc.

Littell, R. C., W. W. Stroup, and R. J. Freund. 2002. *SAS for Linear Models, Fourth Edition.* Cary, NC: SAS Institute Inc.

Hsu, J. C. 1996. *Multiple Comparisons: Theory and Methods.* New York: Chapman & Hall/CRC.

Milliken, G. A., and D. E. Johnson. 1997. *Analysis of Messy Data Volume I: Designed Experiments.* New York: Chapman & Hall/CRC.

For more information about correlation, regression, and regression diagnostics, see the following:

Belsley, D. A., E. Kuh, and R. E. Welsch. 2004. *Regression Diagnostics: Identifying Influential Data and Sources of Collinearity.* New York: John Wiley & Sons, Inc.

Draper, N. R., and H. Smith. 1998. *Applied Regression Analysis, Third Edition.* New York: John Wiley & Sons, Inc.

Freund, R. J., R. C. Littell, and L. Creighton. 2003. *Regression Using JMP.* Cary, NC: SAS Institute Inc.

Neter, J., M. Kutner, W. Wasserman, and C. Nachtsheim. 1996. *Applied Linear Statistical Models, Fourth Edition.* New York: McGraw-Hill.

For more information about tests and measures of association for contingency tables, see the following:

Agresti, A. 2002. *Categorical Data Analysis, Second Edition.* New York: John Wiley & Sons, Inc.

Agresti, A. 1996. *An Introduction to Categorical Data Analysis.* New York: John Wiley & Sons, Inc.

Fleiss, J. L., Bruce Levin, and Myunghee Cho Paik. 2003. *Statistical Methods for Rates and Proportions, Third Edition.* New York: John Wiley & Sons, Inc.

For more information about practical experimental design, see the following:

Box, G. E. P., W. G. Hunter, and J. S. Hunter. 2005. *Statistics for Experimenters: Design, Innovation, and Discovery, Second Edition.* New York: John Wiley & Sons, Inc.

JMP Documentation

The following books are the documentation set for JMP, Release 6. These are also available electronically. In JMP, click **Help→Books**. The list includes all of the following books, plus two quick reference cards. The electronic books are PDF files, so you need Adobe Reader to view them.

JMP Design of Experiments Guide, Release 6

JMP Introductory Guide, Release 6

JMP Scripting Guide, Release 6

JMP Statistics and Graphics Guide, Release 6

JMP User Guide, Release 6

Index

A

B

Books Available from SAS Press

Advanced Log-Linear Models Using SAS®
by **Daniel Zelterman**

Analysis of Clinical Trials Using SAS®: A Practical Guide
by **Alex Dmitrienko, Geert Molenberghs, Walter Offen,** and **Christy Chuang-Stein**

Annotate: Simply the Basics
by **Art Carpenter**

Applied Multivariate Statistics with SAS® Software, Second Edition
by **Ravindra Khattree** and **Dayanand N. Naik**

Applied Statistics and the SAS® Programming Language, Fifth Edition
by **Ronald P. Cody** and **Jeffrey K. Smith**

An Array of Challenges — Test Your SAS® Skills
by **Robert Virgile**

Building Web Applications with SAS/IntrNet®: A Guide to the Application Dispatcher
by **Don Henderson**

Carpenter's Complete Guide to the SAS® Macro Language, Second Edition
by **Art Carpenter**

Carpenter's Complete Guide to the SAS® REPORT Procedure
by **Art Carpenter**

The Cartoon Guide to Statistics
by **Larry Gonick** and **Woollcott Smith**

Categorical Data Analysis Using the SAS® System, Second Edition
by **Maura E. Stokes, Charles S. Davis,** and **Gary G. Koch**

Cody's Data Cleaning Techniques Using SAS® Software
by **Ron Cody**

Common Statistical Methods for Clinical Research with SAS® Examples, Second Edition
by **Glenn A. Walker**

The Complete Guide to SAS® Indexes
by **Michael A. Raithel**

Data Management and Reporting Made Easy with SAS® Learning Edition 2.0
by **Sunil K. Gupta**

Data Preparation for Analytics Using SAS®
by **Gerhard Svolba**

Debugging SAS® Programs: A Handbook of Tools and Techniques
by **Michele M. Burlew**

Decision Trees for Business Intelligence and Data Mining: Using SAS® Enterprise Miner™
by **Barry de Ville**

support.sas.com/pubs

Efficiency: Improving the Performance of Your SAS® Applications
by **Robert Virgile**

Elementary Statistics Using JMP®
by **Sandra D. Schlotzhauer**

The Essential Guide to SAS® Dates and Times
by **Derek P. Morgan**

Fixed Effects Regression Methods for Longitudinal Data Using SAS®
by **Paul D. Allison**

Genetic Analysis of Complex Traits Using SAS®
by **Arnold M. Saxton**

A Handbook of Statistical Analyses Using SAS®, Second Edition
by **B.S. Everitt**
and **G. Der**

Health Care Data and SAS®
by **Marge Scerbo, Craig Dickstein,**
and **Alan Wilson**

The How-To Book for SAS/GRAPH® Software
by **Thomas Miron**

In the Know... SAS® Tips and Techniques From Around the Globe, Second Edition
by **Phil Mason**

Instant ODS: Style Templates for the Output Delivery System
by **Bernadette Johnson**

Integrating Results through Meta-Analytic Review Using SAS® Software
by **Morgan C. Wang**
and **Brad J. Bushman**

Introduction to Data Mining Using SAS® Enterprise Miner™
by **Patricia B. Cerrito**

Learning SAS® by Example: A Programmer's Guide
by **Ron Cody**

Learning SAS® in the Computer Lab, Second Edition
by **Rebecca J. Elliott**

The Little SAS® Book: A Primer
by **Lora D. Delwiche**
and **Susan J. Slaughter**

The Little SAS® Book: A Primer, Second Edition
by **Lora D. Delwiche**
and **Susan J. Slaughter**
(updated to include SAS 7 features)

The Little SAS® Book: A Primer, Third Edition
by **Lora D. Delwiche**
and **Susan J. Slaughter**
(updated to include SAS 9.1 features)

The Little SAS® Book for Enterprise Guide® 3.0
by **Susan J. Slaughter**
and **Lora D. Delwiche**

The Little SAS® Book for Enterprise Guide® 4.1
by **Susan J. Slaughter**
and **Lora D. Delwiche**

Logistic Regression Using the SAS® System: Theory and Application
by **Paul D. Allison**

Longitudinal Data and SAS®: A Programmer's Guide
by **Ron Cody**

Maps Made Easy Using SAS®
by **Mike Zdeb**

Models for Discrete Date
by **Daniel Zelterman**

Multiple Comparisons and Multiple Tests Using SAS® Text and Workbook Set
(books in this set also sold separately)
by **Peter H. Westfall, Randall D. Tobias,**
Dror Rom, Russell D. Wolfinger,
and **Yosef Hochberg**

support.sas.com/pubs

SAS® System for Elementary Statistical Analysis,
Second Edition
by **Sandra D. Schlotzhauer**
and **Ramon C. Littell**

SAS® System for Regression, Third Edition
by **Rudolf J. Freund**
and **Ramon C. Littell**

SAS® System for Statistical Graphics, First Edition
by **Michael Friendly**

The SAS® Workbook and *Solutions* Set
(books in this set also sold separately)
by **Ron Cody**

Selecting Statistical Techniques for Social Science Data: A
Guide for SAS® Users
by **Frank M. Andrews, Laura Klem, Patrick M. O'Malley,**
Willard L. Rodgers, Kathleen B. Welch,
and **Terrence N. Davidson**

Statistical Quality Control Using the SAS® System
by **Dennis W. King**

Statistics Using SAS® Enterprise Guide®
by **James B. Davis**

A Step-by-Step Approach to Using the SAS® System
for Factor Analysis and Structural Equation Modeling
by **Larry Hatcher**

A Step-by-Step Approach to Using SAS®
for Univariate and Multivariate Statistics,
Second Edition
by **Norm O'Rourke, Larry Hatcher,**
and **Edward J. Stepanski**

Step-by-Step Basic Statistics Using SAS®: Student
Guide and *Exercises*
(books in this set also sold separately)
by **Larry Hatcher**

Survival Analysis Using SAS®:
A Practical Guide
by **Paul D. Allison**

Tuning SAS® Applications in the OS/390 and z/OS
Environments, Second Edition
by **Michael A. Raithel**

support.sas.com/pubs

Univariate and Multivariate General Linear Models:
Theory and Applications Using SAS® Software
by **Neil H. Timm**
and **Tammy A. Mieczkowski**

Using SAS® in Financial Research
by **Ekkehart Boehmer, John Paul Broussard,**
and **Juha-Pekka Kallunki**

Using the SAS® Windowing Environment:
A Quick Tutorial
by **Larry Hatcher**

Visualizing Categorical Data
by **Michael Friendly**

Web Development with SAS® by Example, Second
Edition
by **Frederick E. Pratter**

Your Guide to Survey Research Using the
SAS® System
by **Archer Gravely**

JMP® Books

JMP® for Basic Univariate and Multivariate Statistics:
A Step-by-Step Guide
by **Ann Lehman, Norm O'Rourke, Larry Hatcher,**
and **Edward J. Stepanski**

JMP® Start Statistics, Third Edition
by **John Sall, Ann Lehman,**
and **Lee Creighton**

Regression Using JMP®
by **Rudolf J. Freund, Ramon C. Littell,**
and **Lee Creighton**